Frommer's™

The Amalfi Coast
& Bay of Naples

with your family

rom charming resorts to Roman ruins

by Nick Bruno & Shona Main

WILEY

UK Publisher: Sally Smith
Executive Project Editor: Daniel Mersey (Frommer's UK)
Commissioning Editor: Fiona Quinn (Frommer's UK)
Development Editor: Sasha Heseltine
Project Editor: Hannah Clement (Frommer's UK)
Cartographer: John Tulip
Photo Research: Jill Emeny (Frommer's UK)

Wiley also publishes its books in a variety of electronic formats. Some content that appears in
print may not be available in electronic books.

British Library Cataloguing in Publication Data

A catalogue record for this book is available from the British Library.

ISBN: 978-0-470-51999-8

Typeset by Wiley Indianapolis C

Printed and bound in China by

5 4 3 2 1

Portsmouth City Council	
C800375703	
Askews	05-Mar-2009
914.5730493 BRU	£12.99
	9780470519998

Contents

About the Authors

Nick Bruno is a freelance travel writer and journalist. His dad is Neapolitan and he spent his childhood eating his nonna's fried eggs with mozzarella and following his uncle, the well-known crooner Luciano Bruno, around the piano bars of Campania. He spends lots of time in Italy and the rest of the year trying to lose some weight.

Shona Main also peaked too soon as Pop Editor of *Jackie* magazine when just 20. In a naive attempt to change the world she had short and not quite as interesting careers in law and politics. She has since returned to frippery and now writes about Italy, Scotland, art and popular culture.

They both co-authored the *Frommer's with Your Family guide to Northern Italy,* which came runner-up for the 2007 Italian State Tourist Board's Best Travel Guide.

Acknowledgements

Thanks to everyone who helped, including the more charming and courteous cogs in the Neapolitan bureaucracy that enabled us to do our research.

A big thank-you goes to Fiona Quinn, Mark Henshall and Jill Emeny at John Wiley. Also to: Giovanna Raffone and Albert, Mariano e famiglia, Massimo Di Porzio (vice president of the Associazione Verace Pizza Napoletana and a good man), Mimmo e Mamma, i pizzaioli Mariano e Gaetano, Ernesto Cacialli, Anna Scrocca, Gabriella Russo, Giuseppe Cafora, la famiglia Scotti, Domenico Di Meglio, Roberto Addeo and the Presidio Vulcano Vesuvio, Giovanni Visetti, Enzo and Peppino at La Tagliata, la famiglia Gargano, Giovanni Benvenuto, Napoli Sotterranea and Giuseppe Lauro.

The Mains and the Eames. Ma Bruno. Papà e Anita. Barbara e Pietro. Dave and Black Salt. A special thanks to Michelle and Indra for their loveliness and to Umberto Benvenuto, who is a real gentleman.

An Additional Note

Please be advised that travel information is subject to change at any time and this is especially true of prices. We therefore suggest that you write or call ahead for confirmation when making your travel plans. The authors, editors and publisher cannot be held responsible for experiences of readers while travelling. Your safety is important to us however, so we encourage you to stay alert and be aware of your surroundings.

Star Ratings, Icons & Abbreviations

Hotels, restaurants and attraction listings in this guide have been ranked for quality, value, service, amenities and special features using a star-rating system. Hotels, restaurants, attractions, shopping and nightlife are rated on a scale of zero stars (recommended) to three (exceptional). In addition to the star rating system, we also use 5 feature icons that point you to the great deals, in-the-know advice and unique experiences. Throughout the book, look for:

FIND	Special finds – those places only insiders know about
MOMENT	Special moments – those experiences that memories are made of
VALUE	Great values – where to get the best deals
OVERRATED	Places or experiences not worth your time or money
GREEN	Attractions employing responsible tourism policies

The following abbreviations are used for credit cards:

AE	American Express
DC	Diners Club
DISC	Discover
MC	MasterCard
V	Visa

A Note on Prices

Frommer's provides exact prices in each destination's local currency. As this book went to press, the rate of exchange was €1=£0.79. Rates of exchange are constantly in flux; for up-to-the-minute information, consult a currency-conversion website such as www.xe.com.

In the Family-friendly Accommodation section of this book we have used a price category system.

An Invitation to the Reader

In researching this book, we discovered my wonderful places – hotels, restaurants, shops and more. We're sure you'll find others. Please tell us about them, so we can share the information with your fellow travellers in upcoming editions. If you were disappointed with a recommendation, we'd love to know that too. Please email: frommers@ wiley.co.uk or write to:

Frommer's *The Amalfi Coast & Bay of Naples with Your Family,* 1st Edition
John Wiley & Sons, Ltd
The Atrium
Southern Gate
Chichester
West Sussex, PO19 8SQ

PHOTO CREDITS

Cover Credits

Main Image: © Cristina Fumi Premier Collection / Alamy

Small Images (L-R): © Mark Dyball / PCL; © Tim Hill / Alamy; © David Young / Fotolibra; © David Young / Fotolibra.

Back Cover: © Jon Arnold Images Ltd / Alamy.

Front Matter Credits

Pi: © Cristina Fumi Premier Collection / Alamy; piii/piv: © Mark Dyball / PCL; © Tim Hill / Alamy; © David Young / Fotolibra; © David Young / Fotolibra.

Inside Images

All images: © Nick Bruno with the following exceptions:

© Damiani: p109.
© Fototeca ENIT: p1, p4, p98, p103, p123, p134, p149, p179, p197, p209.
© Umberto D'Aniello: p10, p86.
Courtesy of Alamy: p89, p100 (© Adam Eastland).
Courtesy of Bridgeman Art Library: p74 (Credit: St. Jerome Removing a Thorn from the Lion's Paw, c.1445 (oil on panel) (see

1 Family Highlights of the Amalfi Coast & Bay of Naples

Campania Felix (*Happy Land* to the Romans) has always been popular with epicureans and families after the good things in life. Its flavoursome mix of relentless life, fabulous food, entwined layers of history and cultural treats is intoxicating. This crater-full of ancient and modern attractions spills out of an Arcadian landscape dominated by the ominous presence of a dormant volcano, Vesuvius (in Italian Monte Vesuvio), a reminder of nature's awesome power and its irrepressible inhabitants' precarious position.

The Amalfi Coast and Bay of Naples have some of the most well-known archaeological sites and natural wonders on the planet. When Vesuvio erupted in AD79 towns and villas were buried deep below volcanic debris. Their discovery provides captivating time capsules of Roman life. A visit to Pompeii and Herculaneum is the nearest thing to time-travel, while Paestum is an unforgettable vision of a lost civilisation.

The Campi Flegrei (Fiery Fields) – an area filled with volcanic craters, eerie lakes and the sulphuric vapours of Solfatara – was the entrance to the mythical Underworld. It was the most fashionable Roman resort, where Brutus and Cassius plotted Caesar's Ides of March. Families can paddle where Cleopatra enjoyed a spa getaway and stand above the underground cages where lions roared into the cauldron of Pozzuoli's amphitheatre.

Family trips to the islands of Capri, Ischia and Procida begin with a sea-breezy glide over azure waters. Each island has its own take on the Neapolitan-style *dolce vita*: Capri has the jet-set glamour, plunging cliffs and hidden marine grottoes; Ischia has thermal springs, tropical gardens and gorgeous beaches; while Procida prospers from its scruffy charm of peeling pastel houses nestled around intimate harbours.

For the ultimate family drive, take the SS163 along the Amalfi Coast – youngsters will gasp at the soaring limestone cliffs above and the limpid greenish blue *Mar Tirreno* way below. The Sorrentine peninsula and Costiera Amalfitana are studded with seaside resorts, intimate beaches and idyllic coves for splashing-good fun. Picturesque hamlets including Positano and Ravello tumble down mountainsides.

And finally, Napoli should not be missed in any lifetime. Families will be mesmerised by its layers of history and atmospheric sights. The dark, mysterious Città Antica – the Ancient City – gets under your skin.

Neapolitans are renowned for their warmth, sense of humour and joy in eating the fabulous fruits of the land and sea together in large and boisterous family groups – sometimes for hours! Eating out here as a family feels so natural – pizza, pastries and ice creams tend to go down well with everyone.

Here is a selection of our favourite family-friendly attractions to whet your appetite for a thrilling journey. *Buon Viaggio*!

BEST FAMILY EXPERIENCES

Best Ancient Towns Let your imaginations run wild walking the furrowed ancient flagstones and contorted mosaic floors of the ill-fated and endlessly fascinating Roman towns. Herculaneum was a well-to-do resort where priceless papyrus scrolls were found in a library that is still yielding its ancient secrets. Sprawling Pompeii is a must-see in any lifetime. Prepare for the whole family to be flabbergasted by the monumental scale of the ruins, exquisite artwork and fascinating glimpses into the life of a Roman town and its tragic burial. See p. 129.

Best Ascents A trip to the summit of the dozing menace, Vesuvius, that is mainland Europe's only active volcano is well worth the toil as the views of the Bay of Naples – on a clear day – are sublime and children get to peer into the steaming crater. See p. 112.

Up and down Monte Solaro. Rise serenely in single-seat chair-lifts above Anacapri on Capri to the island's highest point, where you can recline with an ice-cream cone and survey sparkling blue seas and shimmering coast-lines merging with hazy sky-scapes. See p. 198.

Best Neighbourhood The narrow Greco-Roman road called Spaccanapoli cuts through the throbbing heart of Naples, buzzing with vespas and Neapolitan life, it overflows with

Herculaneum statue

yummy street food, hidden worlds, mind-blowing art and layers of history. See p. 57.

BEST ART & ARCHITECTURE

Best Family Museums

Museo Archeologico Nazionale (Naples) If it's a monumental palace filled with Roman statues and Pompeian mosaics you're after, then the colossal collection at the Museo Archeologico Nazionale in Naples will keep you busy for hours. See p. 72.

Museo di Capodimonte (Naples) An elevated royal palace amid a wonderful park is pretty good to start with. Even better if you chuck in some of the most alluring Renaissance and

3

Neapolitan paintings anywhere, an observatory and a man selling *granita*: crushed ice with freshly squeezed lemon juice. See p. 73.

Best Contemporary Art

PAN (Naples) Naples's most welcoming and swanky contemporary art gallery is housed in the handsome 18th-century Palazzo Roccella in chic Chiaia. See p. 75.

Best Roman Treasures

Baia (Campi Flegrei) The Romans' most decadent resort and its once-sumptuous villas, spas and lavish knick-knacks can be viewed on glass-bottomed boats in the Parco Monumentale and in the Museo Archeologico dei Campi Flegrei – housed in the imposing Castello Aragonese, Baia. See p. 98.

BEST HISTORICAL ATTRACTIONS FOR FAMILIES

Best Caves

Scavi di Cuma (Campi Flegrei) An idyllic park containing Greek ruins and a creepy cave, where the mythical soothsayer Sybil used her magic powers, will spike the imaginations of wannabe wizards and witches. See p. 103.

Best Churches

Il Duomo (Naples) The colossal cathedral, deep in the dark heart of the Citta Antica, contains an ampoule of blood allegedly belonging to San Gennaro, the patron saint of Naples. It's the focus of frenzied praying, parading and shaking twice a year to ensure that the magic blood liquefies, as superstitious Neapolitans believe that should it fail to go gooey, catastrophe will befall the city once again. See p. 59.

Santa Chiara Cloisters (Naples) Take a breather from Spaccanapoli streetlife and discover a serene Franciscan world of Gothic arcades, wisteria-covered pergolas and vivid majolica-tiled pastoral scenes. See p. 63.

Santa Maria del Soccorso (Ischia) Linger outside this cute whitewashed church overlooking the sea at Forio and watch the sun melt into the Mar Tirreno. See p. 203.

The Duomo (Amalfi) Amalfi's 11th-century Duomo is a

The ornate Duomo, Amalfi

Byzantine beauty with a towering campanile and imposing façade covered with a mesmerising mosaic of gold-leaf and majolica tiling. Children love walking up its entrance steps and inside there are breathtaking cloisters and a chilling crypt with the remains of Sant'Andrea (Saint Andrew). See p. 169.

Best Greek Ruins

Paestum (near Salerno) Down the coast near Salerno are some of the best preserved and most evocative Greek ruins left standing. Pythagoras may even have discovered pi while hanging out at one of the temples here. See p. 174.

Best Time for Visiting the City of Naples

During **Maggio dei Monumenti**, see lots of historic sights opened that are rarely seen by the public alongside family-friendly musical and dance performances around the city. May of Monuments includes *Vietato Non Toccare* (It's forbidden not to touch): an initiative to encourage curious children to play games and learn. See p. 55.

Best Value Sightseeing Deal

Campania ArteCard allows you to see the city and region's attractions at a discounted price, and throws in access to all the public transport to boot. See p. 53.

BEST FESTIVALS & EVENTS

Best Religious Festivals

Festa della Madonna del Carmine (Naples, 15th–16th July) Piazza del Carmine is the focus for celebrating the Feast of the Madonna del Carmine. A procession of a pious relic around the Piazza Mercato area is followed by spectacular fireworks around the Madonna del Carmine belltower. See p. 55.

Festa di San Gennaro (Il Duomo, Naples) Fireworks and colourful processions make this festival a family favourite. The protector saint of Naples's blood must liquefy or all hell will break loose and another catastrophe is sure to hit the city! Three times a year – on the Saturday preceding the first Sunday in May, 16th December and on the saint's day of 19th September – a solemn ceremony and much fondling of the phial containing San Gennaro's blood is followed by a frenzy of emotional outpouring by the faithful imploring a miracle. See p. 19.

Best Foodie Festival

Pizzafest (Mostra d'Oltremare, Campi Flegrei) Pizza is eaten in copious amounts, *pizzaioli* (pizza makers) compete in various competitions and popular Neapolitan tunes such as 'O sole mio' are performed at this calorific celebration of Napoli's most famous export. See p. 94.

Best Island Festival

Settembrata Anacaprese

(Anacapri on Capri) The town's four *quartieri* (districts) come together in a fun, themed competition – each district's *cittadini* (citizens) pit their wits against the others in sporting, gastronomic and other eccentric contests. See p. 196.

Best Musical Festivals

The Ravello Festival and I Suoni degli Dei (The Amalfi

Coast) Classical music has never been so sexy. One of the many highlights is *Il Concerto all'Alba* (Dawn Concert: on 10th August – the Feast of San Lorenzo) when a full symphony orchestra, suspended on a cliff-top stage plays while the sun rises over the bay. Late June to October.

The Suoni degli Dei (Sounds

of the Gods) is a free series of outdoor concerts in spectacular

Preparing Napoli's famous dish at PIzzafest

settings along the Trail of the Gods. Although not suited for littl'uns, older children are bound to be swept away by the spectacular settings, atmosphere and musical drama. May to October. See p. 159.

BEST EXPERIENCES FOR ACTIVE FAMILIES

Boat Trips Whether it's bombing off a yacht anchored near a Caprese cove, enjoying a cool breeze on the ferry deck returning to Naples or fishing with Ischia's *pescatori* (fishermen), there's nothing quite like the salty taste and vivid shades of blue-green of the Tyrrhenian Sea. See p. 200.

A Mini-Trek up Mount

Epomeo (Ischia) Fleet-footed or mule-mounted families will have a hoot ascending this dead volcano way above Ischia's crowded beaches and spas. An easy scramble over smooth and sculptural ancient lava shapes rewards you with summit views of the verdant slopes of the *L'Isola Verde* (Ischia is known as 'The Green Island') and beyond. See p. 213.

Walking on the Sorrentine Peninsula & Amalfi Coast

Seasoned trekkers and occasional ramblers have a surfeit of trails to explore: where the eagles fly above limestone pinnacles, amid the olive and lemon groves on mule trails or down by the shore squawking at the gulls. The Trail of the Gods has various sections while the less demanding Valle dei Mulini walk passes waterfalls and old mills near Ravello. See p. 159.

BEST BEACHES

Marina Piccola (Capri) is a shingly beach surrounded by fabulous restaurants with views of the Fraglioni rocks. If you prefer more space for splashing in the limpid waters, head to the Bagni di Tiberio (Capri) – reachable by small boat from Marina Grande just around the corner.

The best way of arriving at the Maronti beach (Ischia), with its natural thermal springs and tranquil beach bars is by boat from alluring Sant'Angelo. See p. 201.

BEST ATTRACTIONS FOR YOUNGSTERS

Best Animal Magic

Agriturismo Farmyard Fun (Around Vesuvius & Sorrentine Peninsula) Children can feed horses, goats and chickens and sing *Vecchio Macdonald* (Old MacDonald) at *agriturismi* (farm restaurants) Bel Vesuvio, Il Cavaliere and La Ginestra. After playing in the fields and petting the animals you can kick-back on the porch and savour a hearty Neapolitan-style ranch meal. See p. 115.

Lo Zoo di Napoli (Campi Flegrei) Naples's zoo survived a threatened closure recently but still pulls in families who come for the tigers, leopards, pelicans, flamingos, deer, buffalo and Indian elephants. Youngsters can also pet and feed various farmyard animals including goats, chicks, ponies and rabbits. See p. 97.

Best Interactive Museum

La Citta della Scienza (Bagnoli) has lots of interactive exhibits for all ages and stimulating themed sections including a Science Workshop for littl'uns, digestible knowledge-nuggets about nutrition and a Planetarium. See p. 95.

Best Theme Parks

Edenlandia (Fuorigrotta) Napoli's long-established theme park has dozens of rides and attractions for toddlers and older children including dodgems, a flight simulator and bowling alleys. See p. 96.

Magic World (Licola, Campi Flegrei) A grinning genie welcomes families to this park with water slides, pools, go-karting, log flumes and a mini-train. Blue-faced *Puffi* (Italian Smurfs) including Grande Puffo (Papa Smurf) show youngsters around their *villaggio*. See p. 97.

BEST ATTRACTIONS FOR TEENS

Bacoli Beach Beguiling bars, including DJ-favourite Nabilah, make this curvy stretch of the Fiery Fields *molto cool* for older teens. After a paddle and play on Bacoli's beach, children can enjoy granita while the elders sip an *aperitivo della casa* (house aperitif), and soak up the atmosphere. See p. 99.

Napoli Sotteranea The old city's underground world is the stuff of legend: naughty Nero's theatre can be seen, home-grown plants thrive under lights and a narrow passageway walk with flickering candles takes you to a hidden cistern. See p. 58.

Scavi di Pompeii (Pompeii Excavations) Perhaps the most stimulating history lesson they'll ever have. Youngsters will be blown away with the scale, detail and ingenuity of this Roman town. A spine-tingling glimpse into the last moments of AD79's victims can be seen in the poignant plaster casts. See p. 129.

Best for Footie Fans

SSC Napoli A game at the Stadio San Paolo is always a passionate Neapolitan affair and a must for *calcio* (soccer)-crazy children of all ages. Pick up a replica *azzurro* shirt from the fabled 84–91 Maradona era outside and soak up the drama of a Serie A fixture. See p. 75.

BEST FAMILY DINING EXPERIENCES

Eating Seafood by the Mar Tirreno Fish and chips will never be the same after a *frittura di mare* – crispy medley of fried seafood – eaten at a seaside eatery like Neptunus, near Sant'Angelo, Ischia. See p. 222.

Scavi di Pompeii

La Tagliata (Amalfi Coast) High above Positano, this rustic trattoria serves flavoursome Amalfitana dishes served by the most jovial hosts. Oh, and the views of the Li Galli islands from the *bagno* window will linger like the aromas from *la famiglia Barba* kitchen. See p. 183.

Picnics al Fresco Pack your haversack with local *alimentari* and *paneficio* goodies like mozzarella cheese, piennolo or San Marzano tomatoes, traditional Neapolitan bread, some *Colline Salernitane* olive oil, *sfogliatella* pastries and luscious fruits for a feast in the park, by the sea or on ancient stones: Capodimonte in Naples, Spiaggia di Maronti or Villa Jovis on Capri, perhaps.

Pizza in Naples Children will be raving about margheritas and mozzarella after visiting the best pizzerias known to man or yeast. Our favourites are Pizzeria di Matteo, Da Umberto and Ciro a Mergellina, all in Naples, the city. See p. 80.

Best Sweet Treats

Ice Cream Naples has delish *gelati* (ice cream) but you won't find the striped pale "Neapolitan" version here. Vivid colours and lots of delicious natural flavours like *amarena* (cherries) and *malaga* (rum and raisin) tempt all the family. Ciro Chalet at Mergellina and Buonocore in Capri town are just two of the

Mini Babà al rhum

many lip-smackingly good *gelaterie* in the Bay of Naples and the Amalfi Coast. See p. 78.

Most Refreshing Drink Arabs brought the tradition of flavouring ice to Sicily then Naples and it lives on today in the simple and oh-so-refreshing *granita al limone* – slushy ice flavoured with freshly squeezed lemons and sugar. See p. 81.

Pastries & Cakes The region's famed *pasticcerie* like Scaturchio in Naples create the yummiest pastries including horn-shaped *sfogliatelle* – crunchy, delicate layers of pastry with a candied fruit centre – and the spongy *babà al rhum* which is soaked in rum.

Salvatore De Riso in Minori makes *la delizia al limone* – a round, creamy cake infused by the Costa Amalfitana's lemons. See p. 79.

BEST ACCOMMODATION

Best Urban Bases

B&Bs (La Bouganville & Casa Mira) These family-run B&Bs in Posillipo and Mergellina provide more than just excellent value for families visiting Napoli. A stay at a B&B is a great way to get a taste of the warm Neapolitan hospitality. See p. 87.

Constantinopoli (Naples) Deep in the throbbing heart of the Citta` Antica, this Liberty-style palazzo-turned-luxury hotel has a gorgeous courtyard and a pool. See p. 87.

Micalò (Naples) Oodles of art and charm make this boutique hotel a most stylish city haven. It's particularly suited to families travelling with design-conscious teens who will adore the high ceilings, mezzanines, curvy walls and artwork. See p. 85.

Best Rural Retreat

La Ginestra (Sorrentine Peninsula) High up in the hills above Vico Equense this *agriturismo* is a superb place to relax for parents and fabulous for children who adore farmyard animals. See p. 188.

Best Island Retreats

Hotel La Vigna (Procida) looks like a little castle and is set within vineyards in the midst of Procida's market gardens. Luxury family suites and spa facilities make it one of our favourite island retreats. See p. 228.

J.K. Place (Capri) is a new boutique hotel straight out of a film-set and trendy design magazine shoot. It may be pricey, especially for a family, but you get what you pay for: the most luxurious, coolest and relaxing place to stay on one of the most beautiful islands anywhere. See p. 225.

Best Resort Hotel

Oleandri Resort (Paestum) Children will love the palm-fringed pools, gardens and shaded playground at this resort which resembles one of those sprawling resorts on the Red Sea. See p. 186.

The stylish Micalò, Naples

2 Planning a Trip to the Amalfi Coast & Bay of Naples

THE AMALFI COAST & BAY OF NAPLES

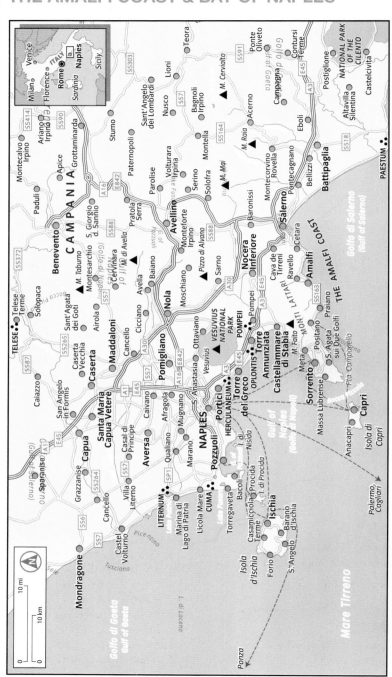

Thankfully, you are highly unlikely to be caught out by volcanic eruptions like the unlucky inhabitants of Pompeii in AD79, but to avoid other mishaps you'd best equip yourself with some extra knowledge; this chapter will give you and your family the essential information for planning an affordable, safe and fun family holiday.

VISITOR & PLANNING INFORMATION

Tourist Offices

A bit of web research before you go will help you to separate the wheat from the chaff. **ENIT** (Ente Nazionale Italiano per il Turismo) (1 Princes Street, London W1B 2AY (*0207 399 3562/0207 408 1254; www.italian tourism.com*) is a useful starting point. From there, visits to the region's tourist boards and their websites (**APTs**: Aziende Provinciale per il Turismo) will help you get a better feel for what suits your time and circumstances.

Amalfi APT: *www.amalfitourist office.it*

Campi Flegrei AACST: *www.infocampiflegrei.it/*

Capri APT: *www.capritourism.com/*

Caserta EPT: *www.eptcaserta.it*

Ischia & Procida APT: *www.infoischiaprocida.it*

Napoli APT: *www.inaples.it*

Salerno APT: *www.turismoin salerno.it*

Sorrento APT: *www.sorrento tourism.com/*

Alas, many of the local APT websites have ridiculous translations and are not very useful. The local tourist boards do have small information offices (*Ufficio d'Informazione*) where you can pick up a free local map, flyers and purchase cumulative tickets for sights and transport.

Advice for Family Travel

There are a number of websites giving advice to families travelling with children. For general advice about flying while pregnant, car seats and holiday first aid, try *www.family-travel.co.uk*; *www.travellingwithchildren.co.uk*; *www.travelforkids.com*; *www. babygoes2.com*. Guardian columnist Dea Birkett has an extremely useful *Travelling with Kids* forum on her website, *www.deabirkett.com*. The Italian website *www.bambinopoli.it* has lots of useful listings for parents and even has a list of babysitters. Handy books include *Take the Kids Travelling* by Cadogan and *Your Child's Health Abroad: A Manual for Travelling Parents* by Bradt. Families with children who have special needs may like to contact parents whose children have similar conditions to swap travel tips at: *youreable.com* and *disabledfriends.com*. Prepare an identity bracelet that has all the details of a child's medical condition, required treatments and doctor's name at *medicalert. org.uk*.

ENTRY REQUIREMENTS & CUSTOMS

Entry Requirements

EU and EEA (EU plus Iceland, Liechtenstein and Norway) nationals need only produce a valid passport or national identity card to be admitted to Italy. Either is acceptable. No visa is required.

Note that babies and children up to 16 not already on a parent or guardian's passport now need their own child passport. These last for five years (three for under-3s in Ireland). If your child is already on your passport they can continue this way until they turn 16, your passport runs out or they need to get their own.

All other visitors must have a passport valid for at least three months beyond the proposed stay. If you are a US, Canadian, UK, Irish, Australian or New Zealand citizen and, after entering, find you want to stay more than 90 days, you can apply for a permit for an extra 90 days. As a rule this is granted immediately. Go to the nearest *questura* (police headquarters) or your home country's consulate. If your passport is lost or stolen, head to your consulate as soon as possible to arrange a replacement.

Customs

What You Can Take into Italy

If you are bringing in tobacco products and alcoholic beverages for personal use there should be no problem. It might be worth noting that cigarettes and alcohol can both be bought very cheaply in Italian supermarkets. EU passengers cannot buy duty-free cigarettes.

What You Can Bring Home from Italy

Citizens of the UK should contact HM Customs & Excise (📞 0845 010 9000; from outside the UK, 📞 020 8929 0152), or consult their website (*www.hmce. gov.uk*). The general rule is that all alcohol and tobacco must be for your own use and be transported by you. Here are the figures for the amount of alcohol and tobacco products you can bring back to the UK from Italy: 3200 cigarettes, 200 cigars, 400 cigarillos, 3kg tobacco, 110 litres of beer, 90 litres of wine, 10 litres of spirits, 20 litres of fortified wine (such as port or sherry). Irish citizens should contact Irish Customs & Excise (📞 067 632 23 or the LoCall number 📞 1890 666 333; from outside Eire call 📞 00353 1647 4444 or negotiate their website (*www. revenue.ie*).

MONEY

The currency in Italy is the **euro** (€). A euro is divided into 100 cents, and there are notes for 5–500€ and coins for 1¢ to 2€. Withdrawing euros using your debit or credit card is easy. There are ATMs (*bancomat* in Italian) everywhere. Some banks and travel agencies offer commission-free exchange, but shop around to find the best rates. If you are travelling from the UK, the Post Office offers a great service, allowing you to order in person or online and pick up later (📞 *08457 223 344*; *www.postoffice. co.uk*).

Euros to the Pound

£1 = 1.25€ or 1€ = £0.79 (though it may have changed by the time you read this)

To convert the price of something in euros into pounds, just take off a fifth. For example, a plate of pasta that costs 5€ is roughly £4. For current rates and a handy converter, see *www. xe.com*.

Travellers' Cheques

Few people use these nowadays, but they are still useful if you want a mix of cash and cheques and some extra security. Banks and travel agencies in the UK and Ireland provide them for a small fee. They can be cashed in Italian banks, cambios and by bigger hotels (the latter is an expensive option). Keep a note of the serial numbers in case they get stolen. Just remember that dealing with banks in Italy can be slow and bureaucratic. They also close for very long lunches. For hours, see Banks p. 41.

ATMs

You can use your card in most of the 24-hour ATMs (called bancomats) in Italy, with most offering an 'English' option button. Italian banks charge a small fee for using their ATMs.

Credit & Debit Card Safety & Security

If you intend to use your credit and debit cards abroad, it's wise to let your card providers know before you go. This means they won't become suspicious when they are used in an unusual location, and refuse a withdrawal. If your card is rejected, phone your provider.

It's a good idea to take more than one card with you. They have been known to get lost, stolen, swallowed up or just not

---

 'Where is the nearest ATM?'

C'è un bancomat qui vicino? (Cheh oon ban-coh-mat, qwee vee-chee-noh)

Hopefully the answer will involve pointing!

What Things Cost in Naples	€
Taxi from Capodichino Airport to city centre	28.00
Tram or bus ride (90 min. travel) – adult or child	1.00
Panino from café	3.50
Espresso standing at bar in café	0.80
Caffe latte sitting outside a café	3.50
500ml bottle of water (take-away) from café	2.00
Two scoops of ice cream in a cone	1.50
Slice of pizza Margherita to take away	2.50
Pizza Margherita sitting down in pizzeria	6.00
Pack of Mister Baby nappies (*pannolini*)	5.00
1 litre of ready mixed infant formula	3.00
Plasmon Pear Baby Food 2X80g	1.50

work, so this saves disasters and exorbitant money transfers from home. Most *bancomats* in Italy offer a choice of languages.

Be vigilant when using your card. It's a good idea to take someone with you when you go to an ATM on a busy street or even a quiet area. As a matter of course, check that the ATM has not been tampered with before you use your card. Look to see if a device has been placed into the card entry slot of a cash machine to capture card details. And cover your hand when typing your PIN. When using your credit or debit card in shops or restaurants, don't let it out of your sight. As a precaution, use cash rather than cards in smaller shops or in less desirable neighbourhoods. Chip and Pin is slowly being rolled out in Italy.

What to Do if Your Bag or Wallet is Lost or Stolen

As soon as you discover your wallet is lost or stolen, contact your bank and/or card provider and report your loss at the nearest police station. Your credit card company or insurer may require a police report number. They may be able to send a cash advance immediately or deliver an emergency credit card within a day or two.

Keeping Costs Low

Travellers who remember Italy before the euro will recall a country that was very affordable to visit. However, the new currency's introduction was poorly managed and resulted in huge price rises. These inevitably were passed on to tourists. Italy is as expensive as the UK with the exception of fresh produce, public transport and accommodation in rural areas. Remember to ask for children's discounts (*sconto per bambini*), especially in museums and galleries. Under-18s get free admittance to many museums and galleries. Children under a certain height travel free on trams and buses.

There is much you can do to keep costs down. *Supermercati* – supermarkets (Italian high-street faves are Standa, Billa, Coop, De Spar, Conad and Sigma) – are a great place to buy water, meat and cheese, snacks, nappies (avoid pharmacies for these) and many items you would usually get in Boots. The main piazza or tourist hotspot in any city or town will always have the most expensive cappuccino, *gelato* and *panini* so refresh off the main thoroughfares. Picnics are great if you're budgeting and the availability and quality of the simplest food in Italy makes it easy to picnic like a prince. See the relevant chapters for daily and weekly food markets and recommended delis.

WHEN TO GO

Southern Italy is a fabulous destination all year – you don't really need good weather to enjoy a visit.

However, if you want to see what the country has to offer rather than jostle with the crowds, avoid July and August (*le ferie*, Italians' holiday month).

Not only are these peak season (and so the priciest for hotels) but they are the hottest. Chaotic Naples in 40 degrees with a couple of toddlers is no fun. Furthermore, many shops and restaurants close in August.

The tyranny of school holidays makes you think this is the only time you can go. But is it? It's cheaper, cooler and less packed during Easter, half-term and, for Scottish families, the "tattie holidays". Even in October, it is still delightfully warm and sunny.

Child-friendly Annual Events

For an exhaustive list of events (*manifestazioni*) check out **www.whatsonwhen.com** and the Italian websites: **www.giraitalia.it** and **www.eventiesagre.it**

January

Epiphany Celebrations Nationwide. All cities, towns and villages in Italy stage Roman Catholic Epiphany observances, processions and fairs.
From Christmas to 6th January.

Useful Credit Card Numbers

American Express ☏ *+44 845 456 6524* and reverse the charges
Barclaycard ☏ *+44 1604 230 230*
MasterCard ☏ *800 870 866* (an Italian number – no code needed)
MBNA ☏ *+44 1244 672 111* and reverse the charges
Visa ☏ *800 819 014* (this is an Italian number and doesn't need a code) or reverse the charges to ☏ *+01 410 581 9*

February

Carnevale The period before Lent sees float parades, feasts and flamboyant shows throughout Campania.

The two weeks before Ash Wednesday.

March

Galassia Guttenburg (Naples) This celebration of fiction and storytelling will spark the imaginations of children with its multimedia events and book fair. *www.galassia.org*

Festa Tradizionale dell' Annunziata (Paestum) Market stalls and events within the ancient town walls showcase the area's bountiful local produce. A procession the next day sees locals offer thanks to an 18th-century statue of the Madonna.

24th and 25th March. ℂ *0828 811016*

April

Good Friday and Easter Week, nationwide Processions and age-old ceremonies – some dating from pagan days, others from the Middle Ages. It begins on the Thursday or Friday before Easter Sunday.

Processione dei Misteri (Procession of the Mysteries) (Procida) This famous procession of historic statues and contemporary depictions of scenes from the Passion of Christ takes place on *venerdì santo*

Good Friday

Comicon (Napoli) *www.comicon.it* Fans of animation and comics gather at Castel Sant'Elmo each Spring. There are many exhibits suited to youngsters, although some of the peculiarly Italian-style drawings are quite graphic and more suited to older teens and adults.

Usually last weekend of month, with exhibition open throughout May.

May

Festa di San Costanzo, Capri. The island's patron saint and protector is celebrated with a flower-strewn procession and cultural events.

14th May, ℂ *081 837 0686 www.capritourism.com*

Maggio di Monumenti, *Napoli.* Each May, Napoli's *centro storico* and historic sites roundabouts stage special cultural events, including free access to fascinating

Average Daily Temperature & Monthly Rainfall in Naples												
	Jan	Feb	Mar	Apr	May	June	July	Aug	Sep	Oct	Nov	Dec
Temp. (°F)	50	54	58	63	70	78	83	85	75	66	60	52
Temp. (°C)	9	12	14	17	21	26	28	29	24	19	16	11
Rainfall (in.)	4.7	4	3	3.8	2.4	.8	0.8	2.6	3.5	5.8	5.1	3.7

private collections, concerts and guided walks.

June

Concerti al Tramonto, Anacapri
Each June to September, the Foundation Axel Munthe organises a programme of classical sunset concerts at the Villa San Michele.

www.sanmichele.org

Regatta of the Great Maritime Republics
Every year, the four medieval maritime republics of Italy celebrate their glorious past with a boat race that rotates between Venice, Amalfi, Genoa and Pisa. In 2009 it's Amalfi's turn.

First Sunday of June.

July

Festival di Ravello (Ravello)
For jazz, classical and arts fans, there is no more spectacularly placed festival.

☏ 089 858 422. www.ravellofestival. com

Festa di Sant'Anna (Ischia)
Colourful processions, eccentrically adorned floats, fireworks and feasting take place under the Castello Aragonese, to celebrate the island's patron.

26th July. www.festadisantanna.it

August

Estate Amalfitana (Amalfi)
Musical, gastronomic and other events staged in and around Amalfi span the summer months.

June to September. ☏ 089 871 107.

Festa della Assunta (Positano)
The 9th- and 10th-century Saracen invasions are commemorated with spectacular re-enactments, music and fireworks on the water.

14th and 15th August. ☏ 0898 75067 www.aziendaturismopositano.it

September

Festa di San Gennaro, *Naples.*
Neapolitans implore the 'miracle of San Gennaro (see p. 61)' in and around the cathedral: if the liquid (supposedly the blood of the martyr) contained in the ampoules promptly liquefies there is much rejoicing, as it is a good omen for the city.

19th September.

Pizzafest (Naples)
Sample the very best mouthfuls of the world's fave fast food in the town that invented it. Usually takes place in early September at the Oltremare exhibition centre.

www.pizzafest.info

October

Sagra della Castagna, *Campania.*
All over the region, the harvest of sweet chestnuts is marked with street parties and food markets. At San Cipriano Picentino they even have a *Palio del Ciuccio* (Donkey race).

Last weekend of October.
www.lasagradellacastagna.net

November

Pane e Olio in Frantoio (Campania)
Local producers of extra virgin olive oil and bread promote their goods at numerous tasting gatherings across the region.

Last weekend of November.
www.cittadellolio.it

Festa di Sant'Andrea (Amalfi)
A statue of the town's protector is carried by local fishermen to the Duomo, where they offer fresh and ornamental fish to the saint. Fireworks and festivities follow.

30th November. ☎ *089 871 107.*
www.amalfituristoffice.it

December

Sagra della Salsiccia e Ceppone (Sorrento).
A massive fire is prepared on the 12th December, and the following night the Feast of Santa Lucia is celebrated with copious amounts of barbecued sausages and local vino.

☎ *081 807 2590 www.turismo regionecampania.it*

Presepi di Natale, *Campania.*
Campania is famous for its lavish and often eccentric nativity scenes (presepi). There's even a "living nativity" at Forino in the provincia di Avellino.

Late December to mid January.
www.presepeviventeforino.it

Public Holidays

Offices and shops in Italy are closed on the following dates: **1st January** (New Year's Day), **6th January** (Epiphany or *La Befana*; Italian children's real Christmas Day), **Easter Sunday, Easter Monday, 25th April** (Liberation Day), **1st May** (Labour Day), **15th August** (Assumption of the Virgin, or *ferragosto*) **15th–30th August** (Italy's summer holidays – yes, the whole nation takes a break!), **1st November** (All Saints' Day), **8th December** (Feast of the Immaculate Conception), **25th December** (Christmas Day) and **26th December** (Santo Stefano). Italians' Christmas holidays last from **24th December to 6th January**.

Closings are often observed on feast days that honour a patron saint of a town; in Naples, **19th September** is La Festa di San Gennaro.

WHAT TO PACK

The seasons are fairly reliable in southern Italy but if you're travelling at the cusps (April or October), we recommend you bring some cosy socks and jumpers.

If you plan to eat in more salubrious restaurants, men will need to bring a smart shirt and trousers.

The Italian sun is strong so bring hats for children – and anyone with a bald pate!

Don't forget to bring travel adapters.

Italy doesn't have Boots or Superdrug or even an equivalent: you'll have to try numerous pharmacies and supermarkets to find cosmetics, toiletries and over-the-counter medicines. It's a good idea to bring your own favourite brands.

A small first-aid kit is useful: bring sterile wipes, plasters, tweezers and tablets for tummy upsets, allergies and headaches. It could save you a lot of money and effort.

Sun creams and anti-mosquito bite preparations are much easier – and cheaper – to buy back home. Plug-in mosquito repellents (with enough tablets or liquid for your stay) are worth their weight in gold. If you're booking more than one room, bring one for each.

A bag with water, juice, snacks, tissues, wet wipes, nappies (if you need them) and sun cream will be invaluable. A collapsible cool-bag will be perfect for picnics.

A small oscillating fan might sound a bit unnecessary, but if you've ever tried to get children off to sleep in a sweltering room with no air conditioning, this could be the holiday saver. You can pick these up for around 35€ in Italy or bring your own.

Packing for Planes & Cars

For a Plane Trip

Be sure to check both your children's and your own pockets and hand baggage for those objects which must be put in the hold: boy scouts' pocket knives, your favourite nail scissors, crochet hooks, etc. If these are not revealed until going though the security check, you'll never see them again.

When travelling with youngsters, it is well worth packing the following in your carry-on bag (just in case):

• The number of nappies your child wears in a day, plus a few extra.

• A changing mat.

• A minimal number of toys: a book, some crayons and a stuffed toy is plenty.

• Bottles for infants, an 'anyway-up cup' and snacks for toddlers.

• A bag of tricks, for those moments where you have to pull something out of the bag. Perhaps an mp3 player, books or someone's favourite dinosaur.

For more advice on flying with children, see 'Getting There', p. 29.

For a Car Trip

If you are hiring a car, enquire about reserving an age-appropriate child safety seat; most major rental agencies have these available for a small fee. (Avis, for example, charges £3 per day for safety or booster seats). Alternatively, take booster seats on the plane as hand luggage.

Long-distance car travel with children presents a completely different packing challenge. Pack the following to help your trip go smoothly:

- A cooler with drinks, snacks and fruit. You can buy one from a supermarket for around 20€.

- Window shades for the sun.

- Talking books or your child's favourite music (your ears will become immune to McFly after the eighth listen, don't worry).

- Other items to consider include a first-aid kit, a box of wet wipes, toilet paper, blankets, plastic bags for motion sickness and a change of clothes. Always have a mobile phone in case of emergencies.

- The RAC website has lots of car games you can download for free. See *www.rac.co.uk/web/knowhow/going_on_a_journey/games.*

- In addition, you can download the Frommer's activity pack from *www.frommers.co.uk/withyourfamily/funpack.html*

HEALTH, INSURANCE & SAFETY

Travel Insurance

Check your home and/or health insurance policies before you buy travel insurance to cover trip cancellation, lost luggage, medical expenses or car rentals. You may have partial or complete coverage. But if you need some, a simple search with MoneySupermarket (📞 *0845 345 5708*; *www.moneysupermarket.com*) allows you to compare benefits and prices. The good news is that such is the competition for your business, it's a buyer's market. You can get cover for all the family at a reasonable price. More dangerous activities are likely to be excluded from basic policies, but are you really going to be paragliding with the children? Always, *always* check the small print before you sign; more and more policies have built-in exclusions and restrictions that may leave you out in the cold if something does go awry. Protect yourself further by paying for the insurance with a credit card – by law, consumers can get their money back on goods and services not received if they report the loss within 60 days of their credit card statement.

The European Health Insurance Card (EHIC) (formerly an E111)

UK and Irish residents can obtain free or reduced cost medical treatment when temporarily visiting another EU country such as Italy, but you must have an EHIC to qualify. You can apply for your EHIC by picking up an application form from your local health centre or post office. In the UK, the Post Office charges a fee of £2, and your EHIC card will be posted to you within 21 days. For more information see *www.ehic-card.org* or call 📞 *090 7707 8370*.

While this covers medical care, it does not cover lost

baggage, cancellation, the costs of accidents, repatriation or several other mishaps covered by purchasing travel insurance.

Disabled Travellers

When you book your flight be sure to let the airline know if you or your child has mobility problems and will require assistance. If using airport car parks, contact the airport to see if they have any disabled long-stay spaces available.

All new public buildings in Italy are obliged to be accessible for the disabled. Older buildings may be less easy to get into and around. More hotels are recognising the need to make things easier for customers with mobility problems. Contact them before you book. For help with booking accommodation contact Tourism For All (☎ 0845 124 9971; *www.tourismforall.org.uk*).

For information, advice and links see the 'door to door' section of the Disabled Persons Transport Advisory Committee's website (*www.dptac.gov.uk*), the BBC's Ouch (*www.bbc.co.uk/ouch*) and the Disabled Parent's Network (*www.disabledparents network.org.uk*).

Before You Go

If you have any worries about your health go to see your doctor before you go. Similarly, if you have toothache, sort it out before you get on the plane.

Find out if you or the children require any vaccinations or boosters before you travel. Pack prescription medicines in your carry-on luggage and keep them in their original containers with the pharmacy labels. They won't make it through airport security otherwise. Also bring copies of your prescriptions. Italian pharmacies may fill them for you. Don't forget an extra pair of contact lenses or prescription glasses.

It is also a good idea to know the name and location of the hospital with accident and emergency facilities in your destination. These are called *emergenza*. They can be located by Googling "*emergenza*", "*pronto soccorso*" and the name of the district you are staying in (e.g. Vomero). The general Tourist Board website has a handy list of contact numbers to print out: *www.inaples.it/eng/numeri.htm* Having this information to hand could be priceless.

Emergency Numbers

☎ *113* Police
☎ *112* Carabinieri (who also deal with crimes)
☎ *115* Fire department
☎ *118* Medical emergency

Helpful Phrases in an Emergency

Aiuto! **Help!** *Ayee-oo-toh!*

Puo aiutarmi, per favore? **Could you please help me?** *Pwo ay-oo-tar-mee pehr fah-vor-eh?*

Pronto soccorso **first aid** *pron-toh soh-kohr-soh*

Ambulanza **ambulance** *am-boo-lan-dza*

Ospedale **hospital** *oz-peh-dah-leh*

Un medico **doctor** *oon meh-dee-ko*

Mi fa male qui **It hurts here** *mee fah mah-leh kwee*

Una ricevuta, per favore **Invoice/receipt please** *oona reech-eh-voo-tah pehr fah-vor-eh*

C'è una farmacia qui vicino? **Is there a pharmacy near here?** *Cheh oona farm-ah-chee-ah kwee vee-chee-noh?*

Al fuoco! **fire!** *Al fwoh-ko!*

Ferma! Al ladro! **stop! thief!** *Fur-mah! Al lah-droh!*

At the *Farmacia*

Most common medicines found in a chemist back home have an equivalent in the Italian *farmacia*. A handy painkiller for minor ailments, containing paracetamol, is *Tachipirina*. For a list of minor ailments in Italian, refer to the Appendix of this book.

What to Do if You Become Ill

In most cases, your EHIC will ensure you get treated swiftly. However, costs will still be incurred.

When you see the doctor, take the EHIC and any travel insurance documents with you. Be sure to ask for a receipt if you make any payment. You can use this receipt to make a claim on your return. If s/he gives you a prescription, ask for directions to the pharmacy.

If you or your child's illness is so severe that you need to go straight to the hospital, again take both the EHIC and your insurance documents.

Staying Safe

Italy is a comparatively safe country. There are, of course, thieves everywhere, so don't invite them to steal. Naples has a bit of a reputation for its cunning pickpockets and con-artists, so be wary. Don't leave bags unattended in your hire car and take everything out of the boot at night. Exercise good sense when walking around: avoid unlit streets and ensure your wallet isn't easily accessible (or keep it in a money belt). Mobile phones, cameras, jewellery and mp3 players are obvious targets, so keep these out of sight. And if someone offers you what seems like a bargain (camcorders are the favourite bait) on the street, say "*no grazie*" and walk away swiftly. And make sure you've got adequate insurance in case of theft (p. 22).

Legal Advice While in Italy

See Embassies & Consulates in Fast Facts section (see p. 42).

PLANNING YOUR TRIP ONLINE

Surfing for Airfares

There is only one airport in the region: Aeroporto Internazionale di Napoli, called Capodichino Airport by the locals. Alitalia.com, British Airways (ba.com), AerLingus. com, FlyBMI.com and Easy Jet.com all fly to Naples. Online travel agencies that sell air tickets are **Expedia.co.uk, Lastminute.com, Opodo.co.uk and Travelocity.co.uk**. Each has individual deals with airlines and may offer different fares for the same flights, so shop around. Travel agencies such as **ThomasCook.com and Thomsonfly.com** also sell cheap flights to the area but have less of a range. **Cheapflights.com and LowFareFlights.co.uk** do comparisons and will direct you to the airline website to book.

Don't forget to check regular airline websites: you can get great deals by side-stepping travel agency commissions. For contact details for airlines that fly to the Naples area, see Appendix (p. 237).

If, for whatever reason, your child between 5 and 14 years old is to travel alone, ask about whether your airline operates an unaccompanied minor service, and what this costs.

Surfing for Hotels

It is a good idea to spend some time researching hotels and shopping around. Booking directly is often the best bet and if things go pear-shaped, it is often good to have a direct relationship with the hotel. It's a good idea to print off the confirmation of the *prenotazione* (booking) to have something to cling to if you're met with blank looks or increased rates when you check in.

If you book over the Internet make sure you get a confirmation number and make a printout of your online booking transaction.

When booking a hotel through a site such as **Lastminute.com**, remember the old Latin maxim, *caveat emptor:* let the buyer beware. Companies like Lastminute act as a third party, selling hotel bookings for partner agencies. This doesn't really matter unless things go wrong. If you arrive and find that the hotel and/or room is mouldy, vibrating with Euro House music or overrun with ants, the chances of being relocated to another, better hotel or getting your money back are thin. If this does happen, your best bet is to keep your cool, complain until every avenue of restitution is exhausted, take photographs and document the problems for future use. If you are very lucky, you will be relocated. If not, write the letter of complaint of your life to the partner agency when you return, in the hope of getting some money back. **HolidayTravel Watch.com** provides invaluable advice on how to complain.

You can reduce – but not eliminate – the risk of booking a dodgy hotel by using websites like **Holidays-uncovered.com, HolidayWatchdog.com, Trip advisor.com** and **Virtual tourist.com.** These use readers to rate hotels and can offer helpful insights and candid reviews.

What to Look For

The Italian rating system for accommodation doesn't appear to be based on fieldwork. Five-star hotels can be wonderful but some shabbier ones seem to make the grade on the strength of a murky pool alone. Levels of service, the things that make or break a hotel have no bearing on their grading, which means you can have a 4-star hotel with misery-making, rubbish service and a 2-star that treats you like kings.

An **albergo** is the old name for a hotel. **Locanda** once meant an inn or carriage stop, though it's now sometimes used to refer to a place with charm. A **pensione** is a bit like a guesthouse. You usually have to share the bathroom. They are often the cheapest and most cheerful, and perfect for children. You can now book 'il **Bed and Breakfast**' (try *www.bbitalia.com*) and, in rural parts, an **agriturismo.** This is a broad term for a rustic B&B, sometimes run by farmers trying to diversify. Within this term you will find a group of agriturismo purists who only serve locally produced food and drink. There are several websites to help you find an agriturismo: try *www. agriturist.it*; *www.agriturismo.net*; *www.agriturismo.com*; *www. terranostra.it*; and *www. turismoverde.it*.

TIP ➤➤ **Saving Money on Airfares** ◄◄

- Book well in advance, stay over a Saturday night or fly midweek to give you a bigger chance of bagging the lowest fares.
- Register with the airline's website to receive updates on fare sales and special offers. Gather intelligence on the range of prices offered by the airlines themselves, Internet agents like Travelocity, Expedia and Opodo and high-street agents.
- Look out for promotional specials or fare wars, when airlines lower prices on their most popular routes. Check out the Sunday papers' travel sections. Sometimes newspapers run special offers: it may mean you have to buy one for a week or two to collect the coupons, but it could save you money.

- With a bit of charm and negotiation you may be able to lower the price of your room:
- **Ask about special rates and other discounts** – dial the hotel direct to ask the price of a room and tell them you're looking for a *sconto* (discount). Ask if children stay free in the room (and clarify at what age they become adults). If not, is there a special rate?
- **Seek deals** – see what price the hotel is offering and check if any Internet sites have it cheaper. Many hotels offer Internet-only discounts, or supply rooms to Lastminute or Expedia at rates much lower than those available from the hotel direct.
- **High season means higher prices** – off- or mid-season means lower prices and more room for negotiation.
- **Ask for a long-stay discount** – if you're planning a long stay (at least 5 days), you might qualify for a discount. If you don't ask, you won't get it.
- **Avoid excess charges and hidden costs** – when you book a room, ask whether the hotel charges for parking. Use your own mobile, pay phones or prepaid phone cards instead of dialling direct from hotel phones, which have rates to make you wince. Eschew the minibar: 3€ for a tiny bottle of water? Finally, ask about additional charges for the room (balcony, view, cot, air conditioning, etc.). It all adds up.
- **Full- or half-board or B&B?** Many Italian hotels, especially in high season, only offer full- or half-board. Full-board is great if the food is lovely but can leave you feeling trapped. Is there a choice of places to eat nearby? What is the cost of eating out? If staying half-board, can you choose to have lunch or dinner? Would going out for dinner each night be difficult with a young child?
- **Book an apartment** – a room with a kitchenette allows you to shop for groceries and cook your own meals. This is a big money saver, especially for long stays and, despite it being a holiday from all things mundane, you'd be surprised how enjoyable cooking with Italian market fresh fish and vegetables can be.

Happy **campers** will find lots of places to pitch up under the stars, with a number of them able to rent you the tent and the gear that goes with it. The Italians are wholehearted about camping provisions: it's not unusual to find swimming pools, saunas and lush gardens on-site. To find the best campsites in Italy check out the Touring Club Italiano guides (*www.touringclub. it*) or the Federazione Italiana Campeggiatori (📞 *055 882 391*; *www.federcampeggio.it*). Useful websites for comparing facilities are *www.easycamping.it*, *www. camping.it* and *www.campeggi. com*. British-based companies like Eurocamp (📞 *0870 901 9410*; *www.eurocamp.co.uk*) offer camping packages.

Planning Your Trip Online

Booking a Tour or Package Holiday

For those who can't be bothered with the faff of doing it yourself or the risk of booking a package holiday, a number of independent tour operators offer a huge range of holidays to Naples and the Amalfi Coast, including activity or specialist breaks. So if you want to factor in some *parliamo Italiano* lessons, do a cookery course or learn to paint, a search in Google or a leaf through the back pages of the broadsheet newspapers will throw up a variety of operators. Alternatively, and for a safer bet, the Association of Independent Tour Operators Limited **AITO.co.uk** have a handy search engine with a 'child/family friendly' indicator to help you find the kind of holiday that will suit your family.

There are a number of **youth hostels** across the region. These vary in size, but are wonderfully economical and a great way to meet other families. Contact the Associazione Italiana Alberghi per la Gioventu (☎ *06 4890 7740 www.ostellionline.org*). To obtain an International Youth Hostel Federation membership card see ☎ *01629 592 700*; *www.yha.org.uk*

If you like to come and go as you please, it might be an idea to rent your own apartment. There are a few really good websites dedicated to renting apartments including: *www.homelidays.com* and *www.italianlife.co.uk.* To weigh up the many options Google your destination, 'appartamento' and 'vacanze', and take your research from there.

Surfing for Rental Cars

Cars from **Avis, Budget, Easy Autos** and **Hertz** (for contact details see Appendix p. 240) can all be booked before you go. Make sure you book a car with enough space and – if you plan a lot of driving – doors (some children hate being trapped in a

3-door car). It's wise to book any child seats or boosters in advance. If you decide to hire these when you arrive, they will be more expensive.

As always, check the car before you drive off if you want to avoid paying for someone else's scratch. If you plan doing a lot of miles, there is a chance that the odd carton of juice may be spilt on the upholstery. If you are taking a break from cleaning up horrible messes, contact a car valeting service. Hotel receptions and petrol stations can find you the nearest one: just point at the spillages and throw *macchina* and *pulizia* at them, or tell them that you're looking for someone to clean your car: *Cerco qualcuno per pulire la mia macchina per favore.*

21st-Century Traveller

Without Your Own Computer

Naples and the surrounding hotspots have a pretty decent number of Internet cafes these days. However, in rural areas you might find it hard to find anywhere to log on. Under Italian anti-terrorism laws, every Internet cafe must photocopy the passport of non-Italian nationals and log your usage, so come prepared.

With Your Own Computer

WiFi (Wireless Fidelity) is increasingly available in Naples itself. If it's not available in your hotel, they may have dataports for laptop modems. Failing that, most will have a couple of computers with Internet connections for guests' use. You might find a global WiFi hotspot locator like JiWire (*www.jiwire.com*) useful.

Remember to bring a connection kit with the right power and phone adapters, a spare phone cord and a spare Ethernet cable. The electric current in Italy is 220V, 50Hz. Some older hotels may still use 125V. Italians use power sockets with two or three holes, and these do not have their own switches. Make sure you take plug adapters with you.

Using a Mobile Phone

Most UK and Irish mobiles are GSM world-capable multiband (Sony Ericsson, Motorola and Samsung models are), so you can make and receive calls across much of the globe. Call your network provider and ask for "international roaming" to be activated. Unfortunately, per-minute charges can be high – usually £1–1.50 in mainland Europe.

There is a cheaper (albeit bureaucratic) way of making mobile calls when you're over there. If you have an "unlocked" GSM phone, you can take out your Sim card and buy a new Italian one for about 15€ (show your phone to the salesperson; not all phones work on all networks). You will have to display your passport and fill in a form, but your Italian number will have much lower calling charges. To unlock a locked phone, just call your mobile provider and tell them you are going abroad for several months and want to use your phone with a local provider. The main networks in Italy are TIM, Vodafone, Wind and 3. These have stores in most major towns. An alternative is to pick up a Sim card for use in Italy (£30) before you go from providers like *www.0044.co.uk*.

GETTING THERE

Before opting for the aerial route or taking a vehicle, you might want to explore the greener option...

By Train Go green, take the train! It may sound like a slog and can be pricey but by taking the train, you could stop at places of interest on the way. For example, take the Eurostar from St Pancras to Paris Nord and enjoy a few days in France (Euro Disney anyone?) before catching the Sleeper from Paris Bercy to Milan or even Rome. A less green option might involve using up some carbon and booking a swifter flight home. For more info check out: *www.raileurope. co.uk* and see **Responsible Tourism** in the Appendix.

Italy's nationally owned train network is comfortable, regular and reliable. It's also incredibly good value. For example you'll pay about 12€ for a journey between Naples and Salerno.

If you are intending to use the train, before you leave for Italy visit the Trenitalia website (*www.trenitalia.com*) or the new version for English speakers (*www.italiarail.co.uk*), to check routes, timetables and fares.

There is little difference between first and second class, the only real benefit being more space if you're travelling overnight. If you avoid rush hours you are sure to get a seat. However, on the faster routes between cities, you will need to book a seat to ensure you are all together. *La Ferrovia Italiana* has quite a few different types of train:

ES (Eurostar) are fast trains connecting major Italian cities.

EN (Euronotte) are the overnight version of these, with sleeping cars or couchettes.

EC (Eurocity) are high-speed international trains connecting main European and Italian cities.

IC (Intercity) trains are similar to *Eurocity* trains, in that they offer both first- and second-class travel and require a supplement, but they never cross an international border.

E (Espressi) stop at all major and most secondary stations.

IR (Interregionale) make more stops than the *Espressi*.

R (Regionale) stay within a region (e.g. Campania) and stop at every station.

A D (Diretto) not what they sound like – they stop at virtually every station.

L (Locale) stop at every small station, and sometimes just stop!

When buying a regular ticket, ask for either **andata** (one-way) or **andata e ritorno** (round-trip). If the train you plan to take is an ES/EC or IC, ask for the ticket *con supplemento rapido* (with speed supplement) to avoid onboard penalty charges.

Most importantly, **stamp your ticket in the little yellow box** on the platform before you board. It is not unheard of for tourists to get a hard time from guards for unstamped tickets.

Children under 12 always travel half-price, and those under 4 travel free. If you are under 26, you can buy a 26€ **Carta Verde** (Green Card) at any Italian train station. This gets you a 15% discount on all FS (State Railway) tickets for 1 year. Over-60s can get discounts by buying a **Carta d'Argento** (Silver Card).

The **Trenitalia Pass** is similar to the Eurail pass, in that you have 2 months in which to use the train on a set number of days. The base number of days is 4, and you can add up to 6 more. For example, for adults, the first-class pass for 4 days costs £151 and £75 for a child; the second-class version is £112 for adults and £56 for a child.

You can get different deals or buy extra days and get savings if two adults travel together. You must buy this before you go to Italy: contact **Rail Europe** *www. raileurope.co.uk*).

When you get to Italy, you can make use of Trenitalia's offer for family groups made up of 3–5 people (where there is at least 1 adult and 1 child under 12). This can be used on all trains and allows a discount of 20% (for adults) and 50% (for children) from the standard fare. Book as far ahead as possible as these fares are subject to availability.

Timetables for all routes are displayed on posters in stations. Useful schedules for all train lines are printed biannually in booklets available at any news-stand. You can also get official schedules (and more train infor-mation, some even in English) on the web (see *www.trenitalia. com*).

Stations tend to be well-run and clean, with luggage storage facilities at all but the smallest and usually a good bar with surprisingly palatable food. *Binario* means platform. If you pull into a small town with a shed-sized or non-existent sta-tion, find the nearest bar or *tabacchi* to buy your tickets and ask for information.

> **INSIDER TIP**
> Do not leave buying train tickets to the last minute. Queues are long. Tellers take ages. Trains get missed. Tears and tantrums ensue.

By Plane The most convenient airport for access to the Naples area is **Aeroporto Internazionale di Napoli** (or Capodichino to the locals) (✆ 081 789 6259; *www. gesac.it*), which is about 4 miles (7km) from the centre of Naples. There are buses to Naples and to Sorrento from here. Check at the information desk about standard cab fare prices to your destination and agree a fare before getting in the taxi.

There are a number of well-served airports in Italy, including Rome and Bari in the south, with UK/Irish flight connections – so you could fly to one of these and perhaps take a domestic connect-ing flight to Naples, hire a car or take the train –this journey option is bound to be gruelling though!

The principal airlines flying to Italy from the UK and Ireland are: Al Italia (UK ✆ 0870 544 8259/Ireland ✆ 01 677 5171; *www. alitalia.co.uk*); Aer Lingus (Eire ✆ 0818 365000/ UK ✆ 0870 876 5000; *http://www.aerlingus.com/*); British Airways (✆ 0870 850 9850; *www.britishairways.com*); Flybmi (✆ 0870 6070 555/ 01332 64 8181; *www.flybmi.com*); easyJet (✆ 0905 821 0905; *www.easyjet.com*); Jet2 (✆ UK 0871 226 1737/ Ireland ✆ 0818 200 017; *www.jet2.com*).

Top Tips for Flying with Children

If your youngsters have never flown before or were just babies when they did, it might be an idea to introduce them to things they will come across – such as

Shopping at the Airport

Your holiday is over, you've had a great time but, horror of horrors, you've forgotten to buy grandma a present! What can you buy in Naples airport?

- Typical local and Italian delicacies, oils and vinegar.
- Perfumes from Capri.
- Naplesmania gifts with funny Neapolitan sayings (in the main concourse).
- Italian books and newspapers.
- Chocolates and sweets.
- Local and Italian wine and spirits.

Most of these are available in the shops in the departure lounge, which means you can buy them once you've been through security. However, if you have room in your case, much of this can be bought more cheaply in the supermercati. Get yourself some bubble wrap and fill your hold luggage with goodies; anything bought and taken as hand luggage will be seized.

checking in, going though security, the safety talk and dealing with a bumpy ride – by playing 'let's go to the airport'. *www. TravellingWithChildren.co.uk* has lots of useful travel ideas and products.

Use your own methods of persuasion to let them know that they must be on their best behaviour on the plane.

Check with the airline to see if they provide **bolsters or car seats** for under-2s. Some also provide special seatbelts.

Make sure everyone has been to the toilet just before boarding. Always accompany younger children to the toilet onboard.

Read the laminated safety card and know where the exits are. Ditto the lifejackets and oxygen masks.

There are pros (more legroom) and cons (no baggage during take-off and landing) to booking a row where the emergency exits are.

Be sure to pack **water, snacks and a few toys** for your children in your carry-on luggage. See 'Packing for Planes & Cars', p. 21.

Make sure your child's **seatbelt remains fastened** properly: turbulence can happen at any time.

Seat your child by the window or between two parents; it is harder for them to wander off.

When you board, ask a flight attendant if it is possible that your **children are served their meal first**, especially if they are very young or seated at the back of the plane.

Yes, some folk are just grumpy when it comes to young children, but if you have a particularly boisterous or restless child, do bear in mind other passengers' comfort. Watch out for your child constantly kicking the back of someone's seat. Keep international relations cordial by stopping it and apologising.

Getting Through the Airport

The golden rule for happy check-in is 1 hour before a domestic flight and 2 hours before an international one. It's always better to leave plenty of time when travelling with children, and be aware that security checks take a while. If you are running late, phone the airline (take a note of the local number before leaving). If you turn up late, don't just join a queue: let the airline staff know and give them as great a chance as possible to get you on the plane.

Make one person responsible for keeping the tickets and passports.

Different airlines offer different check-in arrangements, particularly for those carrying just hand luggage.

Make sure you have checked what you can carry on and what you can't. The terrorist threat in the UK has meant that government regulations are liable to change depending on the level of threat. Recent rule changes have involved the carrying of liquids on planes. At the very least, don't pack anything sharp or even thin and made of metal. It's also worth knowing that Italian security won't let you board with cigarette lighters on the way back.

As for cabin baggage, most airlines have agreed to one bag sized 56cm x 45cm x 25cm and one briefcase, laptop bag or equivalent. However, there may be tougher regulations in force at the time of flying.

By Car Italy is best explored by car, but you'll need to be unflappable to cope with Italian driving, some of which is downright dangerous. Driving around Naples can feel as chaotic as a bumper car ride. Everyone seems to beep their horn –each klaxon is more of an involuntary action that can be translated as "I'm here –careful!" rather than the aggressive "Oi! Get out of it!" of the Anglo-Saxon nations. Car theft is also a big problem in the region. You should consider using public transport over a car, unless you are planning to visit some of Campania's mountainous corners.

Hiring a Car

Remember your driving licence. You must have had a full licence (i.e. passed your driving test) for two years. When booking or picking up you'll also need your passport and a credit card (this will save you making a hefty deposit). Insurance on all vehicles is compulsory; though check the excess and what is not covered.

Driving Rules

Italians drive on the right-hand side of the road. If a car comes up behind you and flashes its lights, that's the signal for you to let it pass. Stay in the right lane on highways; the left is only for passing or those in a hurry.

Autostrade are superhighways, denoted by green signs and a number prefaced with an "A", like the A1 from Naples to Milan. Those not numbered are called *raccordo,* a connecting road between two cities. On longer stretches, *autostrade* often become toll roads. *Strade statale* are state roads, usually two lanes wide and indicated by blue signs. Their route numbers are prefaced with an SS or an S, but like the *autostrade*, they don't always have numbers; you'll just see blue signs listing destinations by name.

Signage on roads, particularly minor ones, is dismal, with little or no warning for smaller towns. It is also inconsistent, sometimes listing everything within a 50-mile radius, sometimes forgetting to mention a turnoff. Get a good map (the spiral-bound *Michelin Italy Tourist and Motoring Atlas* is good).

INSIDER TIP »

The best thing about the *autostrade* is the **Autogrill** service station. If you're expecting an Italian version of stewed tea, all-day-grease-on-a-plate and damp sandwiches, you are about to be stunned. Autogrill is irrefutable proof that culinary standards need not plunge just because you're beside a motorway. They are superb: freshly made pizzas, well-filled *panini* and chunky salads at reasonable prices; shops selling deli-foods; and toilets that are pleasant to use.

Taking Care & Precautions

Always tuck in your mirror after parking to make sure it's not missing when you return. Avoid leaving valuables in the car even in remote places. The lure of a romantic and dramatic drive along the Amalfi Coast shouldn't blind you to the fact that many stretches are narrow, you will require Formula-One standard reflexes at times and traffic is constant at busy times.

Driving Rules & Regulations

Drink Driving The permitted UK level of alcohol is 0.8mg of alcohol per ml; in Italy it's 0.5mg. Don't risk it: imprisonment is a regular punishment.

Fines Where it's a minor contravention, these are on the spot. Make sure you get a receipt!

Fuel Unleaded petrol is called *benzina*; diesel is called *gasolio*. Make sure you put in the right one. Almost all stations are closed on Sundays, but many will have a pump fitted with a machine that accepts bills and credit cards.

Seat Belts These are **compulsory.** Children under 4 must have a suitable seat or bolster, whilst those between 4 and 12 cannot travel in the front unless suitably restrained (exactly how depends on the size of your child).

Speed Limits Motorway: 80mph (130kph); dual carriageway: 68mph (110kph); open

Parking

To park your car either find a *parcheggio* (car park) or park on the street. White lines indicate free public spaces and blue lines paying public spaces, usually marked by a *pagamento a sosta* (pay to park) sign. Find a meter, punch in how long you want to park for, then stick the ticket somewhere visible. If you park in an area marked *parcheggio disco orario*, look for the cardboard parking disc in your hire car's glove compartment (or buy one at a petrol station). Here you just dial up the hour of your arrival and display it on the dashboard. You're allowed *un ora* (1 hour) or *due ore* (2 hours) of free parking depending on the sign. **Car parks** have ticket dispensers and/or manned booths. You pick up your ticket as you drive in, and pay at the booth or automated machine as you leave.

space: 56mph (90kph); town: 31mph (50kph)

Visibility Vests Along with warning triangles, these are usually in the boot of hire cars, but check before driving off. If you break down on the motorway or dual carriageway, you cannot get out of your car unless you have a visibility vest. You will be fined if you fail to wear one.

Warning Triangle These are also compulsory and must be erected just up the road from where you have stopped. Remember, if you're travelling through France on the way to Italy you are required to display a GB sticker and have headlamp deflectors fitted. Carrying spare headlamp bulbs is strongly advised.

Road Signs

Speed limit a black number inside a red circle on a white background.

End of a speed zone black and white, with a black slash through the number.

Yield to oncoming traffic a red circle with a white background, a black arrow pointing down, and a red arrow pointing up.

Yield ahead a point-down red-and-white triangle.

Pedestrian zone in town, a simple white circle with a red border or the words *zona pedonale* or *zona traffico limitato*. You can drop someone off, however.

One-way streets a white arrow on a blue background. Also the sign *senso unico*.

No entry a red circle with a horizontal white slash.

Not allowed like the UK, any image in black on a white background surrounded by a red circle indicates you can't do it.

No parking a circular sign with a red circle and slash.

By Bus Regional buses are called *pullman,* though *autobus,* the term for a city bus, is also sometimes used. It's not easy getting hold of an oft-free *orario* timetable for local buses, but ask in the tourist office or the *tabacchi* nearest your stop. A town's bus stop is usually either the main piazza or on the outskirts. The nearest newsstand or *tabacchi*, or sometimes a bar, will sell you tickets. Remember to stamp these using the machine on the bus.

By Boat Naples is a fine seafaring nation, which is handy as that's the only way to get to the islands of Capri, Ischia and Procida (unless you are Naomi Campbell and go by helicopter). From February 2008 the ferry operators have been using the **Porta di Massa** dock, leaving **Molo Beverello** and **Mergellina** to handle the faster hydrofoils. For example, the large ferries (*navi*) that operate out of Porta di Massa take about 80 minutes to reach the Marina Grande, the main port in Capri. TMVs or *Traghetti Veloci* (fast ferries) take about 50 minutes, while the *aliscafi* (hyfrofoils) take about 35 minutes. During the *Stagione Alta* (high season) one-way adult prices to Capri are around: 6€ for the ferry, 11€ for the fast ferry and 17€ for the hydrofoil. Most of the carriers offer child discounts (under 5s often go free if they don't take up a seat and under 13s travel for about two-thirds of the adult fare) – ask for a *"sconto per bambini"*.

Some of the carriers offer discounts for return tickets (*andata e ritorno*). Check the back pages of the free bimonthly *Qui Napoli* tourist booklet or the local paper, *il Mattino* for the latest seasonal timetables.

> **INSIDER TIP** »
>
> Molo Beverello can get very busy in the summer and there can be quite a few dodgy characters hanging around so be especially careful with your valuables here. For a less stressful and potentially more enjoyable voyage it's best to use Mergellina, along Via Francesco Caracciolo.

By Taxi Beware Neapolitan taxi drivers. Like the UK, licensed taxis have regulations. Unlike the UK, many drivers pay little regard to them. If you find a great taxi driver, tip him well. It helps if you have an idea about what sort of fare to expect before you climb in. At an airport, ask at the information desk how much your journey is likely to cost. A rough figure can be helpful when faced with a brazen driver who insists on three times the price. To help you out, here are five golden rules:

- **Always** ask how much the fare is likely to be or fix a price before setting off.

- **Always** check the meter is on.

- **Always** ask to see the laminated price list for supplements (extra people, baggage, after midnight, weekend/holiday

TIP ›› **Top Tip for Island Hoppers** ‹‹

Do not presume you can easily hop from island to island. Such services exist in high season but are infrequent. Check the timetables to see if this can be done, but there is a chance you will have to take a detour via Naples, particularly if you are visiting out of season.

rates, etc.). There is still a chance you might get ripped off, but letting them see you're on the ball can help.

- **Always** try to carry smaller denomination notes. Sometimes the cheekier chancers supposedly have "no change".

- **Always** be prepared to stand your ground. Some taxi drivers just like to see how much nonsense they can get away with. You'll know you've 'won' when they matter-of-factly shrug their shoulders and smile.

Only in the bigger cities can you hail a cab – elsewhere find a taxi rank or call one. Information is provided in the relevant chapters.

TIPS ON EATING OUT

You'll start the day with **colazione**, or breakfast. This is usually orange juice and croissants (*cornetti*) filled with marmalade, chocolate or custard (*crema*), all washed down with milky caffè latte or cappuccino. Supposedly it's just not form to drink either of these after midday but, you're in Italy, so make like the Italians and ignore the rules if you feel like it. You often

get cold meats and cheeses at the breakfast buffet, which can be tucked into a brioche, wrapped in a napkin and smuggled out of the breakfast room for later.

If you stand at a bar – *al banco* – you'll be charged the minimum for your drinks, ice cream or *panini*. If you sit down, you incur a cover charge and heftier prices for exactly the same food. Sit outside the bar and you pay even more. A simple *panino* (flattened, toasted bread with a cheese, ham or vegetable filling) can cost anything from 1.50€ to 5€.

Pizza will be the thing your children most remember about their trip. If you want to sit down and pay a bit extra, a **pizzeria** will prepare your favourite toppings. Check to see it has a wood-burning oven if you want something close to the original Neapolitan. A **rosticceria** is the same type of place with chickens roasting on a spit in the window.

Pranzo (lunch) or **cena** (dinner) consists of **antipasti** (appetizers), **primo** (first course) of pasta, soup or risotto, and **secondo** (second course) of meat or fish, possibly accompanied by a **contorno** (side dish) of veggies, finished off with **dolce** (dessert) and a **caffè** (espresso coffee).

Handy Phrases for the Bus

I'd like to find out about the bus timetable please. **Vorrei sapere gli orari del Pullman per favour.** *Voh-ray sa-peh-reh yee o-rah-ree dehl pool-man pehr-fah-vor-eh.*

I'm getting off at Mergellina. **Scendo a Mergellina.** Shehn-doh a *Mehr-jeh-lee-nah*

Can you let me know when we approach Mergellina please? **Mi fa sapere quando si avvicina a Mergellina per favore?** *Mee fay sa-peh-reh kwan-doh see a-vee-che-na a Mehr-jeh-lee-nah pehr fah-vor-eh?*

It's the next stop/ Is it the next stop? **E` la prossima fermata (?)***Eh la pross-ee-mah fehr-mah-ta?*

May I please get off? **Posso scendere?** *Poh-ss-oh sh-ehn-deh-reh?*

Are these places free? **Sono liberi questi posti?** *So-no lee-beh-ree kweh-stee poh-stee?*

Don't feel compelled to order every course: *primo* and *dolce* will suffice for most children – and adults. Menus often have English subtitles, but if not don't be afraid to ask. Children's menus are not that common but easy enough to construct yourself. Vegetarians will find lots of options from the many *contorni* (side dishes) available. Some *agriturismi* and a growing number of restaurants specialise in serving only organic produce.

A word of warning: the **pane e coperto** is a bread and cover charge of anywhere from 50¢ to 8€ that you pay for the privilege of sitting at the table, even at a bar. To request the bill, say *"Il conto, per favore"* (eel con-to pehr fah-vor-eh). A tip of 15% is usually included these days, but if unsure ask *"è incluso il servizio?"* (ay een-cloo-soh eel sair-vee-tsee-oh?).

SUGGESTED ITINERARIES: THE AMALFI COAST & BAY OF NAPLES IN 1 & 2 WEEKS

These journeys are designed to give you an idea of what you could do and may not be suited to everyone. Families with toddlers will no doubt prefer a more leisurely itinerary, while the adventurous or energetic could cover different ground. For example, if your family digs the ancient sites, you may want to include a trip to the Greek temples at Paestum. These tours are best done using public transport and include lots of fun boat trips. So gather the family around, get yourself a large map of Campania like the Touring Club Italiano version, delve into this book and plan a route to suit your family's needs.

1 Week Itinerary

Day 1: The Amalfi Coast

Fly into Capodichino Airport and head straight to your chosen resort on the Amalfi Coast.

Days 2 & 3: The Amalfi Coast

Explore the stunning coastline by car or bus, including Positano, Amalfi and Ravello.

Day 4: Sorrento & Pompeii/ Herculaneum

Travel along the coast to Sorrento for some shopping and lunch, and then it's onto Pompeii for a look around the Roman remains before dusk. If you have younger children, Herculaneum is a better bet as it's on a smaller scale. If you love Pompeii you'll be even more impressed with Herculaneum.

Day 5: Naples

The old city may be chaotic but it sure is an exhilarating place to visit and is full of character. Visit the Spaccanapoli district and the Archaeological Museum before heading up to the Museo di Capodimonte, where you can take a breather in the park there. Pick a pizzeria and sample the original and best *pizza napoletana*.

Days 6 & 7: Capri

Take the quick hydrofoil from Mergellina or the scenic ferry trip from Porta di Massa to Capri. Take a boat tour of the island, swim in the azure waters, then take the funicular up to Monte Solaro in the evening before dining in Anacapri.

2 Week Itinerary

Follow the week-long itinerary, spending another night on Capri before heading to Ischia...

Days 8 & 9: Ischia

Take the boat to Ischia from Capri's Marina Grande. Check

Piatti Tipici: Neapolitan Dishes for You & Your Children to Try

Pizza Margherita – the classic Neapolitan pizza is cooked in a wood-fired oven and has a thin, crusty yet moist base, topped with pools of buffalo mozzarella, flavoursome tomatoes and fresh basil.

Fritto misto di mare – the catch of the day (could be small fish, squid, prawns) dipped in flour and deep fried for a few seconds, and served with lemon wedges for that zesty squeeze.

Bucatini alla napoletana – the long chunky pasta with a hole through it is a favourite in Naples and is typically served with a tomato and chilli sauce.

Sfogliatelle – this shell-shaped pastry has many thin crunchy pastry leaves surrounding a sweet filling.

into a family-friendly hotel, then enjoy some seaside fun, visit the island's sites (including Mont Epomeo if you are feeling fit) and eat seafood pizza or local speciality rabbit in the evenings at one of the fab eateries.

Day 10: Procida

Explore this unspoilt island on foot and/or by boat, play on the golden beaches, then enjoy a meal in one of the cater-for-everyone restaurants here.

Day 11: Pozzuoli & the Fiery Fields

Dip into the antiquities of this fascinating area with its mythical sights and volcanic geography. Fire the imaginations of your youngsters with tales of gladiators' heroics in the Roman amphitheatre, the underground world of the Parco Archeologico Subacqueo di Baia and the legend of the Sybil at Cuma. Don't miss seeing the earth huff and puff at the fumaroles of Solfatara.

Day 12: Caserta

The magnificent Bourbon-built Palazzo Reale has lavish salons and extensive grounds with ornate fountains reminiscent of Versailles. And there's plenty of space for children to run around

Days 13 &14: Naples

Head back to Naples to visit more of the city's wonderful sights and to do some shopping.

Make sure you have a meal by the harbour at Castel dell'Ovo or pizza along Mergellina before going home.

GETTING CHILDREN INTERESTED IN THE AMALFI COAST & BAY OF NAPLES

Get the youngsters excited about the trip by watching a few films and suggesting some books to read.

Books *The Adventures of Pinocchio* by Carlo Collodi is a great read for small children. *Tony's Bread* by Tomie dePaola is a sweet tale for littl'uns. *Pompeii...buried alive* by Edith Kunhradt is an account of the AD79 eruption, for early readers. *The Mysteries of Vesuvius* by Caroline Lawrence will fire young imaginations. *Vesuvius Poovius* by Kes Gray is a funny tale about ancient Roman poo.

Films Classic Italian films are a good place to start: *Cinema Paradiso* (the shorter version is the child-friendly one), *Life is Beautiful* and *Pinocchio*.

Music Those who like their holidays to have a soundtrack will love or hate Italian pop: always a winner for a sing-along in the car. You can tune in to a multitude of cheesy radio stations or pick up great-value CDs of Italian hits and Neapolitan songs at any Autogrill motorway services. Fnac, a French shop, similar to Virgin Megastore (Via Luca

Ristoranti, Trattorie, Osterie... What's the Difference?

The boundaries between the different types of eatery may have blurred in recent times, but in general **un ristorante** is the most sophisticated and formal, having a printed menu and wine list. A **trattoria** is a more homely establishment serving fewer dishes, often without a written menu, and the service is less polished. An **osteria** (or Hostaria) is a tavern that serves a limited choice of hearty dishes often in rustic, relaxed surroundings; the meals of the day are displayed on a blackboard. In recent years a new breed of urban wine bar, the **enoteca** has sprung up, offering wine by the glass accompanied by cheese and cold-cut platters, as well as small tapas-like dishes. **Pizzerie** serve pizzas, but increasingly they have other dishes. A **tavola calda** (meaning hot table) is usually a place where you eat standing up and a **rosticceria** has roasted meats and veggies for people in a hurry. A **paninoteca** sells panini and other snacks and a **pasticceria** is a pastry shop that often also has a selection of hot and cold drinks. Italians pop into **un bar** for a quick espresso or cappuccino and sweet pastry in the mornings, and later on for more espressi or a snifter perhaps. **Un caffè** is usually a little more sophisticated, having waiter service as well as tables inside and out.

Giordano 59. ☎ *081 220 1000*. Metro: Piazza Vanvitelli) is the best place to find music. Morricone's soundtracks for the Sergio Leone Spaghetti Westerns are perfect for epic Amalfi Coast drives: children whistling along to *The Good, the Bad and the Ugly* will thank you in years to come. Older teens and parents into music may want to explore Naples's rich musical tradition: including the opera of Enrico Caruso, Pino Daniele's blues (*Tra Music e Magia* collects his best early work) and Almamegretta's trip-hop (the *Sanacore* album was mixed by Adrian Sherwood and they often collaborate with Massive Attack). For classic *piano bar* tunes check out legendary Neapolitan crooner Luciano

Bruno (*www.lucianobruno. com.br*) on the Brazilian Som Livre label.

TV Fans of *Doctor Who* will love the episode 'Fires of Pompeii', when he and Donna travel back in time to the day before the catastrophic eruption.

FAST FACTS

Alcohol There is no minimum age for drinking in Italy. However, unlike our great nation with its strict licensing system, you will hardly see anyone drunk. There are no restrictions on what time you can purchase alcohol in shops either.

Babysitting. The Italian website *www.bambinopoli.it* has a list of babysitters (in Italian only).

Banks Banking hours are normally Monday to Friday mornings from 8.30am to 1pm and for an hour in the afternoon, usually 3 to 4pm. Also see 'ATMs,' p. 15.

Breastfeeding Breastfeeding in public is acceptable but you may get some looks. You are best advised to find an out-of-the-way spot.

Buggies & Wheelchairs
Campania is mountainous so some effort is needed to get around with non-motorized wheels. Some churches and sights are easier to access these days, although the uneven terrain of the archaeological sites make them tough to get around. Also see 'Disabled Travellers,' p. 23.

Business Hours Regular hours are 9am–1pm and 4–7.30pm, or thereabouts. Those who like a little lunchtime shopping will struggle with this.

Car Rental See 'Getting Around', p. 28, 33.

Chemists A chemist (or drugstore in American) is called a *farmacia*. Your hotel will be able to tell you where you can find one and give you the lowdown on out-of-hours opening.

Climate See 'When to Go', p. 17.

Currency The euro. See 'Money', p. 15.

Driving Rules See 'Getting Around', p. 34.

Electricity Like other European countries, Italy uses 220V, 50Hz. Some older hotels may still use 125V. Power sockets have two or three holes and do not have their own switches. Buy an adaptor at home.

Embassies & Consulates The following are in Naples:
British Consulate at via Crispi 122 (℡ *081 663 511*)
Canadian Consulate at Via Carducci 29 (℡ *081 401 338*)
US Consulate at Piazza della Repubblica 2 (℡ *081 583 8111*)
Irish citizens can contact the **Irish Embassy** in Rome at Piazza di Campitelli 3 (℡ *06 697 9121* or the **Irish Consulate** is in Milan at Piazza S. Pietro in Gessate 2 (℡ *02 5518 8848*
Milan is home to the following:
Australian Consulate at Via Borgogna 2 (℡ *02 777 041*)
New Zealand Consulate at Via Arezzo 6 (℡ *02 4801 2544*).

Emergency Numbers
℡ *113* Police
℡ *112* *Carabinieri* (also deal with crimes)
℡ *115* Fire department
℡ *118* Medical emergency

Internet Access It's easy enough to find an Internet café in cities and major towns. Remember to take your passport to ensure you comply with Italian regulations (see p. 28). WiFi isn't quite as widespread as at home, but you'll find a hotspot in most large towns. See also '21st-Century Traveller,' p. 28.

Language English is widely spoken, but where's the fun in that? Marlon Lodge's *Rapid Italian: 200+ Essential Words and Phrases Anchored into Your Long Term Memory with Great Music* (available in audio book or audio CD) is a fun way to learn and, more importantly, have the confidence to speak. If you're really keen, get a copy of *Basic Italian Grammar* by C. A. McCormick. See the Appendix for a glossary of useful words and phrases, p. 230.

Legal Assistance The Italian section on the British Embassy website (**www.britishembassy. gov.uk**) has a list of lawyers, under 'When things go wrong'. Your travel insurance company can also advise on how to get help.

Maps Most car hire companies will furnish you with a decent map of the region, but for more detail and smaller roads (the ones where you are more likely to get lost), get an AA or Michelin map. These cost around 8€ for a fold-up one or 18€ for the hardcover version, and are widely available. See '21st-Century Traveller,' p. 28.

Newspapers & Magazines If it's British newspapers you're after, they don't reach Italian newsstands until the next day. However, yesterday's *Guardian*, *Times*, *Financial Times*, *Mail* and *Mirror* are readily available. Italy doesn't have tabloids, only broadsheet-style dailies like *La Repubblica*, *Corriere della Sera*

and *La Stampa*. *Il Mattino* is the local choice of many Neapolitans and is great for useful info like boat timetables and entertainment listings. There are celebrity-obsessed glossies like *Gente* and reportage-style mags like *Espresso*. Sports fans should check out *Gazzetta dello Sport* and *Corriere dello Sport*.

Passports See 'Entry Requirements & Customs', p. 14.

Post It costs 65¢ to send a postcard (or anything up to 20g) home by *posta prioritaria*. Stamps can be bought in *tabbachi*, some shops, post offices and some hotels.

Radio Italian radio stations all seem to offer generic Europop with a smattering of cheese. Teens might like to tune into Radio Kiss Kiss (**www.kisskiss.it**) at 97–105 MHz on the FM dial.

Registering with the Police Legally, you are required to register with the police within three days of entering the country. However, if you are staying at a hotel, they will do this for you (that's why they take your passports): the police don't pay much attention to this if you're an EU citizen.

Safety & Security Acts of random violence are not as prevalent as in Britain, but Italy, and the city of Naples in particular, is notorious for petty theft, especially pick-pocketing and opportunist snatching. Use a money belt to keep your family's valuable documents in and do not display jewellery or fancy gadgets. Beggars can be insistent – so we always respond strongly with a "no grazie!" if needs be. Anarchic Naples is a nightmare to drive around so you are advised to avoid it. Traffic lights are largely ignored, so crossing the road can take some time. Hold hands and stay very alert. Also see 'Staying Safe,' p. 24.

Smoking Smoking in public places including bars, restaurants, discotheques and offices is banned.

Telephones Public telephones are plentiful and have instructions in English. Calling from your hotel room or from your own mobile can be very expensive, so it will save you money to go out to make that call. If you can't find a phone box, some cafes and bars have a red phone symbol, which means they have a public telephone.

To call an Italian number from the UK: first dial ☎ 00; then ☎ 39; the Italian number. For example, if you wanted to call the Naples tourist office you would dial ☎ 00 39 081 2400914.

To call home from Italy: first dial ☎ 00; and then the country code (UK ☎ 44, Ireland ☎ 353); then the area code (dropping the 0 it begins with); then the number. For example, if you wanted to call British Airways customer services you would dial ☎ 00 44 191 490 7901.

For directory assistance: dial ☎ 12 if you're looking for a number within Italy, dial ☎ 176 for numbers in Europe and

☎ 1790 for numbers outside Europe.

For operator assistance: if you need operator assistance to make a call, dial ☎ 172 0044 to reach BT in the UK or ☎ 172 0353 for Ireland.

For information about mobile phones, see p. 29.

Telephone Cards If you're not taking a mobile phone, buy a *carta telefonica* from a tobacconist for use in public phones. They come in a number of denominations and are easy to use.

Time Zone GMT+1 hour in winter; BST+1 hour in summer.

Tipping Check to see if service is included in the bill. Otherwise 10–15% is the norm. Don't tip bad service but let them know why you aren't.

Toilets & Baby-changing Facilities There are few public toilets, so you're best off making a small purchase at a bar or café and using theirs. Museums and galleries often have toilets, but baby-changing facilities are few and far between. Large bars may only have a fold-down changing table, so carry a changing mat with you.

Water Nobody in Italy drinks tap water, even though it's perfectly safe. Still water is *acqua senza gaz* or *naturale*, whereas sparkling water is *acqua frizzante*. To convert your water bottle straight to baby's drinking water, buy a water bottle teat before you leave *www.babysportonline.eu*.

3 Naples: the City

NAPLES

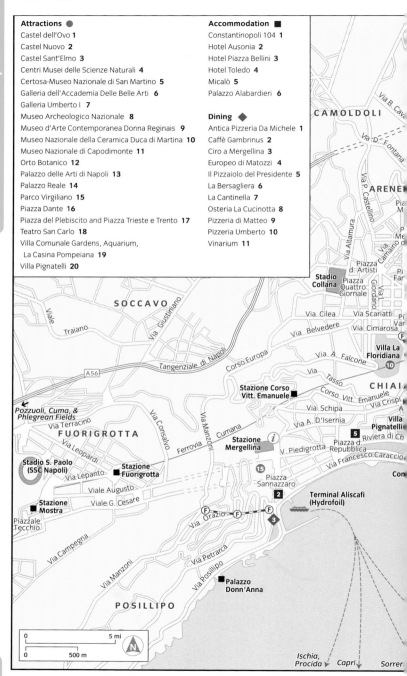

Attractions ●
Castel dell'Ovo **1**
Castel Nuovo **2**
Castel Sant'Elmo **3**
Centri Musei delle Scienze Naturali **4**
Certosa-Museo Nazionale di San Martino **5**
Galleria dell'Accademia Delle Belle Arti **6**
Galleria Umberto I **7**
Museo Archeologico Nazionale **8**
Museo d'Arte Contemporanea Donna Reginais **9**
Museo Nazionale della Ceramica Duca di Martina **10**
Museo Nazionale di Capodimonte **11**
Orto Botanico **12**
Palazzo delle Arti di Napoli **13**
Palazzo Reale **14**
Parco Virgiliano **15**
Piazza Dante **16**
Piazza del Plebiscito and Piazza Trieste e Trento **17**
Teatro San Carlo **18**
Villa Comunale Gardens, Aquarium,
  La Casina Pompeiana **19**
Villa Pignatelli **20**

Accommodation ■
Constantinopoli 104 **1**
Hotel Ausonia **2**
Hotel Piazza Bellini **3**
Hotel Toledo **4**
Micalò **5**
Palazzo Alabardieri **6**

Dining ◆
Antica Pizzeria Da Michele **1**
Caffè Gambrinus **2**
Ciro a Mergellina **3**
Europeo di Matozzi **4**
Il Pizzaiolo del Presidente **5**
La Bersagliera **6**
La Cantinella **7**
Osteria La Cucinotta **8**
Pizzeria di Matteo **9**
Pizzeria Umberto **10**
Vinarium **11**

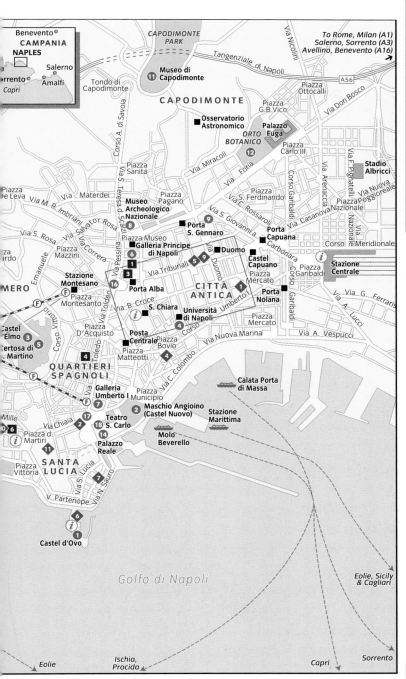

Benevento

CAMPANIA
NAPLES

Salerno

rrento
Capri

Amalfi

CAPODIMONTE
PARK

To Rome, Milan (A1)
Salerno, Sorrento (A3)
Avellino, Benevento (A16) →

Tangenziale di Napoli

A56

11 Museo di
Capodimonte

Via Nicolini

Piazza
Ottocalli

Via Don Bosco

CAPODIMONTE

Tondo di
Capodimonte

Corso A. di Savoia

Via Teresa di Savoia

Observatorio
Astronomico

Piazza
G.B.Vico

ORTO
BOTANICO

12

Palazzo
Fuga

Piazza
Carlo III

Via Arenaccia

Stadio
Albricci

Via F.Pignatelli

Via Miracoli

Piazza
Sanita

Piazza
e Leva

Via M. R. Imbriani

Via Materdei

Via Salvator Rosa

Via S. Rosa

Piazza
Mazzini

Piazza
ardo

Via Correra

Via Foria

Piazza
S. Ferdinando

Via C.Rossaroli

Piazza
Pagano

Via S. Giovanni a

Corso Garibaldi

Piazza
Nazionale

Via Nuova Poggioreale

Via Nuova Nazionale

Museo
Archeologico
Nazionale

8

Piazza Museo
Galleria Principe
di Napoli

6

1
3

Porta
S. Gennaro

9

Via Pessina

Via Tribunali

5 **9**

Duomo

Via Duomo

Carbonara

Porta
Capuana

Castel
Capuano

Corso Meridionale

MERO

Via Emanuele

Stazione
Montesano

Piazza
Montesanto

16

Porta Alba

S. Chiara

CITTÀ
ANTICA

1

Piazza
Mercato

Via Casanova

Corso Garibaldi

Piazza
Garibaldi

Stazione
Centrale

Via G. Ferraris

Castel
Elmo

3

Certosa di
. Martino

5

Via B. Croce

Via Toledo

Via Vittorio

Corso

Piazza
D'Acquisto

Università
di Napoli

Posta
Centrale

4

Piazza
Matteotti

Piazza
Bovio

Corso Umberto I

Porta
Nolana

Piazza
Mercato

Via A. Lucci

QUARTIERI
SPAGNOLI

Galleria
Umberto I

7

Via C. Colombo

Via Nuova Marina

Via A. Vespucci

Calata Porta
di Massa

Mille

6

Via Chiaia

2

17

Piazza d.
Martiri

11

Teatro
S. Carlo

18

Palazzo
Reale

Piazza
Municipio

Maschio Angioino
(Castel Nuovo)

2

Molo
Beverello

14

Stazione
Marittima

SANTA
LUCIA

Piazza
Vittoria

Via Sta Lucia

Via N.Sauro

7

V. Partenope

6

1

Castel d'Ovo

Golfo di Napoli

Eolie, Sicily
& Cagliari

Eolie

Ischia,
Procida

Capri

Sorrento

Napoli is an unrelenting beast of a city – it's a colourful tangled mess, with skeins of history, fabulous monuments and vibrant streetlife. Founded by Greek colonists, it's older than Rome, displaying layers of history and influences from its many rulers: Greek, Arab, Roman, Spanish, Catalan, Norman and the Napoleonic French have all left their mark over 2,500 years. Once you get over the sensory shock and tune into the eccentric and hectic yet laid-back pace, your family may just fall head over heels in love with this deeply flawed, yet compelling and incomparably beautiful city.

Down in the Città Antica, the sticky granite flagstones of ancient lanes of Spaccanapoli and Via Tribunali buzz with weaving Vespas, serenading street vendors and the clipped vowels of Neapolitan dialect. The Spaccanapoli excites with colour and life. Mouthwatering food smells and a mysterious mix of religious sights abound: the intense Sansavero Chapel and lighter Santa Chiara Cloisters live long in everyone's memory. Slurping ice cream on leafy Piazza Bellini by Greek columns, you can glimpse Roman bricks revealed by the crumbling plaster walls of a gorgeous Renaissance palazzo. Graffiti is scrawled on the statue of Vincenzo Bellini and his operatic heroines. That's Napoli. Beautiful and ugly. Just go with the flow...

Should your family tire of royal palaces, artistic treasures and creepy crypts in the Città Antica, there are wonderful green spaces in lofty Posillipo, Vomero and Capodimonte – the views of the crazy city and beguiling bay from the San Martino charterhouse, Parco Virgiliano belvederes and Capodimonte's former royal hunting grounds are divine. And the Bay of Naples has it all within a train ride, boat trip or helter-skelter drive: stunning islands, dramatic coasts, ancient Roman towns and a mighty volcano currently snoozing in the corner of your eye. Oh and don't forget the cornucopia of yummy pizzas, ice-cream scoops and pastries to coax children along.

ESSENTIALS

Getting There

By Plane Aeroporto Capodichino (📞 *081 789 6259*; *www.gesac.it*) is about 7km (4 miles) from the city centre of Naples. Taxis into the city will set you back about 27€. The latest attempt to curb rip-off drivers involves asking the taxi coordinator to direct you to a company that offers fixed rate fares, such as Consortaxi – ask for '*tariffa fissa*'. This is not always possible in the melee outside the airport, so make sure that you agree a reasonable price before setting off or ensure the driver puts his meter on. Prices start at around 10€.

Alibus (📞 *800 639 525*) runs a shuttle between the arrivals concourse and Piazza Garibaldi near Napoli Centrale train station before going on to Piazza Municipio, handy for Beverello port. The service costs 4€ one way and runs every 20 minutes from the airport (Mon–Fri 6.30am–11:30pm; Sat–Sun 6.30am–11.50pm) and from Piazza Municipio (Mon–Fri 6am–12.12am; Sat–Sun 6am–midnight). The new 3T Tourist Travel Ticket (20€ for three days' travel; *www.unicocampania.it*) is good value as it allows travel on Alibus and public transport throughout the Naples area.

By Train There are frequent train services into the city's main train station of **Napoli Centrale** (Piazza Garibaldi, ☏ 081 554 3188) from many Italian and European towns. Below Napoli Centrale station is the Naples underground (*Metropolitana*) and the Circumvesuviana railway (Corso Garibaldi 387; ☏ 081 772 2444), serving Pompeii, the Sorrento peninsula and the Amalfi Coast, as well as the urban railway line (Cumana and Circumflegrea lines; Piazza Montesanto ☏ 081 551 3328), serving the Campi Flegrei area west of Naples toward Pozzuoli and Cuma.

Stazione Mergellina (☏ 081 761 2102) is northwest of the city centre, on Piazza Piedigrotta. This is ideal for visitors staying in Chiaia and Posillipo.

> **INSIDER TIP** ▷
>
> Napoli Centrale has criminal elements working in and around the station: beware of pickpocketers and unregistered taxi drivers. Official Comune di Napoli (Naples Municipality) taxis are usually painted white and carry an official list of fixed rate fares.

By Boat If you are arriving into the Bay of Naples by sea, chances are you will arrive by cruise ship at Stazione Marittima at Molo Angioino. Regular ferry (*nave*), hydrofoil (*aliscafo*) and catamaran (*catamarano*) services run to and from the islands (see The Islands p. 189–228), while services to and from Sicily, Sardinia and the Aeolian Islands also embark and disembark here at Molo Beverello. Hydrofoils and catamarans are swifter and pricier than ferries. If you have young children, they are comfortable, warm and protected from the elements, whereas huge ferries are fun for older children who can get outside on deck and watch the landscape change as your journey progresses.

A new port terminal at Porta di Massa opened in 2008 to handle most of the ferry services, while nearby Beverello handles the other services including hydrofoils and catamarans.

West of the city along the waterfront, the Mergellina quay has far fewer passengers, so is a more civilised place to catch a hydrofoil to the islands. Watch your valuables as pickpockets operate here.

By Car Naples is notoriously problematic for car drivers: car theft, heavy traffic and manic driving involving lots of weaving and speeding are all common-place. Hotels normally offer parking; check arrangements in advance – although it can be very expensive. Unless you are familiar with the city's one-way system and the maze of narrow back-streets, getting around the city may prove nightmarish – traffic lights and rules are seldom abided by here. South of Rome, approaching Naples on Autostrada 1 (A1 motorway) and then the Tangenziale di Napoli (city ring road), the driving style becomes increasingly more fluid, which takes some getting used to.

There are a number of car parks – the most convenient and central is Parcheggio Buono Molo Beverello (℡ *335 499 658; www.parcheggiobeverello.com*; 6am–9pm daily; 16€ per day for a medium-sized car). You'll find it next to the port and Maschio Angioino castle.

VISITOR INFORMATION

Before you set off, check out the new Easy Napoli website, which has links to relevant tourist websites and a downloadable Family Kit: *www.easynapoli.it.*

Naples Regional Tourist Office Board (APT)
Piazza dei Martiri 58 ℡ *081 410 7211*; *www.inaples.it*)
Open *9am–2pm Mon-Fri.*

More convenient and customer-orientated are the following tourist information points:

Capodichino Airport
℡ *081 780 5761*

Piazza del Gesu Nuovo 7
℡ *081 551 2701*

Open *9am–1.30pm and 2.30–7pm Mon–Sat.*

Piazza Plebiscito
Via San Carlo 9 ℡ *081 402 394*
Open *9am–1.30pm and 2.30–7pm Mon–Sat.*

Stazione Centrale
Piazza Garibaldi ℡ *081 268 799*
Open *9am–7pm Mon–Sat*

Stazione Mergellina
Piazza Piedigrotta 1 ℡ *081 761 2102*
Open *9am–7pm Mon–Sat*

Museo Aperto Napoli (M.A.N.)
Via Pietro Coletta 85 ℡ *081 563 6062*; *www.museopartonapoli. com*; runs guided tours of the Città Antica. Also known as MAN, it claims to be the biggest open-air museum in the world, and hires out audio guides, for 5€, to 81 Neapolitan monuments. It's a great place to gather information and also provides a luggage-deposit service.
Open *10am–3pm daily; closed Wed.* ***Admission*** *Free.*

Orientation

Naples' urban sprawl follows the shore of its famous bay and rises up the hills encircling its western flanks. From west to east, the following districts make up the city:

Posillipo has the cliff-top villas and well-to-do residential areas on the hill behind.

Mergellina is centred around the marina and small hydrofoil port – it's popular with Neapolitan families and loved-up couples who enjoy the waterfront promenade and kitschly lit cafés.

Chiaia has the chic shops west of Piazza della Repubblica. The long Riviera di Chiaia faces the Villa Comunale and gardens, popular with joggers and families, and is home to the antiques market. The backstreets behind have interesting shops, galleries, restaurants and clubs.

Vomero sits high above the teeming city and is predominantly a wealthy residential district with stunning views of the bay. Amid its elegant fin-de-siècle *palazzi* and modern apartment buildings are three family-friendly attractions: the Castel Sant'Elmo (see p. 66), Certosa San Martino (see p. 71) and Villa Floridiana (see p. 73).

Santa Lucia is the old fisherman's quarter immortalised in song. The only remnants of its maritime atmosphere are found in the Borgo Marinari near the Castel dell'Ovo (see p. 64), where attractive restaurants look onto a marina. Fancy, oft-overpriced hotels line the 19th-century Via Partenope promenade, where traffic roars past 24/7.

Città Antica is the heart of the city, on the site of the Greco-Roman city Neapolis. Most of Naples' historical monuments and attractions lie here. Its intricate network of streets extends from Piazza Municipio to the Museo Nazionale (see p. 73) going north and the Castel Capuano in the east. This densely populated area is crammed with historic monuments, bars, restaurants, markets and shops.

Quartieri Spagnoli is the area north of Piazza Plebiscito – the city's main ceremonial square. This tight network of narrow streets once housed Spanish soldiers in tall tenements that go up the hill to the west of Napoli's main shopping street, Via Toledo (or Via Roma as Neapolitans call it).

Capodimonte is a residential neighbourhood up in the hills above the city, home of the fabulous Museo di Capodimonte (see p. 73) and gardens.

Getting Around

By Car Drivers weave in and out and appear reckless but they will give way if you make your intentions known.

On Foot The narrow streets of the Città Antica are best explored on foot as major roads around the ancient centre are choked during morning and evening rush hours. Public transport can be pretty reliable although crowded at peak times. With children it's often far more convenient to take a taxi after a long day's sightseeing when little feet are tired.

INSIDER TIP

Traffic lights are often ignored, so take extreme care when crossing the road with children.

By Public Transport Naples has a comprehensive transport system of buses, trams, funiculars and metro trains. All the transport authorities have websites but lack English-language versions – for up-to-date timetables consult the latest *Qui Napoli* booklet available in tourist offices and at various sights. Tickets for public transport are available from *tabacchi* (tobacconists – look out for the big 'T'), ticket offices, some bars and newsstands. UnicoNapoli travel cards provide unlimited travel in the city and beyond over various timescales: 90 mins for 1€; 24 hours on weekdays for 3€; 24 hours at the weekend for 2.50€; 72 hours throughout the Campania region including the islands; and 72 hours in conjunction with the Artecard for 25€ (see p. 53).

The **Metropolitana** is undergoing redevelopment and the new metro system consists of 10 lines, most of which are still being built. Most visitors will need just the two: Line 1 or *Metro d'Arte* runs from Piazza Dante to Vomero – look out for the contemporary art installations. It will eventually run in a circle between Napoli Centrale train station and Capodichino Airport; Line 2 crosses the city from east to west, linking Pozzuoli to Gianturco.

Naples' **buses and tram services** run from 5am to midnight and are notoriously dirty and frequently overcrowded. There are three colour-coded types: red buses (marked by the letter 'R') are supposedly fast and frequent; orange buses are the most common (both run all over the city); while blue buses serve the outlying areas. Night buses (*linee notturne*) are best avoided altogether.

There are four **funicolari** (cable railways) connecting Naples' hills (Vomero and Posillipo) with downtown areas: **Centrale** links Piazza Fuga in the Vomero and the Via Toledo opposite Galleria Umberto; **Montesanto** runs between Vomero and Montecalvario, near Piazza Dante and the Città Antica; **Chiaia** connects Parco Margherita and Cimarosa in the Vomero; and **Mergellina** runs between the waterfront near the hydrofoil terminal and Via Manzoni in Posillipo.

By Taxi Taking *un tassi* is cost-effective and can be entertaining for children to watch Neapolitan taxi drivers negotiating chaotic traffic. Taxis are regulated but some unscrupulous drivers will try and squeeze out an extra euro or ten: if the meter isn't switched on, agree to a fixed price beforehand – and check the flat rate of your journey on the price list in the back of the cab. Official Comune di Napoli (Naples Municipality) taxis are painted white – hail them outside the station at the official taxi rank. Get a taxi at one of 90 city-wide taxi ranks or by phoning one of the following for a 1€ booking fee: Consortaxi (℡ 081 552 5252); Radio Free Taxi (℡ 081 551 5151); Consorzio Taxi Vagando: (Co.Ta.Na) (℡ 081 570 7070; *www. taxivagando.it*).

Campania ArteCard VALUE

The **Campania ArteCard** allows you to see the city and region's attractions at a discounted price, and throws in access to all the public transport to boot.

There are four different cards:

The first *Ordinaria* card allows *"3 days all sites"* of discounted sightseeing for 25€ (18€ 18–25 years) with the first two attractions free (so pick the pricey ones first) and then 50% off entry to other sights, plus free use of all public transport – including regional trains and certain buses during this time. The seven-day version costs 28€ (21€ for 18–25-year-olds), while the 365-day version is 40€ for adults and 30€ for 18–25s.

Finally, the *"3-day Naples and Campi Flegrei"* card (13€ adults, 8€ 18–25 years) gives you the same deal but within Naples and the Campi Flegrei only. The following sights are included in the scheme: Castel Sant' Elmo (p. 66), Certosa e Museo di San Martino (p. 71), Città della Scienza (p. 95), Complesso Museale di Santa Chiara (p. 63), Museo Archeologico Nazionale (p. 72), Museo Civico di Castel Nuovo (p. 65), Museo Nazionale di Capodimonte (p. 73), Palazzo Reale (p. 67) and all five major attractions in the Campi Flegrei (p. 89) (counted as one admission). Many other sights offer small discounts on presentation of the card. It's available at major transport hubs, tourist offices, at participating attractions and at some *edicole* (newsstands). *www.artecard.it*

Planning Your Outing

City Sightseeing Napoli

We found the best way to get to know the city quickly was on an open-top bus tour and children will enjoy hopping on and off at their favourite sights. City Sightseeing Napoli (℅ *081 551 7279; www.napoli.city-sightseeing. it/eng*; tickets valid for all three routes: Adults 22€, Children 6–15 11€, Family ticket for two adults and three children 66€) has three routes departing from Piazza Municipio. Line A takes in the principal artistic attractions (10 stops including Piazza del Gesù and the Museo di Capodimonte (see p. 73)) and

lasts 75 minutes. Line B tours 12 panoramic spots in 75 minutes including Posillipo and the waterfront Castel del Ovo. Line C (weekends only) includes San Martino and the Vomero sights as well as a look at the narrow Greco-Roman *decumani* (streets of the ancient city) and Chiaia's Piazza dei Martiri.

FAST FACTS

Banks There are banks with *bancomats* (cashpoints) throughout the city. Banco di Napoli has a handy branch at Via Toledo 177. There's a Barclays Bank

(📞 *081 704 0111*) at Via San Brigida 43.

Breastfeeding Family-oriented Neapolitans generally have no problem with breastfeeding mums and crying infants – and people are very helpful in providing a quiet corner.

Currency Exchange Try the above or use a *cambio* at the train station, airport or one of the many on Corso Umberto.

Doctor Guardia Medica Specialistica (📞 *081 431 111*) is available 24 hours a day. The consulates have a list of English-speaking physicians.

Embassies & Consulates see Fast Facts in the Planning Chapter p. 41.

Emergencies For an ambulance call 📞 *118*; for the fire brigade call 📞 *115* and for the police call 📞 *113*.

Hospital Ospedale Fatebenefratelli is at Via Manzoni 220 (📞 *081 769 7220*).

Internet Zeudi Internet point is in a pedestrianised stretch of Via Chiaia at number 199/C (📞 *081 251 2250*).

Laundry/Dry Cleaning Get your clothes cleaned and pressed at Lavanderia Helvetica (Via San Mattia 1; 📞 *081 415 635*) or Lavanderia Suprema (Piazza Vittoria 5; 📞 *081 248 1386*).

Maps A more detailed map (*stradario*) with an alphabetical list of streets, published by Touring Club Italiano, Vincitorio and Mini-City can be found at *edicole* (newsstands) or bookshops.

Newspapers & Magazines *Qui Napoli* is a handy listings magazine with useful timetables and maps (*www.innaples.it/quinapoli.htm*). The local paper *Il Mattino* publishes lists of events and boat timetables.

Police Call 📞 *113* (*Polizia*) or 📞 *112* (*Carabinieri*).

Post The Central Post Office (*Ufficio Postale*) is housed in the impressive Fascist-era building at Piazza Matteoti (📞 *081 551 1456*).

Toilets Public bathrooms with baby-changing rooms are few and far between. Your best bet is to buy a coffee and use the *bagno* in a café.

WHAT TO SEE & DO

Children's Top 10 Attractions

❶ **Playing in** the Capodimonte park, p. 73.

❷ **Slurping Napoli's** delicious gelato.

❸ **Seeing the** Santa Chiara majolica tiles, p. 63.

❹ **Creeping around** the Sansevero crypts, p. 59.

❺ **Eating the best pizza** in the world, p. 80.

❻ **Exploring** the Reggia di Caserta fountains and gardens.

For Your Own Safety! ‹‹

Naples is a busy port city with a fair amount of petty crime so you need to be on guard at all times. Don't carry expensive cameras or bags and be especially careful around Piazza Garibaldi and Napoli Centrale train station where the travelling crowds are swelled by a multicultural crowd hanging around the counterfeit goods sold on the pavements, making it a prime site for pickpockets.

Pickpockets operate in squads – often on scooters – so keep your eyes peeled. Use a money-belt for carrying money, cards and passports.

❼ **Shopping for presepi** figurines at Via San Gregorio Armeno, p. 78.

❽ **Looking up at** Roman statues in the Archaeological Museum, p. 72.

❾ **Surveying the Bay** from Parco Virgiliano and Castel Sant'Elmo p. 68.

❿ **Sitting on the dock** of the bay at Borgo Marinari p. 51.

Child-friendly Events & Entertainment

Maggio dei Monumenti
See lots of historic sights opened that are rarely seen by the public as well as lots of family-friendly musical and dance performances around the city. May of Monuments includes *Vietato Non Toccare* (It's forbidden not to touch): an initiative to encourage children to play and learn.
May.

Festa della Madonna del Carmine
Piazza del Carmine is the focus for celebrating the Feast of the Madonna del Carmine. A procession of a pious relic around the Piazza Mercato area is followed

by spectacular fireworks around the Madonna del Carmine bell tower.
15th-16th July

Christmas
Christmas is magic in Naples, particularly around Via San Gregorio Armeno, which is filled with twinkling lights, festive foods and *presepi* (see p. 78). Many churches have their own fantastical nativity scenes and there's an annual manger model exhibition at the Mostra d'Arte Presepiale (see p. 78).

Family-friendly Sights

The rich history of Naples means there is no shortage of fascinating sights. While some families with older children may enjoy visiting the dozens of churches, museums and palaces, other parties will prefer to pick and choose a few of the most stimulating Neapolitan sights.

A Walk Around Spaccanapoli
If you do nothing else in Naples, then you must take a walk along Spaccanapoli (literally: Split Naples), one of the three main east–west streets (*decumani*) cutting through the heart of the

ancient Greek city, Neapolis. Put your valuables away, keep your wits about you and enjoy the vibrant streetlife, artistic treasures and weird Neapolitan sights. Kick off your adventure at **Piazza del Gesù** at the spire Guglia dell'Immacolata, taking in the colourful palaces, studded *ashlar* façade of the **Gesù Nuovo** church (see p. 60) and entrance to narrow Via Benedetto Croce, the first Spaccanapoli street. Check out the church with its thousands of shiny ex-votos devoted to Giuseppe Moscati before heading into the wonderful **Santa Chiara** complex (see p. 63). After visiting the cloisters with their vibrant tiles created by father and son team Donato and Giuseppe Massa, continue along Spaccanapoli, dipping in and out of the eclectic shops selling red horns and other oddball paraphernalia of the superstitious Neapolitans. The grimy old buildings along here have lavish Renaissance interiors and serene courtyards: take a peak into the **Palazzo Filomarino** courtyard at no 12, which was the home of the philosopher and historian Benedetto Croce. You have to sample some of the sublime pastries at **A Sfogliatella Di Ercolano** (Via Benedetto Croce 46) and historic **Scaturchio**, further on at Piazza San Domenico Maggiore 19. It's well worth lingering in the piazza to soak up the atmosphere and to admire the grand buildings, central obelisk and **San Domenico Maggiore** (see p. 61) church.

Take a side street to the east of the piazza to reach the **Cappella di Sansevero** (see p. 59), a family chapel housing the most exquisite sculptures and the dark secrets of a mysterious Prince, Raimondo di Sangro (see p. 60). Head back to Spaccanapoli which now becomes **Via San Biagio dei Librai** where you'll find more intriguing outlets, historic bookshops and antique stalls including **Quagliozza Salvatore** at no 11 which is crammed with junk and treasure, and Ospedale delle Bambole (Dolls' Hospital) at 81.

Piazzetta Nilo has an elegant Egyptian statue brought by Alexandrian settlers, the cute **Sant'Angelo a Nilo** church (contains Cardinal Brancoccio's tomb by Donatello and Tuscan friends) and Bar Nilo – a proper Neapolitan bar for espresso, pop and juice refreshments – outside is a mini-chapel dedicated to Diego Maradona. Dip into the cultural courtyard and chapel of the **Cappella del Monte di Pietà** before losing yourself in the miniature world of presepe (nativity-scene figures) on Via San Gregorio Armeno. Take a peek inside the **San Gregorio church** (see p. 62) and cloisters before heading to **Piazza San Gaetano** where two churches, **San Lorenzo Maggiore** (see p. 63) and **San Paolo Maggiore** (see p. 63) merit attention. If you have a spare 90 minutes, descend into the city's fascinating past at **Napoli Sotterranea** (see p. 58).

SPACCANAPOLI

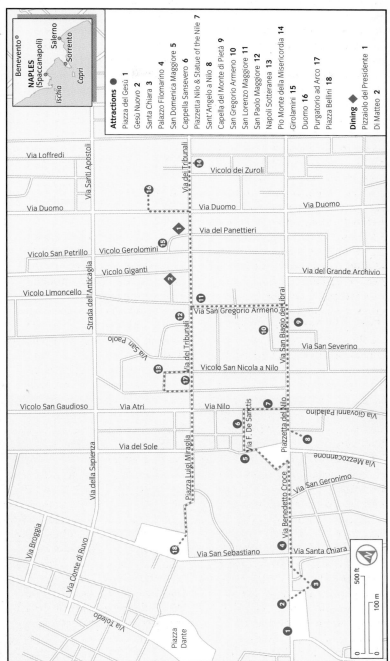

Attractions

Piazza del Gesù **1**
Gesù Nuovo **2**
Santa Chiara **3**
Palazzo Filomarino **4**
San Domenica Maggiore **5**
Cappella Sansevero **6**
Piazzetta Nilo & Statue of the Nile **7**
Sant'Angelo a Nilo **8**
Capella del Monte di Pietà **9**
San Gregorio Armeno **10**
San Lorenzo Maggiore **11**
San Paolo Maggiore **12**
Napoli Sotterranea **13**
Pio Monte della Misericordia **14**
Girolamini **15**
Duomo **16**
Purgatorio ad Arco **17**
Piazza Bellini **18**

Dining

Pizzaiolo del Presidente **1**
Di Matteo **2**

For those with room in their heads for more culture and history, go east along the **Via Tribunali** and take in the artistic treasures at **Pio Monte della Misericordia** and **Girolamini** before making the pilgrimage to the **Duomo** (see p. 59) to see San Gennaro's 1600-year-old blood. Alternatively, head west along edgy Via Tribunali to one of Napoli's best pizzerie at **94** or **120**: **Di Matteo** or **Pizzeria del Presidente** (see p. 81), and then past shiny bronze skulls outside the **Purgatorio ad Arco**. Take a well-earned breather and refreshments at Intra Moenia bar on leafy **Piazza Bellini** overlooking the old Greek city walls. Pick up some arty postcards here and they'll happily call you a cab.

Città Antica: The Ancient City

The energy of Neapolitan streetlife is what most children will be struck by: no other area encapsulates this vibrancy more than the Città Antica, with its medieval atmosphere, eclectic shopping and quirky sights. We start at the Spaccanapoli, an edgy yet enthralling thoroughfare slicing through Naples's ancient heart and comprising two streets: Via Benedetto Croce and Via San Biagio dei Librai.

Napoli Sotterranea ★
AGES 10 AND UP

Piazza San Gaetano 68 ℡ 081 296 944; www.napolisotterranea.it. Bus: R2, R3, C25.

Teens will dig the descent 40 metres into this vast underground city carved out of the volcanic *tufa* rock, although the very young may find the tour too dark, dank, scary, disorientating and long – it takes 90 minutes. For families with older

Paintings for sale, Via dei Tribunali

children, a visit to the cool depths makes a refreshing break on a sweltering day in the Città Antica. Well-informed guides – including the charming and enthusiastic Ilaria – trace intriguing layers of Neapolitan history: the Greek foundations of ancient Neapolis, Greco-Roman aqueducts and a theatre where the Emperor Nero performed Greek tragedies and musical ditties in the first century AD. Five metres of 20th-century rubbish are buried under a vast air-raid shelter. If you don't mind cramped spaces, there is the perfect chance to walk by candlelight through a narrow tunnel to an eerily lit cistern. Prepare to be spooked.

Admission 10€, free under-18s. Reductions with Artecard (see p. 53). Tours depart noon, 2pm and 4pm, Mon–Fri; also 9pm Thurs; 10am, 12pm, 2pm, 4pm and 6pm Sat–Sun. Amenities Shop., Toilets.

Churches

Cappella di Sansevero ★★
AGES 5 AND UP

Via Francesco De Sanctis 19, ☎ 081 551 8470. www.museosansevero.it. Bus: R2, 24, C57.

The stories surrounding the legendary and infamous prince Raimondo di Sangro (see p. 60) will spike the imaginations of *goth* children who will be spooked and inspired by the sight of 250-year-old fossilised flesh and stone. The Prince of Sansavero remodelled this tomb-chapel, decorating it with exquisite sculptures: Giuseppe

Sanmartino's creepily life-like *Cristo Velato* (Veiled Christ) is the centrepiece and was apparently carved from a single block of marble – it is one of the most important and beautiful sculptures ever made. The sensuous *Pudicizia* by Antonio Corradini is dedicated to the patron's mother who died at just 23; *Disinganno* or Disillusion, by Francesco Queriolo honours di Sangro's father, who chose a monastic life – it depicts a man disentangling himself from a rope net, helped by a curious winged youth. Strange Masonic symbols are scattered around the chapel, adding to the mystery. Down in the crypt, a couple of anatomical figures display their cardiovascular systems in gruesome detail.

Open 10am–5.40pm Mon and Wed–Sat; 10am–1.10pm Sun. Admission 6€; 10–25 years 4€. Reductions with Artecard (see p. 53). Amenities Toilets.

Duomo ★★ **AGES 4 AND UP**

Cathedral: Via Duomo 147 ☎ 081 449 097; www.duomodinapoli.it. Museum: Via Duomo 149. ☎ 081 294 980; www.museodeltesorodisan gennaro.info. Metro: Cavour. Bus: R2, E1.

This colossal cathedral will fascinate folk young and old with its gory relics and epic scale. It was begun by Angevin King Carlo I in the late 1200s on the site of a 4th-century Greek temple. Early mosaic floors and Roman relics can be seen in atmospheric excavations below the basilica. The Latin-Cross structure and

What to See & Do

Raimondo VII

Among superstitious Neapolitans, Raimondo di Sangro (1710–1771) is an alchemist who administered a potion that killed two trusty servants and magically preserved their circulatory systems and the sorcerer who could reproduce the miracle of San Gennaro (see p. 61). This maverick figure fascinates children not only for his macabre experiments: his other pioneering projects include a submarine, an eternal lamp, an intricate timepiece and the extraction of phosphorus from urine. While his esoteric exploits brought him infamy, his activity as a Masonic Grand Master led to excommunication by Pope Benedict XIV in 1751.

elaborately painted ceiling are supported by 110 granite columns. Over the main entrance are the tombs of Angevin kings and to the right is the lavishly adorned Cappella di San Gennaro, dedicated to the city's patron saint. Look up at the fresco cycle by Domenichino depicting the life of San Gennaro. Children will be transfixed by the altar tabernacle containing the saint's supposedly supernatural remains: a silver bust protects the skull and two phials are filled with his congealed blood. The oldest baptistery in the Western World, **La Cappella di San Giovanni in Fonte** (4th century) contains vibrant mosaics depicting biblical scenes. The Museum of the Treasure of San Gennaro contains seven centuries of donations, while the Sacristy is filled with frescoes and paintings by Luca Giordano.

Open 8am–12pm and 4.30–7pm Mon-Sat; 9am–1:30pm and 5–7:30pm Sun and holidays. *Admission* Free. *Museum Open* 9am–5pm Tues–Sat; 9am–2.30pm Sun and holidays. *Museum Admission* 6€; 4€ under–18s. Reductions with Artecard (see p. 53). *Amenities* Disabled access. Shop. Toilets.

Gesù Nuovo ★ ★ AGES 4 AND UP

Piazza del Gesu ℂ 081 551 8613. *Bus: C57, 24.*

The piazza of Gesù Nuovo's centrepiece is the Guglia dell'Immocolata (1757), a flamboyant Baroque column modelled on a typical Neapolitan processional object that gave thanks for deliverance from one of the city's many catastrophes and epidemics. Beyond the austere diamond-pointed exterior – the pimpled remains of the Sanseverino Palace – the church of Gesù Nuovo has a 16th-century Greek-cross layout embellished by a riot of frescoes, coloured marble, gilt and stucco from the 17th and 18th centuries.

Unusual votive offerings to renowned doctor and saint, Giuseppe Moscati (1880–1927), fill two side rooms by the Moscati chapel – where queues of pious Neapolitans come to pray to him. Children enjoy looking through the ex-voto metallic hearts and body parts with messages asking for healing. Moscati's office is preserved, complete with the dangling shards of a World War II bomb.

There's not much written about Napoli's patron saint but you can't ignore the impact of the San Gennaro story upon superstitious Naples. Gennaro was born around AD272 and became Bishop of Benevento, only to be condemned to death after the Emperor Diocletian authorised the persecution of practising Christians – he was discovered taking Communion to an imprisoned deacon and decapitated in AD305 near Solfatara. His blood was collected in two ampoules and he was buried nearby. It is said that after Constantine gave Christians their freedom to worship, Gennaro's remains were laid in his family's tomb, whereupon Vesuvius erupted and the dried blood in the ampoules miraculously liquefied. And so the belief grew that the liquefaction was a sign that Gennaro would protect Naples from disaster. His relics were taken to the Duomo in 1497, where they are honoured three times a year – on the Saturday before the first Sunday in May, on his saint's day of 19th September and on 16th December – in a solemn ceremony followed by a frenzy of emotional outpouring by the faithful celebrating the miracle who implore the saint's blood to liquefy. Should the vigil last many hours it is thought to be a bad omen for Naples.

Open *9am–1pm and 4–7pm Mon–Sat; 9am–1pm Sun.* **Admission** *Free.* **Amenities** *Shop.*

Pio Monte della Misericordia ★ AGES 7 AND UP

Via dei Tribunali 253 ☎ *081 446 944; www.piomontedellamisericordia.it. Bus: R2, 24, C57.*

The charitable institution was set up in 1601 by seven noble gents and now contains Renaissance treasures in the first-floor gallery and adjoining church. Our Lady of Mercy's star billing goes to *The Seven Acts of Mercy* (1607) by Caravaggio, on the high altar of the octagonal church, an imposing painting depicting charitable acts with labyrinthine Naples as a backdrop. Keen art aficionados can view 150 canvasses by 17th- to 18th-century Mannerist masters including Vaccaro, Luca Giordano and Ribera. If the artworks don't enthral then the building will impress: light steams into the cavernous space beneath the dome, while upstairs you can take peeks at the towering Guglia (spire) di San Gennaro.

Open *9am–2pm Thurs–Tues.* **Admission** *5€. Reductions with Artecard (see p. 53).* **Amenities** *Disabled access. Shop. Toilets.*

San Domenico Maggiore ★ AGES 5 AND UP

Piazza San Domenico Maggiore. ☎ *081 449 097. Bus: C57, R2, 24.*

The mish-mash of architectural styles that is the rear end of the San Domenico church dominates one of the most attractive squares in Naples. Its centrepiece is the Baroque marble obelisk, La Guglia di San Domenico (1737) built in thanks for the end of a terrible bubonic plague that wiped out 75% of the population. Erected by the Angevins (1283–1324) and much altered after earthquakes and fires, the interior is 76m long and contains 14th-century frescoes in the Cappella Brancaccio by Pietro Cavallini, a Roman artist who influenced Giotto as well as spooky tombs in the ancient Chiesa di Sant'Angelo a Morfisa, the original place of worship here. A copy of Caravaggio's *Flagellation* (1607) is hung in the north transept – you can compare Vaccaro's version with the original in the Museo di Capodimonte (see p. 73). In the Cappellone del Crocifisso, you'll find a reproduction of the 13th-century panel painting through which – legend has it – Christ spoke to the influential theologian

Thomas Aquinas. Aquinas studied at the adjoining monastery – the original seat of the University of Naples – as did the radical philosopher Giordano Bruno who promoted the idea of a solar system and infinite worlds.

Open 9am–noon and 5–7pm daily. **Admission** Free. **Amenities** Disabled access. Shop.

San Gregorio Armeno ★ ★
AGES 5 AND UP

Via San Gregorio Armeno 44. Metro: Piazza Cavour. Bus: C57, R2, 24

Amid child-friendly shops selling nativity scenes (*presepi*, see p. 78) and various amusing tat is this wonderful Benedictine convent built upon the remains of a Roman temple. The reddish-hued Baroque belltower (1700s) looms over the narrow street crammed with pastoral scenes and figurines. The nuns who founded the church in the 8th century brought the remains of the

San Domenico Maggiore

Armenian bishop and saint Gregorio here and named the church in his honour. Along with the nuns and Gregorio, Santa Patrizia – a noble turned nun who renounced wealth and imperial marriage – also ended up in Naples after escaping Constantinople. She died in AD665 and her dried blood is said to liquefy here every Tuesday. Check out the gilt stuccowork, vibrant frescos and carved wooden ceiling in the church before exploring the beautiful cloisters filled with citrus trees, statues and fountains. Legend has it that the well-to-do nuns made lavish ice desserts and invented the *sfogliatella* – the delicious horn-shaped Neapolitan pastry – in the old refectory.

Open *9.30am–noon daily.* **Admisson** *Free.* **Amenities** *Café. Disabled access. Shop. Toilets.*

San Lorenzo Maggiore ★★

AGES 5 AND UP

Piazza San Gaetano ☎ *081 290 580;* *www.sanlorenzomaggiorenapoli.it. Metro: Piazza Cavour. Bus: C57, R2, 24.*

Beneath this beguiling Franciscan church are the remains of the Greco-Roman forum (including ancient market stalls) and the basilica of Neapolis, which are well worth a look. It's undergone many changes since the 6th century: in the 13th century Charles of Anjou rebuilt the church in Gothic style using French craftsmen and it received a 17th-century Baroque makeover after one too many earthquakes. More restoration followed in the 20th century. There is a small museum with a collection of relics and child-friendly historic *presepi* figures (see p. 78), which occasionally make an appearance during temporary exhibitions.

Open *8am–noon and 5–7pm Mon–Sat.* **Admission** *Free.* **Excavations and Museum Open** *9.30am–5.30pm Mon–Sat, 9.30am–1.30pm Sun.* **Excavations and Museum Admission** *5€ adults; 3€ under-18s. Reductions with Artecard (p. 53).* **Amenities** *Disabled access. Shop.*

San Paolo Maggiore ★

AGES 5 AND UP

Piazza San Gaetano ☎ *081 454 048. Metro: Piazza Cavour. Bus: C57, R2, 24*

Piazza Gaetano lies at the centre of Old Neapolis and this 16th-century church stands on the site of a Roman temple dedicated to Castor and Pollux, Zeus's twin sons. The earthquake of 1688 may have destroyed all but two of the original Corinthian columns and much of the façade, but youngsters will enjoy scampering up the Baroque double staircase that took its place. Dip into the cavernous church for a gander at Francesco Solimena's (1689–90) frescos in the sacristy and a couple of flamboyantly decorated chapels replete with mother of pearl, coloured marbles and paintings by Massimo Stanzione.

Open *8am–noon and 5–7pm daily.* **Admission** *Free.*

Santa Chiara ★★★ ALL AGES

Church: Via Santa Chiara 49. ☎ *081 552 6280. Cloisters and Museum: Via*

Fiammetta

It was in the lofty apse of San Lorenzo Maggiore, in 1336, that one of the great love stories in literature was sparked when Boccaccio met his Fiammetta. "Round her red garland and her golden hair, I saw a fire about my Little Flame's head" wrote the poet.

It is believed that Maria d'Aquino, the illegitimate daughter of King Robert of Naples, and Boccaccio's love and muse, perhaps inspired mischievous Fiammetta in Boccaccio's Medieval masterpiece, *The Decameron*. Set during one of the many outbreaks of plague, the book centres around ten people who have fled to the countryside and spend their days telling story after story. Fiammetta is the wittiest teller of tales and spins many a yarn about love, charlatans and naughtiness.

It has been claimed that Maria spurned Boccaccio's advances. Either way when the Black Death rampaged through Naples in 1348, it took Maria d'Aquino with it, leaving Boccaccio broken-hearted.

Benedetto Croce 16 ☎ *081 792 156;* **www.santachiara.info**. *Bus: C57, 24.*

The Santa Chiara complex enchants young and old with its lavish interiors, museum exhibits and charming cloisters. Its tranquil courtyards, filled with shady wisteria, citrus trees and vibrant majolica tiles, are a perfect example of Napoli's hidden courtyard life. Built in the early 14th century, the church's roof and Baroque interior were gutted by World War II Allied bombs in 1943. Take a stroll around the old cloisters behind the church, amid flaky Gothic arcades and dreamlike tiles covering 72 columns, benches and walkways created by Domenico Vaccaro in the 18th century. The whirls of deep blue, green and yellow majolica are an uplifting sight. It's the perfect respite from the Spaccanapoli hubbub. A museum traces the history of the Franciscan complex and has remains of 1st-century AD

Roman baths – it's all quite interesting but too detailed to dwell in for long with children.

Open 9.30–1pm and 4–6pm Thurs–Tues; 9am–1pm Sun. Admission Free. Cloisters and Museum Open 9.30am–6.30pm Mon–Sat; 9.30am–2.30pm Sun. Cloisters and Museum Admission 4€; discount with Artecard (see p. 53). Amenities Baby changing. Café. Disabled access. Shop. Toilets.

Castles & Royal Palaces

Castel dell'Ovo ☆ ALL AGES

Borgo Marinari ☎ *081 240 0055. Museo di Etnopreistoria:* ☎ *081 764 343. Bus: R3, 152, C25.*

The Castle of the Egg lies on the tufa rock of Megaris, an ancient island colonised by the Greeks, who founded Parthenope here. Roman big-wig Lucullus, Saint Basil monks, Frederick II's Hohenstaufen dynasty, Normans, Angevins and Bourbons all made their mark on the castle's colourful history. The iconic structure evolved into a lavish villa, monastery and palace before being transformed into the formidable fortress you see today. Grand castle spaces can be admired in the Hall of the Columns and Loggiato, while outside the towers offer stunning views of the Bay of Naples. What makes it a fab place for families is the nearby Borgo dei Marinari (see p. 51) fisherman's district with its swanky harbourside restaurants, whose lights twinkle in the water at night. Legend has it that the Roman poet Virgil (author of *the Aeneid* and a magician) hung a magic egg within an iron cage under the castle – and if the egg should break all manner of catastrophes would befall the city. There are other more mundane explanations as to how it got this name but this is the one children will enjoy! A small, rather unexciting Museum of Prehistory is also housed here, containing prehistoric tools and ceramics.

Open *8.30am–6pm Mon–Sat, 8.30am–2pm Sun.* **Admission** *Free.*

Museum Open *10am–1pm Mon–Fri by appointment.* **Museum Admission** *Free.* **Amenities** *Shop. Toilets.*

Castel Nuovo (aka Maschio Angiono) ★ AGES 4 AND UP

Piazza Municipio ☎ *081 420 1241. Bus: R2, C25, R3.*

The sturdy bulk of this Angevin-built fortress and its five towers loom over the unrelenting traffic in Piazza Municipio and the harbour. Children will love its sword and swagger history. Angevin monarch Charles I had it built in 1279 and its present shape is down to 15th-century King Alfonso of Aragon. On entering the courtyard, passing the moat that once housed crocodiles, take time to admire the early Renaissance Triumphal Arch to commemorate Alfonso's conquest of Naples in 1443 – above the highest arch the four Cardinal Virtues (Prudence, Justice, Temperance and Fortitude) are depicted. Check out the grandiose Sala dei Baroni

Castel dell'Ovo, otherwise known as the Castle of the Egg

where a mock wedding ensnared some troublesome barons. The 28m (92ft) high-vaulted dome was originally adorned with frescoes by Giotto, sadly lost in a 1919 fire. Look out for the World War II cannonball damage on the imposing bronze door in the Museo Civico here.

Open *9am–7pm Mon–Sat.*
Admission *5€; free for under-18s.*
Amenities *Disabled access. Toilets.*

Castel Sant'Elmo ★★
AGES 5 AND UP

Via Tito Angelini 20 ☎ *081 578 4030. Metro and Funicular: various to Piazza Vanvitelli, Vomero.*

The main reason for a visit to the Sant Elmo Castle is to take in the wonderful views of the bay from the many ramparts and forts atop the Vomero hill. A 10th-century church dedicated to Saint Erasmus (shortened to Sant'Elmo in typically Neapolitan linguistic fashion) stood on the summit here. The original Angevin construction (1329–43) was

transformed into its present star-shaped form by the Spanish Viceroy Pedro Toledo in the 16th century. This former prison and symbol of the short-lived Napoleonic Parthenopaean Republic (1799) now houses temporary art exhibitions.

Open *9am–6.30pm Thurs–Tues.*
Admission *3€; free under-18s.*
Amenities *Picnic area. Shop. Toilets.*

Galleria Umberto I ★ ALL AGES

Four entrances going clockwise from Piazza Trento e Trieste: Via San Carlo, Via Toldeo, Via Santa Brigida and Via Giuseppe Verdi. Bus: R2, R3, C25.

Built in 1887, this Liberty-style shopping gallery looks sadly neglected compared to its swanky Milanese counterpart, the Galleria Vittorio Emanuele II. Despite the scaffolding and grime, and the usual colourful Neapolitan characters hanging around the four grand entrances of this cruciform structure, its glass and iron elegance and colossal cupola leave you gawping.

Castel Nuovo, Piazza Municipio

Apart from taking time to admire the cavernous space, architectural detailing and coloured marble floors there's not much else to detain you: just a couple of elegant but overpriced cafés and a mish-mash of unremarkable shops. Don't miss Napoli's other Belle-époque gallery, Galleria del Principe di Napoli near the Museo Archeologico Nazionale.

Amenities Disabled access.

Palazzo Reale ★ ★ AGES 6 AND UP

Piazza del Plebiscito 1. ☎ 081 400 547/580 8111. Bus R2, R3, C25.

Walk along the façade of this imposing palace to meet the various rulers of Naples down the centuries – grand niches contain eight regal statues in stately attire, showing the odd bulge here and World War II damage there. Gioacchino Murat, Napoleon's brother-in-law, looks particularly fetching and makes an amusing photo backdrop. Unless you have drama-queen teens who swoon at the thought of a costume-drama location, you might want to skim through the umpteen apartments here. "There are only so many tapestries, porcelains and drapes one can take" is oft-heard on the grand staircase. Highlights include the Teatrino di Corte, Studio del Re (kings' study), the Cappella Palatina containing a grand *presepe*, the Hall of Hercules ballroom and dramatic views from the chessboard-tiled roof gardens.

Open 9am–7pm Thurs–Tues.
Admission 4€; free under-18s;

discounts with Artecard. Guided tour by reservation. *Amenities Baby changing. Café. Disabled access. Picnic area. Shop. Toilets.*

Teatro San Carlo AGES 7 AND UP

Via San Carlo 93. ☎ 081 400 300 or ☎ 081 797 233. www.teatrosan carlo.it Bus: R2, R3, C25.

The first opera-theatre in the world (1737) was built for King Carlo I and became the epitome of the city's reputation for glamour, music and worldly pleasures. Musical and ballet-bonkers teens might enjoy the sumptuous spectacle and exceptional acoustics – but maybe not the length of a performance. All the Italian greats have graced the theatre including Rossini, Donizetti, Puccini, Mascagni, Verdi and Pavarotti, as well as foreign composers Mozart and Haydn and the smoothest *castrati* voices Farinelli and Velluti. An impressive façade was added in 1812 before an 1816 fire destroyed much of the interior, including the original Bourbon blue upholstered seats (now in red).

Tours 9am–5.30pm daily except Aug and theatre closing days. Meeting Point: the foyer.

Box office 081 797 2331 (Open 10am–7pm Tues–Sun). Amenities Baby changing. Café. Disabled access. Shop. Toilets.

Open Spaces

In car-crazy Naples it's good to take a breather from the traffic dodging and fumes. As well as the lush park surrounding the

Palazzo Reale terrace

Capodimonte museum (see Museum and Galleries section), there are various green spaces and pedestrianised *piazze* around town. Animal-crazy youngsters go wild for the city's natural history collections and their enormous fish tanks, stuffed animals and dinosaur skeletons. The local council organises family activity days on many weekends (mainly Sundays) throughout the year – look out for info about *Domenica nei Parchi* around town and in the local press.

Orto Botanico ★ ★ ALL AGES

Via Foria 223, 📞 *081 449 759 or 081 445 654;* **www.ortobotanico. unina.it.** *Bus: C57, R4 Metro: Cavour.*

If you and the family have a penchant for plant life, give the botanical gardens a ring to book a visit. 9,000 species and 25,000 plants are secreted from the furious traffic on Via Foria. The 12 hectares contain many different themed areas, from the Arboretum's rare trees to ponds bursting with colourful water

lilies. Don't miss the vast greenhouses with temperate, hot-humid and hot-dry climates. The Monumental Merola, built in 1820, is teeming with tropical and subtropical vegetation. Within the restored rooms of a red-hued castle you can find plant fossils and human inventions crafted from plant materials – get the children to look out for the tiny canoes from Borneo's mangroves, beautifully crafted Amazonian weapons and a giant lute or two.

Open 9am–2pm Mon–Fri by appointment only; Guided visits 9–11am Mar–May by appointment only. *Amenities* Baby changing. Café. Disabled access. Picnic area. Shop. Toilets.

Parco Virgiliano ★ ★ ALL AGES

Viale Virgilio

Off the beaten path in smart Posillipo, this large park has wonderful views and child-friendly spaces in which to let off energy. A series of terraces offer jaw-dropping vistas of the Bay of Naples, the Campi

Flegrei and the islands of Capri, Ischia and Procida. You can also gaze down from dizzying heights at the idyllic Trentaremi Bay while enjoying a picnic or ice cream from the van at the entrance. Youngsters can let off some steam in the playgrounds, running track and sports field, while adults will relish the peace of a sit down amid the shade of Mediterranean pines. There is a small private amusement park with various merry-go-round rides suitable for toddlers for a fistful of euros at Viale Virgilio 10, just outside the park.

Piazza Dante ★ ALL AGES

Piazza Dante, along Via Toledo. Metro: Dante.

Child-friendly festivals, concerts and gatherings often take place in this grand piazza on Via Toledo. Juggling clowns and stalls enliven the large space surrounding a statue of poet Dante Alighieri. If you're into books and antiquarian titles, it's well worth a look at Via Port'Alba, at the entrance to the Città Antica (see 'Shopping' p. 76).

Piazza del Plebiscito and Piazza Trieste e Trento ★
ALL AGES

Off Piazza Trieste e Trento. Bus: R2, R3, C25.

The vast square beside Palazzo Reale is the focal point of the city for Neapolitans, hosting concerts, celebrations, contemporary art installations and state visits. Thankfully it's now closed to traffic, making it possible for children to play football and run around in front of the Pantheon-aping San Francesco di Paola church (1817), with its bulbous dome and grand portico. Youngsters love the languid lions stretching out at the ends of the semi-circular sweep of Doric colonnades and the equestrian statues of Carlo III and Ferdinando IV by Antonio Canova and Antonio Calì. More photo opportunities await at Piazza Trieste e Trento, where you'll find historic Caffè Gambrinus (see p. 79), the Fontana del Carciofo (an unusual fountain with water spouting from a giant artichoke) and views of the Galleria Umberto I and Teatro San Carlo.

Villa Comunale Gardens, Aquarium, La Casina Pompeiana & Villa Pignatelli ★★ ALL AGES

Villa Comunale, Riviera di Chiaia. Acquario ☏ 081 583 111; www. szn.it. Bus: 140, C9, R3.

The public park sandwiched between Via Caracciolo and Riviera di Chiaia is popular with families and joggers, despite it being surrounded by roaring traffic. Walk along the Passeggio Reale (Royal Promenade), designed for the Bourbon king Ferdinando IV in 1780, with its gravel paths dotted with Baroque statues and fountains including the Fountain of The Ducks which is decorated with shells and lounging lions. The park has playgrounds, occasional bandstand performances and a series of Neo-classical buildings containing unusual attractions: **Villa Comunale** houses Europe's oldest aquarium (opened in 1874) replete with leaking tanks filled with Mediterranean marine life, while the elegant **Casina Pompeiana** hosts art shows and cultural events. Every third and fourth weekend of the month, the gardens and surrounding streets are given over to a fabulous antiques market, Il Mercato Antiquariato (see Shopping). Just over the road is the 1820s-built **Villa Pignatelli**, with its Renaissance paintings and collections of porcelain, books and horse-drawn carriages. The real highlight for families is the lush gardens with towering palm trees.

Aquarium Open 9am–5pm Tues–Sun. Admission 2.50€; free for under-18s. La Casina Pompeiana ☎ 081 245 1050. Open 9am–7pm Mon–Sat. Admission Free. Villa Pignatelli Riviera di Chiaia 200. ☎ 081 761 2356. Open 9am–1.30pm Wed–Mon. Admission 2€; free under-18s. Amenities Baby changing.

Café. Disabled access. Picnic area. Toilets.

Museums, Galleries & Attractions

Centri Musei delle Scienze Naturali ★ ALL AGES

Via Mezzocannone 8 ☎ 081 253 5164; www.musei.unina.it Bus: R2.

Animal-crazy children and natural scientists will be fascinated by this collection of animals, minerals and humans. The museums of zoology, mineralogy and anthropology are housed amid the grand halls of the Higher Jesuit College while the palaeontology exhibits are housed in the former monastery of San Marcelliano. Look out for the Indian elephant skeleton, a white whale from the waters near Taranto in Puglia, Bolivian mummies, plaster face casts of African tribesmen, meteorites and half-ton Madagascan quartz crystals.

Villa Comunale Gardens

Open 9am–1.30pm Mon–Fri; plus 3–5pm Mon and Thurs; 9am–1pm Sat and Sun. **Admission** Adults 4.50€ and under-18s 3€ for all 4 museums; 8€ family of 5. **Amenities** Disabled access. Shop. Toilets.

Certosa-Museo Nazionale di San Martino ★★ AGES 4 AND UP

Piazzale San Martino 5. ☎ 081 558 6408. Metro and Funicular: various to Piazza Vanvitelli, Vomero and then Bus V1.

Next to Castel Sant' Elmo, at the highest point of the Vomero, is a sprawling 14th-century monastery that had a Baroque makeover in the 17th century. The enormous wealth of art at the museum and gallery here – one of Napoli's best – may tire young minds after a while, but the atmospheric cloisters and gardens are bound to impress. Through the entrance there is a courtyard and a Baroque church, complete with side chapels filled with inlaid marble and various artworks including statues by Neapolitan masters Cosimo Fanzago and Giuseppe Sanmartino as well as frescoes by Giordano, Caracciolo, Vaccaro and D'Arpino. Children enjoy striking a bearded pose in front of Ribera's *Moses*, who has curious steamy horns of light and is pointing with crooked finger at a mysterious stone tablet.

A stroll around Chiostro Grande (Great Cloister) with its Renaissance flourishes and gardens, along with a visit to the museum, which documents the monastery's history, really gives a feel for the monastic life. Youngsters especially enjoy the collection of *presepi* (nativity scenes) and carriages while older children are drawn to the various views of Vesuvius blowing its top. The north and east wings house exhibitions detailing the history of Naples and Neapolitan theatre. The real show stopper is the terrace with its stunning vistas.

Open 8.30am–7.30pm Thurs–Tues. **Admission** 6€; free for under-18s. Discount with Artecard (see p. 53). **Amenities** Baby changing. Café. Disabled access. Picnic area. Shop. Toilets.

Galleria dell'Accademia di Belle Arti AGES 6 AND UP

Via Costantinopoli 107 ☎ 081 444 245; www.accademianapoli.it Bus C57, R1, 24.

Recently reopened, the Academy of Fine Arts has lots to offer families who appreciate the finer brush strokes of the 17th to 20th centuries. The former 18th-century convent building of San Giovanni delle Monache was turned into the Academy by architect Enrico Alvino in the 1840s. 'Wows!' will accompany a look at the sweeping staircase, which has copies of classic sculptures set on the balustrades. Among the oldest works is *San Girolamo* by Jusepe de Ribera, while in the 19th-century section there are lots of Romantic landscape gouaches and works from the influential Posillipo school of painting: the dramatic pastoral scenes of Gigante, Duclere and Carelli are worth lingering over. The two *Sale Novecento* contain a 20th-century collection that goes right up to the 1960s – highlights include Giarrizzo's Matisse-like works.

Open *10am–2pm Mon–Thurs, 2–6pm Fri.* **Admission** *5€; 3€ under-18s.* **Amenities** *Café. Disabled access. Shop. Toilets.*

Museo Archeologico Nazionale ★ ★ ★ AGES 4 AND UP

Piazza Museo 19 ☏ 081 440 166. Bus: C57, 24, R4. Metro: Museo or Cavour.

Napoli's most famous museum is of international importance – its ancient exhibits make the brain boggle – and is a must-see for anybody. The colossal building houses one of the most important collections of Roman and Greek artefacts in the world. Children particularly enjoy the finds from Pompeii (see p. 129) and Herculaneum (see p. 118), although the sheer scale of it may sap their enthusiasm after a while. To save you trawling around the endless rooms, it's best to find out what your children like and plan your route using the leaflet given out. A comic strip at the entrance starring the cartoon character Napolito attempts to make it fun for youngsters.

On the ground floor you can walk and gawp amid striking statues that once stood in Roman villas, many of which are from the important Farnese Collection – started by a 16th-century pope and ending up in Bourbon Naples via a dowry. You can't miss the Farnese Bull – a 4-m (13-ft) high Roman copy of a 2nd-century BC Greek sculpture from Rhodes – or fail to be wowed by its lifelike dog fur and rope textures honed in marble. Take a break with refreshments in an inner courtyard café while gazing up at towering palm trees. Upstairs there are rooms filled with priceless ancient inscriptions, coins, Pompeian

Roman art, Museo Archeologico Nazionale in Naples

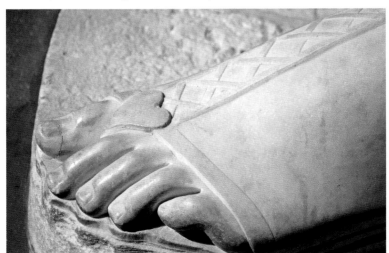

paintings, furnishings, glassware, gems, metalwork and mosaics. If you're planning a trip to **Pompeii** (see p. 129), catch the dancing statuette and mesmerizing mosaics from the House of Faun. Children will love the mysterious mummies and funerary statuettes in the Egyptian Collection. You may want to avert the youngest eyes from the erotic subjects laid bare in the infamous *Gabinetto Segretto* (Secret Cabinet): an eye-bulging glimpse into the Roman world that always stimulates an awkward shuffle and self-conscious snigger from adults.

Open 9am–7.30pm Wed–Mon. *Admission* 7€; 3.50€ under-25s; free under-18s and over 65s. Audioguide in English 4€. *Amenities* Baby changing. Café. Disabled access. Picnic area. Shop. Toilets.

Museo d'Arte Contemporanea Donna Reginais (Madre) ☆
AGES 8 AND UP

Via Settembrini 79 ☎ 081 292 833; *www.museomadre.it.* Metro: Cavour. Bus: 3S, E1.

It may not be located in the most serene part of town, but art-loving families should definitely brave the Piazza Cavour mayhem to see Napoli's newest cutting-edge gallery (fully opened in 2007) housed in the handsome Palazzo Donna Regina, respectfully transformed into a series of white cubes by Portuguese architect Alvaro Siza. Its three floors of thought-provoking exhibits make a refreshing antidote to the ancient treasures in the nearby Museo Archeologico Nazionale and the lavish religious relics of the Duomo. Among the permanent collection highlights are Koons's puzzling play on Pop Art, Richard Long's down-to-earth land art and Anish Kapoor's mysterious biomorphic objects. All this plus changing exhibitions, two large courtyards filled with sculptures, a café, bookshop and a rooftop equestrian artwork should capture children's attention for an hour or so.

Open 10am–9pm Mon, Wed, Thurs and Sun; 9am–midnight Fri and Sat; closed Tues. *Admission* 7€; 3.50€ concessions. Free on Mon. *Amenities* Baby changing. Café. Disabled access. Shop. Toilets.

Museo Nazionale della Ceramica Duca di Martina ☆
AGES 4 AND UP

Via Domenico 77 ☎ 081 478 8418. Funicolare: Piazza Fuga.

The ceramics museum here may not set the children's hearts a-racing, but the shady landscaped gardens of the **Villa Floridiana** are sure to wow them. Children and adults can skip among the camellias, admire the exceptional views from the terrace and play the thespian in the tiny garden theatre, Il Teatrino della Verdura. The 18th-century villa now houses a collection of 6,000 porcelain and pottery pieces – including many a Capodimonte, Wedgwood and Ming – begun by the Duke of Martina as well as 17th- to 19th-century paintings by the likes of Solimena and Vaccaro.

Open 8.30am–1.30pm Wed–Mon; guided tours of museum at 9.30am, 11am and 12.30pm. *Admission*

St. Jerome Removing a Thorn from the Lion's Paw by Colantonio, Niccolo Antonio (fl.1455-62)

2.50€; free for under-18s; discount with Artecard (see p. 53). **Amenities** Baby changing. Café. Disabled access. Picnic area. Shop. Toilets.

Museo Nazionale di Capodimonte ★ ★ ★ ALL AGES

Palazzo Capodimonte, Via Miano 2; or accessed via the park from Via Capodimonte ℓ 081 749 9111; capodimonte.spmn.remuna.org. Bus: R4, 24, M4.

The captivating combination of nature, architecture, history and art make the Palazzo Reale di Capodimonte a favourite. The sprawling complex was commissioned by the Bourbon king, Carlo III, in 1738 as a lavish hunting lodge to entertain and house his mother's – Elisabetta

Farnese – art collection. Children go wild for the 306-acre park, which has five broad avenues fanning out from the Porta di Mezzo. Tall oaks, palms, cedars, pines, eucalyptus, maples and limes offer welcome shade in the summer and vast lawns surrounded by exotic species are perfect for picnics and play. Plan your assault on the miles of gallery by studying the map before you start. Highlights include Renaissance masterpieces by Raphael, Venetian canvasses by Bellini, ceremonial armour, plus Flemish and German paintings including Bruegel's *Misanthrope* (1568). The Farnese Collections are accessed by an epic staircase and housed in the grand salons of the first floor, where you'll also find the Royal Apartments, Armoury and Porcelain collections. Nearly 50 rooms on the second floor trace the development of Neapolitan painting and the Baroque.

A big favourite for children and adults alike – and one that tugs at the heart strings – is Colantonio's *San Gerolamo nello Studio* in Room 67: it depicts St Jerome removing a thorn from the wounded paw of a lion amid the chaotic trappings of study. The third floor contains temporary exhibitions, contemporary art and photography.

Open 8.30am–7.30pm Thurs–Tues. Ticket office shuts one hour before closing. **Admission** 8€; 7€ after 2pm; concessions 4€; free for under-18s and over-65s. **Amenities** Baby changing. Café. Disabled access. Picnic area. Shop. Toilets.

Palazzo delle Arti Napoli (PAN) ★★ AGES 8 AND UP

Via dei Mille 60 ☎ *081 795 8605;* *www.palazzoartinapoli.net. Bus: C22, C25.*

PAN is the city's first public contemporary art gallery. Beyond the perkily pink and grey exterior of the handsomely refurbished 18th-century Palazzo Roccella are three floors of exhibition spaces filled with cutting-edge art that is bound to make a stir with young and old alike – a recent exhibition explored body image, bulimia and plastic surgery.

After taking in the thought-provoking works seek some fresh-ish air in the relatively tranquil courtyard. Teenagers and adults with a passion for art can access PAN's archives and workshops, which cover such diverse subject matter as theatre, photography, design, architecture and comics. A word of warning: some of PAN's temporary exhibitions tackle very adult themes.

Open 9.30am–7.30pm Mon, Wed–Sat; 9.30am–2pm Sun and public holidays; closed Tues. **Admission** 5€; concessions 3€. **Amenities** Baby changing. Café. Disabled access. Picnic area. Shop. Toilets.

For Active Families

You need to head to the hills, away from the worst of the city's traffic and pollution to find suitable places to play sports. The **Parco Virgiliano** (see p. 68) has plenty for sporty children, including a running track. The Capodimonte park (see p. 73) is even better for a kickabout or

 FUN FACT ⟫ **Football-crazy** ⟨

Calcio (soccer)-crazy families will want to see the Stadio San Paolo turf where Diego Armando Maradona created space and a place in Neapolitans' hearts next to San Gennaro. Tickets to see resurgent SSC Napoli play cost around 25€ (the *tribuna laterale* is a good spot along the touchline) and are available from the stadium in Fuorigrotta (Stadio San Paolo, Piazzale Vincenzo Tecchio; *www.sscnapoli.it*).

Galleria Umberto, Via Toledo

game of Frisbee. Tennis players should check out **Tennis Club Napoli** (Viale Dohrn, Villa Comunale. Chiaia. ☏ *081 761 4656*; *www.tennisclubnapoli.it*).

Piscina Scandone is a large swimming pool complex in Fuorigrotta (Viale Giochi del Mediterraneo 20. Metropolitana: Campi Flegrei). Up in Posillipo, **Virgilio Club** (Via Tito Lucrezio Caro 6. ☏ *081 575 5261*; *www. virgilioclub.it*) has a full-size astro-turf football pitch and two *calcetto* (5-a-side pitches), and organises children's soccer schools.

Shopping

Napoli's shopping haunts have a wealth of small independent shops, many of which have been around for decades. You may find the odd chain shop but overall plucky family-run outlets prosper,

making *fare la spesa* (shopping) full of surprises and discoveries. A word of warning: when paying for your goods in the backstreet shops, avoid using your credit card and always use cash. Shops are open Monday to Saturday from 9am to 1pm and then from 4 to 8pm. Most of them close between 1 and 4pm. Sales are held in January and in mid-July to August.

Antiques

Spaccanapoli is the place to find Neapolitan knick-knacks, such as antique little red horns to bring good luck and tin hearts offered to the shrine of Moscato. Real antique collectors will also be amazed by what is still available, although prices are higher these days. **Quagliozza Salvatore** (Via

San Biagio dei Librai 11 📞 *081 551 7100*) and **Orificerie Ferraro** (Via Benedetto Croce 41 📞 *081 552 0201*) are just two of the many dealers to look out for.

Books

If you like to browse around secondhand bookshops and stalls you could easily fritter away a whole afternoon in **Via Port'Alba** just off Spaccanapoli. Being close to the university it has a number of weird and wonderful academic texts as well as prints, photographic books and beautifully illustrated collectables.

Caffè Intra Moenia ★ (Piazza Bellini 📞 *081 290 988*) is an arty hangout, with a goatee-strokingly good selection of Partenopaean black-and-white photographs, prints, postcards and books, all with a historical, cultural slant. **Evaluna** (Piazza Bellini 72 📞 *081 292 372*) is a women's bookshop with regular exhibitions, café bar, live music and a general buzz. **Treves** ★★ (Via Toledo 249–250 📞 *081 415 211*) sells great cookery and guide books, some in English.

Ceramics

If you eschew the mass produced and want to bring home a handmade Pulcinella puppet or a piece of Capodimonte porcelain for Aunt Peggy, try **Spagnuolo** at Via Benedetto Croce 50.

Fashion & Clothes Shopping

Via Toledo is Napoli's Oxford Street and the home of **Galleria Umberto** (see p. 66) – one of the most handsome of shopping malls (shame it doesn't have that much in it). Turn the corner to begin an assault on Via Chiaia that leads to Piazza dei Martiri, Via della Cavalarizza, and Via dei Mille. All of these streets are fashionista shopping heaven, with everything from top designers to carefully curated independent boutiques to affordable outlets for teens.

Home Style

Culti Spacafé ★
Via Carlo Poerio 47 📞 081 764 4619

Sells all things required for a fabulous lifestyle. It also has a spa and *hammam* to ease away the stress involved in being so high-maintenance hip.

Markets

Fiera Antiquaria Napoletana ★★
Via Caracciolo Di Bella is an open-air antique market held on the last two weekends of every month near the Villa Comunale (8am–2pm). From door knockers to votives there are some great bargains and finds to be had.

Mercato di Porta Nolana, Mercato di Porta Capuana & Piazza Mercato are captivating daily markets at the eastern end of the Ancient City, brimming with

fruits of the land and sea and teeming with Neapolitan characters. Keep your valuables safe.

Perfume

Farmaceutica di Santa Maria Novella

Via Santa Caterina a Chiaia 20 📞 *081 407 176*

The local branch of this 800-year-old Florentine pharmacy is on Piazza dei Martiri and a must for lovers of those wonderful herby smells and its most popular almond hand cream.

Presepe ★

If you're looking for a new baby Jesus and shepherds or maybe Diego Maradona or Silvio Berlusconi to grace your nativity set, the presepe shops on Via San Gregorio Armeno in the Centro Storico are teaming with things.

Hardcore fans of *presepe* should visit the annual manger model exhibition during the festive period. Mostra d'Arte Presepiale, Via Santa Maria la Nova 43 📞 *081 252 5711*, held in the rooms of the Provincial Council of Naples.

Cafes, Snacks & Family-friendly Dining

Naples is *paradiso* for foodies and it is one of the many reasons families choose to visit. Caffès and *pasticcerie* are brimming with Neapolitan pastries like *sfogliatelle* and Babà (see p. 79). Most

children have no problems consuming the sweet treats or munching on the pizza. Fired in wooden ovens, their light crusts with Vesuvius-like charred craters combine with flavoursome toppings: start with the classic *Margherita (see p. 83)*. The *frutti di mare* (fruits of the sea) are everywhere, accompanying pasta dishes, in salads, grilled or cooked *all'acquapazza*. Vegetables and fruits from the fertile volcanic soil and cheeses – including Mozzarella *di bufala* – will probably be the most flavoursome you've eaten. Neapolitans are not afraid of fat and gristle so you may find the sausages are chewier than your children are used to!

Dining out is affordable and enriching – restaurants welcome children and menus easily suit their needs – handy when holidaying with fussy eaters. But grown-ups can still try to be a little adventurous. Some of the dishes may look unappetising at first – take for example *polipo affogato* – octopus plonked on a plate and swimming in its meaty juices: the presentation may not grab you at first, but after a few bites chances are you'll be sucked in by its strong natural flavours.

INSIDER TIP ▸▸

Neapolitan family meals go on for hours and consist of many courses – especially on *ferie* (weekends and holidays). Most places don't mind you sharing dishes so ask for extra plates and create a tasting menu (*menu di degustazione*) for your family. There'll be less waste on the plate and you can spend the savings on *vino*!

Sweet Treats

It's hard to say no to the delicious *dolce* of Naples. But what is what in the *pasticcerie*?

Neapolitan Babà is a rum-drenched, bulbous-headed doughnut, often cream-filled and temple-achingly sweet, so be ready for an amazing sugar rush. Many *pasticcerie* now offer tiny versions so you can eat four instead of one!

Sfogliatella means 'many leaves' or 'layers'. These pastries are made up of thin layer upon thin layer of flaky pastry stuffed with ricotta, lightly cooked and dusted with icing sugar. A hazard to eat (especially if you're wearing black) but it's our favourite of all the wonderful *paste napoletane*.

Apollini are similar to *sfogliatelle* but filled with cream instead of ricotta.

Struffoli are made up of tiny fritters stuck together with honey. They are difficult to eat with any grace!

Torta caprese is a traditional baked chocolate-and-almond pie, sometimes made with a liqueur that comes from the island of Capri.

Zeppoli are Neapolitan doughnuts, sometimes with cream but always crusted with sugar (*zucchero*).

You can buy your sweet treats from one of the following pasticcerie:

Scaturchio Via Portamedina alla Pignasecca 22/24 📞 *081 551 3850*
Carfora Via Cupa S.Pietro, 26 📞 *081 596 2579*
Mazzaro Via Tribunali 359 📞 *081 459 248*

Caffè, Pasticcerrie & Gelaterie

Coffee is taken seriously in Naples; dapper *baristi* (coffee experts) deliver your caffè accompanied with a glass of water to wash it down – espressos are syrupy, thick and pack a punch. Italians drop in for a caffè fix throughout the day, especially in the mornings when they grab a brioche or *cornetto* (croissant) filled with *crema* (cream), *cioccolato* (chocolate) or *marmellata* (marmalade). Children love the chatter, clunk and hiss of the Neapolitan bar experience; most of them go mad for a *cioccolato caldo*, a hot, thick dark and creamy chocolate drink. As an alternative to fizzy drinks, ask for a *spremuta d'arancia*, freshly squeezed orange juice. For a cool fizz, add a *lattina di tonica* (can of tonic water) or *acqua con gas* (sparkling water).

Caffè del Proffessore

Piazza Trieste e Trento 46. 📞 *081 403 0410*

Looking over Piazza del Plebiscito, this place does a mean *caffè ai gusti di nocciola e ciocolato:* coffee flavoured with hazelnut and chocolate.

***Open** 7am–2am daily. Toilets. Credit cards.*

Caffè Gambrinus ☆

Via Chiaia 1 and 2 📞 *081 417 582; www.caffegambrinus.com*

Napoli's most famous caffè is the Gambrinus with late Victorian interiors and period paintings.

Order at the sweeping marble bar, pay at the *cassa* and consume at the bar or at one of the posh tables inside or outside (these are more expensive). The leafy terrace looks out onto bustling Piazza Trieste e Trento and the Palazzo Reale. Children will drool over the *pasticcerie* and chocolate cabinets piled high with oh-so-tempting treats including *sfogliatelle napoletane* and Babà al rhum.

Open 7am–2am daily. Toilets. Credit cards.

Chalet Ciro

Via Mergellina 11 081 669 928; *www.chaletciro.it*

For fabulous ice cream, go to Ciro's on the seafront. It's been going strong since the early 1950s, wooing children and adults with millions of *coppe* and *coni* of *gelati*, *semifreddi* e *sorbetti*. Children of all ages love their fantastical *pizza al gelato* (ice-cream pizza). And check out their dozens of different vessels that can be filled with ice cream, including the *Barca Saracena* (a long boat filled with vanilla and chocolate scoops), the massive *Supercoppa* (a huge glass) and the exotic fruit-laden *Coppa Tarzan* (in a coconut).

Open 24hr. Toilets. No credit cards.

Gran Bar Riviera ☆

Riviera di Chiaia 183, 081 665 026

Open 24 hours and famed for its pastries, ice cream and cakes, including a trademark *buondì notte* filled with nutella and *semifreddo* zabaglione.

Open 24 hours. Toilets. No credit cards.

The Best Neapolitan *Pizzerie*

Pizza was invented by poverty-stricken Neapolitans who only had flour, oil, tomatoes and basil to cook with. Fried *pizza a oggi a otto* – meaning a pizza eaten and then paid for eight days later – became a staple. On payment they picked up the next doughy meal from street vendors with mobile ovens and the on-credit cycle continued eight days later.

The golden rules of a perfect Neapolitan pizza are:

* leave the dough to rise for eight to nine hours

* do not use a rolling pin: use your hands to knead air into the dough

* cook the pizza for about 60–90 seconds at 450–480 degrees Fahrenheit (very hot, hot, hot) in a wood-fired oven

* use only natural ingredients.

Antica Pizzeria Da Michele ☆

Via Cesare Sersale 1/3 081 553 9204

Opened in 1888 this ever-popular pizzeria is for the purists: it only serves the Margherita and Marinara. The maxi-size pizza spills over the plate. Children might only be able to manage the small or medium, which are ample enough. Very thin crusts reign supreme here. Be warned it's so packed there is a ticketing

FUN FACT ▶ ## Cibo di Strada: Street Food ◀

Neapolitan street food, like pizza and maccheroni, gained popularity here on the city's crowded 18th-century streets. Most of the city's other traditional *cibo di strada* creations cost just a few euros and appeal to all ages – although not the tripe and offal sellers of the Quartieri Spagnoli, perhaps. Just off Piazza Dante is **Timpani e Tempura** (Vicolo della Quercia 17 📞 *081 551 2280*. Open 10am-9pm daily, closed Sun afternoon), a great place for tasting snacks like fried tempura (lots of tasty Neapolitan veg like aubergine slices and stuffed courgette flowers – known as *sciurilli* or *fiorilli*). The moulded savoury pastries *timpani* are perfect for picnics. Up on the Vomero hill at Via Cimarosa 44, **Friggitoria Vomero** (📞 *081 578 3150*. Open 24 hours) does fried foods including *arancini* (fried balls of rice with various tasty fillings) *pizza fritta* (fried pizza) and *calzone* (pouch pizza). If you can stomach tripe and trotters, check out **Tripperia Fiorenzano** (Via Pignasecca 14, open 8.30am–8pm) which is worth visiting, if only for the display of various innards and lots of lemons! More refreshing uses of the citrus fruit can be found on mobile stalls: children will chill after a slushy *granita* drink – crushed ice with freshly squeezed fruit and sugar.

---

system, but there is a quick turn-around of customers.

Open *10am–10pm Mon–Sat.* **Pizzas** *5€–10€.* **Credit** *No credit cards.* **Amenities** *Highchairs. Reservations not taken.*

Ciro a Mergellina ★ ★ FIND

Via Mergellina 18/21 📞 *081 681 780;* *www.ciroamergellina.it Metro: Mergellina*

Down by the Mergellina water-front – well, over the road – is Ciro, a Neapolitan favourite loved for its pizza as well as its seafood. When ordering you can choose between *pomodorini di Vesuvio* (small tomatoes grown on the slopes of Vesuvius) or regular *passata*. They also do the classic *Marinare*, *Capricciosa* and *ripieno al forno* – filled and folded calzone style and baked in the oven. You'll notice that most of the Napoletani are eating seafood classics like *insalate di mare* (seafood salad)

and *spaghetti alle vongole* (clams). If you're feeling adventurous and particularly hungry order a *polipo affogato* – octopus cooked in its own juices. The jovial waiter service adds to the dining spectacle.

Open *11.30am–11.30pm Tues–Sun.* **Pizzas** *6€–9€.* **Credit** *AmEx, DC, MC, V.* **Amenities** *Highchairs. Reservations recommended.*

Il Pizzaiolo del Presidente ★

Via deí Tribunali 120/121 📞 *081 210 903*

The Pizza Maker of the President, Ernesto Cacciali thrust a *pizza-piegata* in the hands of Bill Clinton in 1994 when he visited Di Matteo down the road. Canny Signor Cacciali gained worldwide fame and opened this no-nonsense pizzeria nearby. After a walk around the captivating Città Antica, drop in and sit at paper-clothed tables in the beguiling basement with lots of

Neapolitans tucking into the classics including their *pizza fritta* (fried pizza).

Open *12.30–3.30pm, 7.30pm–midnight Mon–Sat.* **Pizzas** *4€–7€.* **Credit** *No credit cards.* **Amenities** *Highchairs.*

Pizzeria di Matteo Via Tribunale ★★

Via dei Tribunali 94 – Vico Giganti 94
📞 *081 455 262*

It's always packed and it's not surprising – the pizza is delicious with lots of flavoursome bubbles on the *cornicone* (rim) and the prices won't burn a hole in your pocket. Children go mad for the *ripieno al forno* – a folded calzone filled with lots of gooey goodies – while older palates may like to try one of the *margerita biancas*: one is topped with mozzarella, prosciutto crudo and rocket. President Clinton dropped in during the G7 summit of 1994 – the event is remembered with framed

photos and newspaper cuttings on the walls of the very basic but relaxing dining rooms. Children will enjoy the pizza-making action by the beehive-shaped oven at the front.

Open *9am–11pm Mon–Sat.* **Pizzas** *3.50€–7€.* **Credit** *AmEx, DC, MC, V.* **Amenities** *Highchairs.*

Pizzeria Umberto ★★

Via Alabardieri 30/31, Chiaia 📞 *081 418 555*

Umberto's has been run by the di Porzio family for three generations. It's in the posh Chiaia area and its large *saloni* often host cultural events. Take the children to the long bar between the main room and the frescoed *salone* to the rear for a sneaky peak at the *pizzaoili* (pizza makers) Gaetano and Mariano working their magic by the wood-fired inferno. The pizza bases are thicker here and delicious. The Doc features the tastiest San Marzano tomatoes from

Il Pizzaiolo del Presidente, Via dei Tribunali

Royal Pizza

Pizza Margherita was named in honour of Queen Margherita, wife of King Umberto I and first Queen of Italy who visited Naples in 1889: its colours – green (basil), white (mozzarella) and red (tomato) are those of the Italian flag and pay homage to the first queen of the new Italian state.

the slopes of Vesuvius and mozzarella *di bufala* from Agerola.

Open 12.30–3.30pm, 7.30pm–midnight Tues–Sun. **Pizzas** 6€–12€. **Credit** AmEx, DC, MC, V. **Amenities** Highchairs.

FAMILY-FRIENDLY DINING

INEXPENSIVE

Osteria La Cucinotta ★ VALUE

Via G. Bausan 32, Chiaia, 📞 *081 405 400 Metro/Funicular: Amedeo.*

Down some steps in the backstreets of Chiaia, opposite some antique shops, these two dark yet cosy *saloni* are well worth seeking out: families on a budget will especially appreciate the *Menu del Giorno* (dish of the day) dishes which start at 3.50€ for a *primo piatto* (a simple pasta dish like rigatoni with a meaty ragu sauce that children will devour or linguine with squid), rising to a whopping 4€ for a secondo – a fish or meat dish. A family of four dining on a dish plus one drink and dessert each shouldn't be out of pocket more than 35€ – *che affare*!

Open Noon–3pm, 7pm–midnight Mon–Sat. **Main Courses** 4€–9€. **Credit** DC, MC, V. **Amenities** Highchairs. Reservations recommended.

Vinarium

Vico Santa Maria Cappella Vecchia 7 📞 *081 764 4114*

It's a little tricky to find but well worth the effort as this buzzing eatery-cum-wine bar is fab for families. At the front a small bar and *enoteca* serves wine with benches filled by chatty Neapolitans enjoying the epicurean experience. There's normally more room at the rear of the narrow dining area. The informal atmosphere makes family dining a joy although it can get a little busy and cramped. Nevertheless it's a fun venue for families to sample great value Neapolitan dishes that seldom make it onto tourist menus elsewhere in the city. A simple sheet with the day's choices is given out and includes pasta dishes children enjoy (huge tube-shaped rigatoni in a meaty sauce is a favourite), heaped salads and lots of seafood and the classic pasta *frittata*: a kind of Neapolitan tortilla which is very filling. Yummy desserts include an almond *semifreddo* cake with hot chocolate sauce.

Open 11am–4pm, 7pm–2am Mon–Sat. **Main Courses** 5€–10€. **Credit** AmEx, DC, MC, V. **Amenities** Highchairs. Reservations recommended.

Europeo di Matozzi

Via Marchese Campodisola 4 📞 *081 552 1323.*

La Cucina Napoletana is taken to new heights of epicurean perfection at this venerable establishment, which was opened in the 1930s. The vibrant ceramics and old prints in the dining room and the exquisite food befit a special family occasion. *Le pize* are placed on some of the poshest plates in town. Amongst their perennial favourites are *pasta e patate con provala* (pasta and potatoes with smoky melted cheese from the Campania region) and polpo in cassuola (an octopus casserole). Babà and pastiera cake are on the *dolci* list. It's on the corner of Piazza Bovio – the old financial district.

Open *Noon–3.30pm Mon–Sat and 7.30pm–11pm Thurs–Sat.* **Main Courses** *12€–19€.* **Credit** *AmEx, DC, MC, V.* **Amenities** *Highchairs. Reservations recommended.*

La Bersagliera

Borgo Marinari 10/11 📞 *081 764 6016*

A great location on the water near the Castel dell'Ovo (see p. 64), *fabulous* food and plenty of history make this a firm favourite of families. Opened in 1919, La Bersagliera has drawn many famous diners to its simple Neapolitan classics and portside location: Sophia Loren has been, Pavarotti popped in when he was in town to sing at San Carlo. Plates of seafood like *insalata di polipo* – chunks of octopus dressed with a simple lemon squeeze –

may not float the boat of youngsters but the *frittura di paranza* (lightly fried and crispy catch of the day) should get them hooked. If you enjoy seeing a wedding celebration you are likely to be treated to a show – it's a favourite reception venue and spot for Neapolitan wedding photos.

Open *Noon–3pm, 7pm–midnight Wed–Mon.* **Main Courses** *9€–20€.* **Credit** *AmEx, DC, MC, V.* **Amenities** *Highchairs. Reservations recommended.*

La Cantinella ★

Via Cuma 42 📞 *081 245 1987*

Three restaurants in one along the waterfront, offering different family dining experiences, La Cantinella is a kind of posh house of bamboo – the décor has a whiff of the exotic and the *cucina* is experimental Neapolitan: they do a pilaf of curried prawns for example. This is one for a special family occasion, perhaps when dining with older teens. Nearby at no. 38 is La Cantinella Club (📞 *081 764 0663*), which serves similar food and features live piano music, so you can enjoy your pizza and *pappardelle* with courgettes, prawns and tomatoes while listening to *O Sole Mio*. Further along the Lungomare di Santa Lucia is la Piazzetta (Via N. Sauro, 21/22. 📞 *081 764.6195*) which has a colourful interpretation of Capri's main square inside. Good-value pizza and a casual atmosphere make this great for eating with young children. Try their *pizza al largo dell'Angelo* with pomodorini (little tomatoes) from Vesuvio, aubergines, provolo cheese and basil leaves.

Open *12.30pm–3.30pm and 7.30pm–midnight Mon–Sat.* **Main Courses** *18€–32€.* **Credit** *AmEx, DC, MC, V.* **Amenities** *Highchairs. Reservations recommended.*

FAMILY-FRIENDLY ACCOMMODATION

The best places to stay for families are around Chiaia (see p. 51) and Mergellina (p. 51) – decent services, restaurants and transport links are within reach and it's a relatively safe part of town. Unless you need a convenient one-night stay close to the Alibus stop and train connections, avoid hotels around seedy Piazza Garibaldi and the train station, although, if needs must, your best family-friendly bet here is **Hotel Clarean** (Piazza Garibaldi 49, Naples 80100. ☎ *081 553 5683.* 75€ double, 85€ triple. *www.clarean. hotelsinnapoli.com*), which offers enough comfort, quiet and value to help you forget about the pandemonium outside.

Check that your accommodation has easy access: some hotels, particularly in the Città Antica, are in old apartment buildings with old lifts or a mere stairwell) and that your room is not right next to a busy road (hard to avoid in Naples!). Remember some parts of the Città Antica and Quartieri Spagnoli are dodgy – especially after dark – and should be avoided. Up in the hills of Vomero and Posillipo,

traffic, crime and pollution are less of a problem but you're further from the sights.

Most of Napoli's large hotels are more geared to business travellers and old couples rather than families and are overpriced. We have selected smaller, friendlier hotels and B&Bs to stay in. Another option, if you are staying in the city for more than a few days, is to rent an apartment from an agency like **My Home Your Home** (Via Duomo 196, 80138 Napoli. ☎ *081 195 65835; www.myhomeyourhome.it*).

Chiaia, Santa Lucia & Mergellina

Hotel Ausonia

Via Caracciolo 7, 80122 Napoli. ☎ *081 682 278; www.hotel ausonianapoli.com*

Children will love the nautical theme throughout and parents will appreciate the location – handy for the Mergellina hydrofoils, station, Villa Comunale and Castel d'Ovo. Don't be put off by the faceless entrance – once inside the grand palazzo facing the Via Caracciolo waterfront and its thunderous traffic, all is safe and quiet. As a memento of your cabin kitsch stay, they often hand out maritime-themed keyrings. The only downside is that doubles are on the small side and bathrooms are a little cramped.

Rooms *19.* **Rates** *110€–130€ double; 140€–170€ triple; 160€–200€ quad.* **Credit** *AmEx, DC, MC, V.* **Amenities** *Café. Cots free. Disabled access. Dry cleaning service.*

*Internet. Non-smoking rooms. **In room** A/C. Fridge. Shower. TV.*

Micalò ★ ★ ★ FIND

Riviera di Chiaia 88, 80122 Napoli.
℡ 081 761 7131; www.micalo.it

For families seeking an exceptional boutique hotel with oodles of art and charm, the newish Micalò should prove to be an exceptional find. Older children and teens will go gaga for the cool curvy walls, cavernous rooms with marbled mezzanine bathrooms and stylish Art Bar replete with beguiling works by emerging Neapolitan artists. The Anglo-Italian owners have created a lovingly crafted world with the help of a talented young architect, on the second-floor of a 17th- century palazzo, opposite the Villa Comunale Gardens and historic Aquarium. The helpful and knowledgeable staff enthuse about Chiaia's shops, galleries, restaurants and lesser-known local attractions. Handy transport links are within easy reach. After a mind-expanding day exploring crazy Naples, Micalò's serene yet stimulating atmosphere is just the tonic.

*Rooms 9. Rates 165€–200€ double; 200€–400€ family-friendly suite. Discounts for under-12s. **Credit** AmEx, DC, MC, V. **Amenities** Bar. Beauty treatments and massage on request. Concierge 24-hr. Cots. Disabled access. Dry cleaning service. Extra bed. iPod stations. Non-smoking rooms. Parking. **In room** A/C. Fridge. Plasma TV with Sky Italia. Safe. Shower/bath. TV. WiFi Internet.*

Palazzo Alabardieri ★ ★

Via Alabardieri 38, Chiaia, Naples 80121. http://www.palazzo alabardieri.it/

Teens may like the chic shops near this finely attired establishment in Chiaia (see p. 51). Adults will appreciate the luxury, excellent service and relatively tranquil position, and it's close to the sights and Pizzeria Umberto (see p. 82). The soundproofed rooms are elegant, spacious and

Boutique hotel Micalò

Bed & Breakfasts *alla Napoletana*

For a genuine taste of Neapolitan family life try a Neapolitan B&B – you and your family get to sit around the family table, eat fab food and discover the eccentricities of life in the crazy lane. **La Donna Albina** ★ FIND (Via Donna Albina 7. *www.donnalbina7.it*. ☎ 081 195 67817. 85€ double, 100€ triple. 10€ extra bed) has six unfussy, contemporary style rooms and offers hotel-like facilities and services like free WiFi in the Città Antica.

Right next to the Madre contemporary gallery, near the Via Foria cacophony, is a crumbling old 14th-century convent complex containing the art and antique-filled **Donna Regina** (Via Luigi Settembrini 80. ☎ *081 442 1511*. 70€–100€ double, 100€–130€ triple 140€–160€ quad). Due to the tricky access (on the fourth floor) and hectic neighbourbood, it's more suited to those travelling with teens.

The ever-creative Raffone family also have a B&B, **Posillipo Dream** (via Manzoni 214/O, 4b Parco Flory Palazzina. ☎ *081 575 6000; www. posillipodream.it*. 100€ double, 120€ triple) with a flowery terrace up in the more serene heights overlooking the Campi Flegrei. Giovanna, a crafty *cuoca* who runs cookery classes, and her engaging husband, Yorkshireman Albert who does guided tours, have a couple of immaculate rooms in a spacious modern apartment. Just up the road nearer the funicular stop is **La Bouganville** VALUE ★★ (Via Manzoni 155. ☎ *081 769 2205; www.labouganville.com*. 65€ double. 90€ triple, 120€ quad) which has great-value accommodation and a fab host Giuliano.

generally spotless with plenty of options for families.

Rooms *33.* ***Rates*** *140€–165€ double; 220€–280€ suites. Under-3s free. Discounts for under-12s.* ***Credit*** *AmEx, DC, MC, V.* ***Amenities*** *Babysitting service. Bar. City tours. Cots. Disabled access. Dry cleaning service. Extra bed. Internet. Laundry services. Non-smoking rooms. Restaurant. Room service. Safe.* ***In room*** *A/C. Fridge. Safe. Sat TV. Shower/bath.*

Città Antica & Near Via Toledo

Constantinopoli 104 ★★ FIND

Via Santa Maria di Costantinopoli 104, 80138 Naples. ☎ *081 557 1035; www.costantinopoli104.com*

This handsome Liberty-style palazzo has a hidden garden with Baroque flourishes, which is sure to make a splash with children – deep in the ancient and crowded historic centre, it has a pool. The luxurious accommodation mixes classic with contemporary. Napoli's ancient sites are right on the doorstep.

Rooms *19.* ***Rates*** *220 € double; 250€ suite.* ***Credit*** *AmEx, DC, MC, V.* ***Amenities*** *Babysitting service. Bar. City guides. Cots. Extra bed. Internet. Laundry. Massages available. Non-smoking rooms. Parking.* ***In room*** *A/C. Fridge. Plasma sat TV. Safe. Shower/bath.*

The Kitchen at La Donna Regina

Hotel Piazza Bellini

Via Costantinopoli 101, 80138 Napoli.
📞 *081 451 732; www.hotelpiazza*
bellini.com

Contemporary design and
vibrant modern artworks make
for a stylish stay in Boho Piazza
Bellini, with its laidback arty
bars, Greek ruins and edgy vibe.
It's great for families with teens
as you are in the heart of La
Città Antica action and its
multilayered historic charms.
The helpful staff is up-to-date
with the city's cultural events
and reckon the nearby Pizzeria
Di Matteo (p. 81) makes the
best Pathenopaean pie.

***Rooms** 10. **Rates** 75€–130 € dou-
ble; 90€–150€ triple. **Credit** AmEx,
DC, MC, V. **Amenities** Bar. Cots.
Extra bed. Internet. Non-smoking
rooms. Parking. **In room** A/C. Fridge.
Plasma sat TV. Safe. Shower.*

Hotel Toledo

*Via Montecalvario 15, 80134
Napoli.* 📞 *081 406 800; www.hotel
toledo.com*

Looking for a budget option?
Dip your toes in the lively
Quartieri Spagnoli backstreets
in this safe haven off the busy
Via Toledo (see p. 77) shopping
street. Children will enjoy break-
fasting on the leafy roof terrace
and checking their email in the
café. Rooms are a little dated but
generally comfortable – and
there are good options for different family groups. Anyone for
ping pong on the roof?

***Rooms** 33. **Rates** 80€–100 € dou-
ble; 110€–130€ triple; 140€–160€
suite. **Credit** AmEx, DC, MC, V.
Amenities Bar. Cots. Disabled
access. Extra bed. Internet. Non-
smoking rooms. Table tennis. **In
room** A/C. Fridge. Safe. Sat TV.
Shower. WiFi.*

4 Campi Flegrei: the Fiery Fields

CAMPI FLEGREI

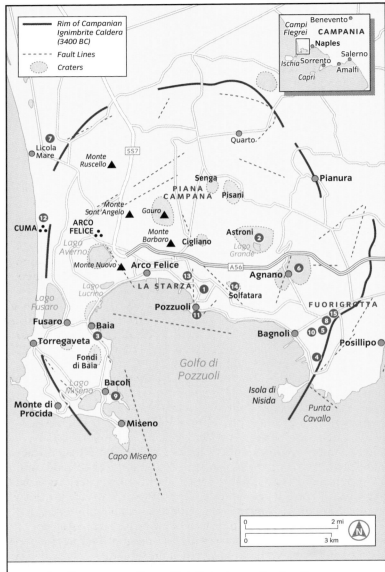

Rim of Campanian Ignimbrite Caldera (3400 BC)

Fault Lines

Craters

CAMPANIA

Benevento

Campi Flegrei

Naples

Ischia Sorrento Salerno

Capri Amalfi

Licola Mare ⓻

Monte Ruscello

SS7

Quarto

Pianura

Senga

PIANA CAMPANA

Pisani

Monte Sant'Angelo Gauro

CUMA ⓬

ARCO FELICE

Astroni ②

Lago Averno

Monte Barbaro Cigliano

Lago Grande

Monte Nuovo Arco Felice

A56

Agnano ⑥

⓭

LA STARZA ①

⓮

Lago Lucrino

Pozzuoli Solfatara

⓫

FUORIGROTTA

⑮

Lago Fusaro

Fusaro

Baia ③

Bagnoli ⑧ ⑤ ⑩

⑨

Posillipo

④

Torregaveta

Fondi di Baia

Golfo di Pozzuoli

Bacoli

⑨

Isola di Nisida

Monte di Procida

Lago Misero

Punta Cavallo

Miseno

Capo Miseno

0 2 mi

0 3 km

N

Attractions ●

Anfiteatro Flavio **1**

Astroni Nature Reserve **2**

Baia's Archaeological Sites **3**

Città della Scienza **4**

Edenlandia **5**

Horse and Chariot Racing at the Agnano Crater **6**

Magic World **7**

Naples Zoo (Lo Zoo di Napoli) **8**

Piscina Mirabilis **9**

Piscina Scandone **10**

Rione Terra **11**

Scavi di Cuma **12**

Serapeo (Tempio di Serapide) **13**

Solfatara **14**

Stadio San Paolo (SSC Napoli) **15**

The *Campi Flegrei* (Phlegrean Fields, "Fiery Fields" or "Burning Fields") west of Naples, is an area that sparks the imagination with its volcanic menace and ancient mysteries. The beaches are not the bonniest in the bay but there are fascinating ancient ruins and smouldering volcanic remnants to keep adventurous families happy. It must be said that the Arcadian landscapes that once inspired classical poets and artists have been largely lost, leaving the sublime and the scruffy to clash throughout the region. Dip into the area for a couple of days – as a mini family adventure – to explore Greco-Roman ruins, steaming volcanic craters, eerie lakes and fun theme parks. Everyone is sure to enjoy discovering the dastardly deeds and hedonistic antics that brought this coastline infamy.

The Phlegrean Fields were mythologised in classical times by Homer and Virgil as containing the entrance to Hades – the Underworld – while being conversely depicted as a heaven on earth, the timeless idyll – a bucolic paradise known as the Elysian Fields. This idealised landscape became the favourite Roman resort of Emperors and their tight curly big-wigged entourage, where historic plots were hatched in lavish palaces of pleasure. It's where Brutus colluded with Cassius and Octavian to plot Julius Caesar's assassination on the Ides of March. Pliny the Younger was at his uncle's Misenum villa during the infamous eruption of Vesuvius in AD 79.

A dozen craters lay testament to the area's seismic episodes. Many of them are filled with water now and were used by colonising Greeks and Romans for such diverse applications as oyster farms and military harbours. Virgil described one such lake, Avernus (Averno as it's known today) in his epic poem *The Aeneid*. Avernus derives from the Greek name Aornus meaning "without birds", alluding to the eerie landscape and noxious fumes that at one time suffocated birds flying over the lake. Agnano, the oldest volcano, was also once a lake and a Roman thermal bath complex – it's now home to horse and chariot racing.

The area contains mainland Europe's newest mountain, Monte Nuovo, and the eerie sulphurous fumaroles of a semi-extinct volcano at Solfatara. At one time Roman Puteoli, modern-day Pozzuoli, was the empire's most important commercial and military port. Its seafaring citizens' brave deeds and loyalty to Rome were rewarded with the construction of the Roman Empire's third largest amphitheatre.

Baia, Bacoli and Miseno have piles of intriguing archaeology to interest budding ancient scholars – some of the great Roman plots were hatched and many a drama took place in the sumptuous imperial villas and military bases along this stretch of coastline. At Cuma, where Greek colonists first based themselves, there is a vast archaeological site to explore including the mythological and mysterious Sibyl's Cave. Who knows, maybe one of you will meet the old soothsayer, fall into a trance and descend into the underworld...

ESSENTIALS

Getting There

By Train Fuorigrotta, Edenlandia, Bagnoli, Agnano, Pozzuoli, Lucrino, Baia, Fusaro and Cuma can be reached on the Circumflegrea and Cumana railway (which will eventually form part of the Metro): it starts at Montesanto.

By Metropolitana Line 6 of the Metropolitana stops at Mostra, by the San Paolo stadium and Mostra d'Oltremare exhibition centre. The true gateway to the Campi Flegrei's ancient and volcanic wonders is Pozzuoli, a bustling harbour town pretty much swallowed up by the urban sprawl of Naples. Metropolitana line 2 runs between Gianturco and Pozzuoli, stopping at Bagnoli-Agnano Terme – you can catch it at one of the city centre stations including Garibaldi Centrale, Piazza Cavour, Montesanto, Amedeo or Mergellina.

By Bus For the cheapest fare, take the no. 152 bus along the long, dusty and winding road from Piazza della Repubblica terminal, outside the Napoli Centrale train station in Naples – be warned this can be tortuous in summer though, due to the heat and traffic fumes.

By Taxi The most comfortable ride is in a taxi, especially during the week, when public transport is less reliable – catch a cab in Naples or reach Pozzuoli via public transport (Metro Line 2) and then a cab from the taxi rank at Piazza della Repubblica in Pozzuoli ☎ 081 526 5800 to reach the other Phlegrean sights.

VISITOR INFORMATION

The 24-hour Easy Napoli Family kit (*www.easynapoli.it*) is valid for two adults and three children up to the age of 18 years staying at participating hotels on a weekend – it includes reduced admission to the Città della Scienza, the Zoo, Edenlandia, reduced fares and other vouchers. It's only available from participating hotels.

The main tourist office for the Campi Flegrei is in Pozzuoli at Via Matteoti 1. ☎ 081 526 6639. *www.icampiflegrei.it*, *www. infocampiflegrei.it*. There is also an office in Baia at Via Risorgimento 28 (☎ 081 868 7541).

FAST FACTS

Banks There are lots of banks with *bancomats* (cashpoints) throughout the Campi Flegrei. Banco di Napoli has a handy branch near Pozzuoli port at Piazza della Repubblica (☎ 081 526 1386). Near the amphitheatre there is a branch of the Banca Credito Italiano (Via Oberdan 1/b, Pozzuoli ☎ 081 303 1292).

Chemist Farmacia Carella is at Via Terracciano 69, Pozzuoli, ☎ 081 526 1162.

Hospital & First Aid Ospedale Santa Maria delle Grazie is just outside Pozzuoli at La Schiana (Via Domiziana (☎ 081 855 2111) and first aid is administered at Via Solfatara (Parco D'Isanto, Pozzuoli ☎ 081 526 6954).

Maps & Leaflets Decent maps and the *Welcome to the Campi Flegrei* listings leaflet are available from the tourist office (see p. 92).

Newspapers & Magazines *Qui Napoli* is a handy listings magazine with useful timetables and maps (**www.innaples.it/ quinapoli.htm**). The newspaper *Il Mattino* publishes lists of events and boat timetables.

Post There's a post office in Pozzuoli at Corso Umberto 1 63 (☎ 081 526 1560).

Toilets Public bathrooms with baby-changing rooms are few and far between. Your best bet is to buy a coffee and use the *bagno* in a café.

CHILD-FRIENDLY FESTIVALS

Neapolis Festival
Piazzale Tecchio in Fuorigrotta, www. neapolis.it

Southern Italy's premier indie-alternative music event is a must for music mad teens and adults. R.E.M., Soulwax, Editors, Massive Attack and the Bristolians' Neapolitan pals,

Almamagretta, made recent appearances.
3rd week in July.

Palo a Mare
Ferragosto.

Daredevil types walk along a slippery wooden pole smothered in soap suspended over Pozzuoli harbour to retrieve the small flag at the end of it. Spectators fill the shoreline and hundreds of boats, cheering on their friends and celebrating the failures of their rivals as they splash into the sea.
15 August

Pizzafest ★★
www.pizzafest.info

All things to do with the humble doughy Neapolitan creation that has conquered the world are celebrated at this annual festival at the Mostra d'Oltremare exhibition centre at Fuorigrotta.
September

PLANNING YOUR TRIP

This oft-neglected area is well worth exploring – especially if you have older children who appreciate steamy geological phenomena and atmospheric, unusual sights with lashings of history thrown in. Two days should cover the most important sights with a bit of beach relaxation thrown in.

WHAT TO SEE & DO

Children's Top Attractions

❶ Freaking out in Sibyl's Cave, p. 103.

❷ Stomping around Solfatara's hollow ground dodging the whiffy fumarole steam, p. 104.

❸ Playing the mad professor at the Città di Scienza, Bagnoli p. 95.

❹ Feasting your eyes on the flapping fish in Pozzuoli, p. 98.

❺ Walking in the footsteps of Roman Emperors at Baia, p. 98.

❻ Spotting birds and other animals at Astroni Nature Reserve, p. 95.

❼ Riding the ghost train and ten-pin bowling at Edenlandia, p. 96.

❽ Cheering on I ciucciarelli (the little donkeys) of SSC Napoli at the San Paolo Stadium p. 75.

Campi Flegrei & Bagnoli

Beyond the hill of Posillipo, going west along the coast, are the less-than-picturesque areas of Campi Flegrei and Bagnoli. The **Campi Flegrei** is worth a visit for an AC Napoli game at the Stadio San Paolo (see p. 8, 75) or to visit its theme parks and leisure facilities. Despite its shabby appearance – the area is being rejuvenated after years of neglect – there are some fine attractions once you escape the exhaust fumes: the Fascist-era Mostra d'Oltremare exhibition centre has re-emerged and there are family-friendly theme parks

nearby, including Edenlandia (see p. 96) and Lo Zoo di Napoli (see p. 97). The long straight coastline at **Bagnoli** is poised to be resurrected from recent industrial ruin: this former beauty- and bathing-spot was blighted by the largest steel and chemical works in Southern Italy. It is now being decontaminated and spruced up and is very slowly being transformed back into a family-friendly resort with theme parks and luxury spa facilities. It may be quite a few years before it is completed (this is Naples after all!), but Bagnoli is a stimulating place to visit, especially if you're a science fanatic, with the superb Città della Scienza (see below) in the town.

Nearby are two old volcanic craters, Agnano and Astroni: one contains a racecourse and the other a World Wildlife Fund nature reserve teeming with birdlife. Ancient attractions with mysterious origins and intriguing histories abound along the coast.

Family-friendly Sights, Theme Parks & Activities

Astroni Nature Reserve ★
AGES 3 AND UP

Via Agnano agli Astroni, Napoli 80125. ☏ *081 588 3720; www. wwfnapolinord.it Tangenziale di Napoli (Naples circular) - Agnano exit – then in direction of Pianura for 1 km. Bus C14 from Pianura circum-flegrea train station.*

Verdant forests and lakes make up this 300-hectare World Wildlife Fund nature reserve that lies in the once-quaking roots of a long-deceased volcano that last erupted some 4,000 years ago. A network of paths takes you around these former Bourbon royal hunting grounds and three hills – Imperatrice, Rotondella and Pagliaroni – all of which are abundant in rare plants, birdlife such as herons and geese and mammals including wolves, rodents and reptiles. Keep your eyes peeled and ears pricked up for the woodpeckers, the symbol of the park. The visitor's centre offers guided tours – phone for latest seasonal details

Open *10am–4.30pm daily.* **Amenities** *Picnic area. Toilets.*

Città della Scienza ★★
ALL AGES

Via Coroglio 104, Bagnoli. ☎ *081 735 2111; www.cittadellascienza.it Cumana railway to Bagnoli then bus C9 or Metropolitana to Campi Flegrei then bus C10.*

Bagnoli's regeneration is embodied in this multimedia science museum and planetarium. The former Italsider factory was once the home of heavy industry and has been reborn as an impressive series of family-friendly exhibition spaces. Science-mad youngsters can spend time learning and being entertained in the Children's Workshop, as well as in the themed rooms – Signs, Symbols & Signals, Science & Nutrition and the Planetarium – and in the (so-called) Science Gyms. Children of all ages are spellbound by the celestial show projected onto a large cupola in the Planetarium. Another section explores the relationship between art and science – the centre hosts temporary exhibitions and permanent displays by contemporary artists like Sol Lewitt and Dani Caravan.

Open *9am–5pm daily (closed Mon during the winter months)* **Admission** *7€; children 0–3 years free.* **Amenities** *Baby changing. Café. Disabled access. Picnic area. Shop. Toilets.*

Edenlandia & Bowling Oltremare ★ **ALL AGES**

Via J. F. Kennedy 76, 80125 Napoli. ☎ *081 239 1348; www.edenlandia.it Cumana Railway stop Edenlandia or Metropolitana to Campi Flegrei*

Napoli's long-established theme park is mainly geared to younger children so don't expect many white-knuckle rides. Alongside the classic fairground fishing-for-ducks, dodgems, ghost house and carousels there's a soaring Star Wars ride, flight simulator and the heart-pounder Dominator revolving and tilting swing. Other rides for thrill-seekers include some small rollercoasters, water flumes and a sharp plunge to earth from The Tower. If the heavens descend upon you there are always the indoor attractions: arcades full of video games and a nearby ten-pin bowling alley (12 Viale Kennedy ☎ *081 624 444; www.bowlingoltremare.it*) with over 30 lanes. Littl'uns enjoy the choo-choo train that tours the park and takes in the fantasy castle – Il Castello di Lord Sheidon – belonging to that er... well-known knight of the realm. A pizzeria serves family-friendly fare.

Open generally 3–8pm weekdays, 10.30am–12am weekends and holidays. *Admission* 2.50€; children under 110cm free; 2€ per ride or 10€ for a bracelet that allows unlimited rides.

> **INSIDER TIP** ›
> Rainy days are best spent around Fuorigrotta where the family can enjoy Edenlandia's 3-D cinema and ten-pin bowling at Bowling Oltremare

Horse and Chariot Racing at the Agnano Crater
AGES 7 AND UP

Via Raffaele Ruggiero, 80125 Napoli. 📞 *081 735 7111; www.ippocity.info Tangenziale di Napoli (Naples circular) – Agnano exit – follow signs for Ippodromo. Bus C2 or train to Agnano.*

Once the home of lavish Greco-Roman spas, this old volcanic crater became a malaria-ridden lake – don't worry, it's been drained and is now the home of horse and chariot racing or as they call it in these parts, *gallopo* and *trotto*. There are occasional meetings dedicated to Neapolitan children's racing chariots harnessed to cute ponies and four thrilling meetings per week: consult the calendar on the website or give them a ring for all the latest. If you get bored of following dusty clouds around the track, visit the contemporary art gallery, which continues the equine theme and is housed in the Hippodrome complex.

Admission tickets from 12€ from the ticket office. *Amenities* Baby changing. Café. Disabled access. Picnic area. Shop. Toilets.

Magic World ALL AGES

Via S. Nullo, Napoli 80014. 📞 *081 854 6789; www.magicworld.it -Cumana railway to Licola.*

A grinning blue genie welcomes lots of lively Neapolitan families to this theme park in the sticks. For older children, lots of amusement park rides, a quad bike track, go-karting, log flumes and a terrifying-looking ejection seat that propels you into the air on bungee cords will keep them occupied for hours. Younger ones can pootle about on a mini-train, play in the *Villaggio dei Puffi* (that's a Smurf Village) and keep going back for more on the small rides – going round and round on the magic carpet carousel with Aladdin keeps them busy for hours. The adjoining Acquapark is awash with pools, fountains and water slides for all ages, and has an Area Baby that allows toddlers to splash in safety.

Open Apr, May, Sep and Oct 4–10pm Sat; 10am–10pm Sun; Jun–Aug 10am–10pm daily. *Admission* 3€; unlimited rides 10€. *Amenities* Baby changing. Café. Disabled access. Picnic area. Shop. Toilets.

Naples Zoo (Lo Zoo di Napoli) ★ ALL AGES

Via J. F. Kennedy 76 – 80125 Napoli. 📞 *081 610 7123; www.lozoodi napoli.it Cumana railway to Edenlandia – Zoo or Metropolitana to Campi Flegrei*

It may not be quite as professionally managed or imaginatively landscaped as some top-notch zoos, but an outing to Lo Zoo di Napoli makes for an enjoyable family day out. Among the exotic animals on show are lions, tigers, leopards, deer, buffalo, llamas, Indian elephants and bears as well as dozens of bird species including pelicans and flamingos. Children especially enjoy a trip to the *fattoria* (farm) where they can pet and feed goats, baby chicks and ponies and cuddle rabbits.

Open *9.30am–6pm daily Apr–Oct, 9.30am–4pm daily Nov–Mar.* **Admission** *5€; children under 80cm free.* **Amenities** *Café. Disabled access. Picnic area. Shop. Toilets.*

Piscina Scandone AGES 7 AND UP

Viale Giochi del Mediterraneo, 80125 Napoli. ☎ *081 570 2636. Cumana railway stop Edenlandia or Metropolitana to Campi Flegrei.*

If the weather is poor, or even if it is too hot to be outside, check out this Olympic-size pool – great for strong swimmers and with diving areas that should keep water-babies busy for a couple of hours. Curious sports-mad families can see games of *pallanuoto* (water polo) that are played here regularly.

Amenities *Baby changing. Café. Disabled access. Picnic area. Shop. Toilets.*

Pozzuoli, Solfatara, Baia, Bacoli, Miseno & Cuma

Pozzuoli:18km (11 miles), Baia 25km (15 miles) west of Naples

The bustling town of **Pozzuoli**, rich in Roman ruins, has a port with ferry links to the islands (very handy for Ischia (see p. 204) and Procida (see p. 215)) and a grimy charm all of its own. The childhood home of Sophia Loren (see p. 104) merits half a day's visit in order to view the boats in the harbour, clamber over Roman ruins – including the impressive Flavian amphitheatre – and to experience the other-worldly landscape of nearby Solfatara – a budding vulcanologist's must see-and-sniff. The National Park of the Phlegrean Fields is a largely dormant volcanic caldera containing numerous craters now filled with water – these eerie lakes (Averno, Lucrino,

Pozzuoli

Fusaro and Miseno) entered ancient mythology and inspired poets before the ever-practical Romans transformed them into a system of inland harbours and military strongholds.

Further west around the bay is **Baia**, once the most magnificent and infamous Roman resort whose opulent villas, fecund terraced gardens and thermal baths are now largely submerged under the sea: diving trips and glass-bottomed boats uncover some of the secrets of its past. If your family enjoys Roman history, a visit to the Castello Aragonese and the Museo Archeologico dei Campi Flegrei housed within its colossal walls is a must. With a car or a driver it's well worth exploring the archaeological sites, extraordinary feats of Roman engineering (including the Piscina Mirabilis, the Cento Cammerelle and Arco Felice) as well as all the volcanic natural wonders in the area.

It may not be as plush and the beaches may not be as clean as the days when Romans sauntered around these parts, but modern-day **Bacoli** still attracts families and weekend hedonists. Among the swanky beachside bars and *molto-cool* clubs, the one most Italian clubbers head for is Nabilah ★, Via Spiaggia Roma 15, Bacoli. *www.nabilah.it*, open Fri–Sun. Although the bar scene is perhaps more suited to clubbers and families with older teens, everyone can get a little taste of sand, salty water and an *aperitivo* along the Bacoli prom.

At the head of the promontory is Capo Miseno (known to the Romans as Misenum), 78m high with dramatic cliffs and a 19th-century lighthouse that overlooks Lake Miseno (aka Mare Morto or Dead Sea) – once the home of the Roman fleet and its admirals, including Pliny the Elder, when the Portus Julius at Baia silted up. Adventurous families could easily spend half a day here, playing on the Miliscola beach – one of the best along the Phlegrean coastline. On the western side of the promontory is the less child-friendly Spiaggia (beach) di Torregaveta, strewn with boulders and overlooked by cliffs of volcanic tufa rock that resemble honeycomb. A concrete pier juts out into the sea nearby.

In the Greek ruins at Cuma, children can enter the chamber where, as legend has it, the sacred priestess, the Cumaean Sibyl, carried out magic deeds.

The best **beaches** for youngsters are at **Miseno** and **Cuma**, while **Bacoli** has a lively stretch for older teens and partying parents who like swanky bars. Be prepared for the odd piece of rubbish on the beaches.

Anfiteatro Flavio ★★★
AGES 3 AND UP

Via Terracciano 75, Pozzuoli. ☎ 081 526 6007. Metro Line 2 or Ferrovia Cumana to Pozzuoli-Solfatara station.

Children will be wowed by the imposing Roman structure that looms out of a busy road junction in the top part of Pozzuoli. Within the grounds surrounding

Roman Romps

Ancient Baiae was a favourite enclave of the Roman elite and was the stage of many a classic historical drama: Nero murdered Agrippina here, Hadrian died at his villa in 138AD, Caligula built his three-mile famous bridge of boats here and rode across it on horseback and Cleopatra was in a Baiae house while Julius Caesar was murdered on the Ides of March (the 15th) in 44BC. Indeed, many of the emperors' colourful lives ended in a sticky mess: Augustus's (who ruled from 27BC to AD14) last words, having perhaps been poisoned, were "Did you like the performance?"; decadent Tiberius (AD14–37) was suffocated at Misenum; Caligula (AD37–41) was stabbed by conspirators; Claudius (41–54AD), who loved gladiatorial battles and executions, was poisoned with a dodgy mushroom; and the cruel thespian Nero (54–68AD) committed suicide.

the amphitheatre, toppled columns and ancient fragments – including the odd oversized foot from a statue – are strewn around next to overflowing dustbins and clumps of grass, adding to the bizarre scene. Wander around the open corridor and peer into the rectangular ditch at the amphitheatre's heart, then imagine caged cubicles filled with wild beasts hoisted into the fray. In late antiquity the theatre was neglected and then partially buried by volcanic debris from Solfatara. Luckily this ash preserved and protected the underground chambers' architectural features from looters, giving us insight into the mechanics of the performances. Since Vespasian completed its construction in AD67–79, the 40,000-capacity amphitheatre has witnessed many a gruesome drama. In 305AD San Gennaro (see p. 61), patron of Naples, was imprisoned here along with another half- a-dozen Christian martyrs before being decapitated at Solfatara; Nero lanced a bull

and some scholars reckon that the arena was flooded for mock sea battles.

Open *9am–1 hr. before sunset Wed–Mon, closed Tues. Closed 1st Jan, 1st May and 25th Dec.*
Admission *4€; includes admission to four sights: Il Serapeo in Pozzuoli, the Museo acheologico and zona archeologica di Baia and the Scavi di Cuma in the Flegrea area in two days; 2€ 18–24 years; free under-18s and over-65s.*

Baia's Archaeological Sites ★★ AGES 4 AND UP

There are rich pickings for families into ancient archaeology at Baia (Baiae), which from the second century BC to the end of the Roman Empire, was the most fashionable and decadent of all Roman resorts. Most of the grandiose villas now lie under the sea at the **Parco Archeologico di Baia** (Porticciolo di Baia. ℂ *081 524 8169; www.baiasommersa.it*. Admission 10€ 20% discount with Artecard (see p. 53) and 10% on scuba equipment hire; 4–12 years 9€; under-3s free Mid-Mar to Mid-Nov Tues–Sun

Archeologico dei Campi Flegrei, Castello Aragonese

9.30am–1.30pm and 3.30–7.30pm). Older children with scuba and snorkelling skills can take the plunge and explore the excavated area, including the villa of Lucius Piso, father-in-law of Julius Caesar. Otherwise you can view the site in one of the specially designed boats, such as the Cymba with an underwater viewing gallery. (Book in advance for a place on one of the trips which depart at 10am, noon and 3pm Tues–Sun). Safely above water, sitting in a commanding position above the Baia promontory is the **Castello Aragonese**, which houses the **Museo Archeologico dei Campi Flegrei** (Via Castello 45, Baia. (*081 523 3397* or (*848 800 2884*. Admission 4€; 2€ 18–25s; free for under-18s and over-65s; includes admission to Zona Archeologica di Baia, Anfiteatro Flavio, the Serapeo and Scavi di Cuma within two days. 9am–3.45 pm Tues–Sun. Closed 1st Jan, 1st May and 25th Dec. Cumana railway to Arcofelice or Lucrino): highlights include the Sacellum (shrine) of the Augustali (dedi-cated to the emperor's cult and found at Misenum), Sala dei Gessi, which contains plaster-casts of celebrated Greek statues, and the sweetly named Ninfeo di Punta Epitaffio. After the tour, head out to the panoramic terrace and imagine the most idyllic Roman stage scene: terraced gardens and villas filled with scented flowers, spa pools, fountains and the ancient VIP-set relaxing, cavorting and scheming.

There are more ruins of an imperial pad and verdant parkland to skip around at the 34-acre **Parco Monumentale**, Via Bellavista, Baia. (*081 523 3797*. 9am–1hr before sunset daily. Closed 1st Jan 1st May and 25th Dec). Free admission. Also worth a gander is the colossal complex of buildings that is believed to have been an imperial residence, built by Ottaviano in the 1st century BC that is now the **Parco Archeologico Terme di Baia**, Via Sella di Baia 22, Baia. (*081 868 7592*. 9am to 1 hr before sunset Tues–Sun. Closed 1st Jan, 1st May and 25th Dec. Admission 4€;

Sibyl!

The legend of the Cumaean Sibyl is tied up with Virgil's 1st-century epic poem *The Aeneid*, in which Trojan hero Aeneas visits the Sibyl, who falls into a prophetic trance and reveals that Aeneas will be the glorious founder of Roman civilization. With the help of the Sibyl, he descends into the underworld at Cuma (p. 103) and talks to his father. Imagine a tiny, old and shrivelled woman ensconced in her Cuma chamber, using magic powers to guide a Greek hero on his glorious path.

Keep this quiet from the children until after the visit or for a later date. In truth *The Aeneid* was written to create a myth that attached the legends of Troy to the Roman Julio-Claudian dynasty, by claiming descent from Aeneas's son Ascanius. This bolstered the imperial claim of Julius Caesar's heirs by making them out to be from good Greek stock. Sibyl's Cave was more likely to have been used for military or funerary purposes than as the venue for dark arts performed by a wrinkly, immortal woman. The question remains: if the Sibyl didn't exist then did a character like her?

includes admission to Museo Archeologica di Baia, Anfiteatro Flavio, the Serapeo and Scavi di Cuma within two days. 2€ under 25s; free for under-18s and over-65s. It is accessed via a downhill path from Esedra, from the Parco Monumentale. Follow in the footsteps of wealthy Romans who came to remedy their ailments in the thermal springs of the Venus, Sosandra, Mercury and Diana baths here. In the 13th century Frederick II reopened many of the establishments as did the Spanish viceroys in the 1800s – unfortunately the land has subsided and little hot water remains.

Amenities Picnic area. Toilets.

Piscina Mirabilis ★
AGES 6 AND UP

Via A. Greco 10, Bacoli. 081 523 3199

A couple of miles along the coast in Bacoli is an oft-overlooked subterranean Roman reservoir structure whose scruffy exterior amid nondescript flats hardly hints at the cathedral-like wonders within – it's well worth the extra effort needed to see it – opening times are sporadic though and you may need to track down the key holder (at time of publication: Giovanna 081 523 3199), who lives nearby. The largest freshwater reservoir built by the Romans was hewn out of the soft tufa rock and has some impressive stats: it's 15 metres high (45 feet), 72 metres long (220 feet) and 25 metres wide (75 feet), with a capacity of 12,000 cubic metres (around 36,000 cubic feet). Lavish Roman villas, gardens and the sailors in the Imperial fleet required lots of water, which came from 100 miles away in the mountains near Avellino, via the Aqua Augusta, aka the Serino Aqueduct. Numerous branches of this incredible feat of engineering served numerous towns on the way, including Pompeii, Pozzuoli and Naples. Now the water has drained away, you can admire the colossal structure – its vaulted ceilings and 48 pillars create an atmospheric space with eerie light effects and unusual acoustics. Children will love the spooky light streaming from the roof way above them and the haunting echoes when they speak.

Open phone Giovanna the custodia (caretaker) to confirm that she will be around to let you in. The opening times are generally 9am–dusk Mon–Fri.

INSIDER TIP ❯❯

After a morning exploring the ancient ruins of Baia head down the coast to Bacoli to hear spine-tingling echoes at the Piscina Mirabilis and then have a seafood lunch at Garibaldi (See p. 106) overlooking the intimate bay.

Rione Terra ★ AGES 3 AND UP

Largo Sedile di Port, Pozzuoli. 📞 848 800 288. Metro Line 2 or Ferrovia Cumana railway to Pozzuoli station.

The oldest part of Pozzuoli and its ancient Acropolis were abandoned in the 1980s as the area was sinking under the sea. It was resurrected as a destination a decade later when excavations uncovered underground Roman streets, replete with shops and fountains. Phone in advance to book a place on a fascinating tour tracing the Decumanus (the main east–west high street) and exploring side street taverns, gladiator quarters and grain

stores. Bring warm clothes as it can get chilly down here. If the children are gagging for some more Roman finds from the Rione, check out the Museo Archeologico dei Campi Flegrei at Baia (see p. 100), which contains handsome sculptures and other ancient treasures.

Open 9am–6pm Sat and Sun. *Admission* 3€; 2€ children 6–18 years; under-6s and over-65s free. Cumulative ticket including Museo Acheologico di Baia, Anfiteatro Flavio and Serapeo in Pozzuoli and Scavi di Cuma 6€ and valid for two days. Guided tours (45 mins.) 4€. *Amenities* Picnic area. Toilets.

Scavi di Cuma ★★
AGES 4 AND UP

Via Monte di Cuma 3, Cuma. 📞 081 854 3060. Bus from Circumflegrea station to Baia or Fusaro.

In 730BC the ancient Greeks chose Cuma as their first colony in the Western Mediterranean – the crumbling remains of the ancient city now sit within wild parkland which will capture the imagination of youngsters, especially the spine-tingling Toblerone-shaped tunnel, Antro della Sibilla. Set aside a few hours for a leisurely stroll around the large archaeological site taking in the various architectural remnants – they may look like heaps of stones but they conjure up some magic nonetheless, telling the story of Cuma's various inhabitants and invaders. Perched on an outcrop is the Acropolis – two huge temples (Apollo and Jupiter), which were transformed into churches in the 5th and 6th centuries. 10th-century Saracen raids toppled these basilicas and most of the ruins here date from Roman and early Christian times. An overgrown and very old amphitheatre (2nd century), where many a gruesome act took place, spikes the imagination as does the spooky Antro della Sibilla (Sibyl's Cave): take a walk along the angular-shaped tunnel hewn out of the tufa rock that ends in a three-room chamber, believed to be the seat of the Cumaean Sibyl, a kind of ancient witch-cum-prophetess. Long before Basil Forte trembled on hearing those ominous words "ohhhhhhh I knnnnnow" uttered by Sybil at the Fawlty Towers reception desk, *la Sibilla* was synonymous with sooth-saying powers.

Open 9am–1 hr. before sunset daily. Closed 1st Jan, 1st May and 25th Dec. *Admission* 4€ includes admission to Museo Archeologico, Zona Archeologico Terme di Baia, the Anfiteatro Flavio and the Serapeo; 2€

Apollo's Temple, Cuma

18–25s; free under-18s and over-65s. *Amenities* Café. Toilets.

Serapeo (Tempio di Serapide) ★ AGES 3 AND UP

Via Roma 10, Pozzuoli. 📞 *081 526 6007. Ferrovia Cumana to Pozzuoli station.*

The Egyptian god Serapis gives its name to this Roman *Macellum* meat market area as a statue of the deity was found here – its cult was all the rage under Emperor Vespasian – and its remains lie at the centre of this impressive and photogenic heap of architectural fragments. Look out for the small holes on the columns made by marine molluscs – evidence that the site once lay under the sea and an example of the bradisism (alternating subsidence and uplift of the earth's surface) that affects the Campi Flegrei.

Open 9am-1 hr before sunset. Wed–Mon, closed Tues. Closed 1st Jan, 1st May and 25th Dec.

Sophia Loren – Pozzuoli's Finest Daughter

"Everything you see, I owe to spaghetti!"

Sophia Loren, Italy's best-known movie star and one of the 20th century's most unconventional beauties, came from humble beginnings indeed. Born Sofia Villani Scicolone in Rome on 20th September 1934 her father refused to marry her mother, so she took the newborn and her little sister to live with their maternal grandmother in rough and tumble Pozzuoli, near Naples.

When she entered a Miss Rome beauty contest she missed out on the title but she won the attentions of one of the judges, anti-establishment film director Carlo Ponti. She was renamed Sophia Loren and her career took off.

She starred in *Gold of Naples* (1954), *The Pride and the Passion* (1957) with Cary Grant (who fell in love with her), *Houseboat* (1958) and The Millionairess (1960) with Peter Sellers (who fell in love with her). *The Fall of the Roman Empire* (1964) is considered her most commercially successful film but Sophia's big moment came in *La Ciociara /Two Women* (1961) for which she won an Oscar.

Sophia and the already-married Carlo Ponti's meeting in 1950 began one of the most scandalous, dramatic but enduring love stories of the

---

Admission *4€; 2€ 18–25s; free for under-18s and over-65s: includes admission to Museo Archeologico e Zona Archeologica di Baia, Anfiteatro Flavio and Scavi di Cuma.* **Amenities** *Picnic area. Toilets.*

Solfatara ★ AGES 4 AND UP

*Via Solfatara 161, Pozzuoli. ☎ 081 526 2341; **www.solfatara.it** -Metro to Pozzuoli–Solfatara and then bus P9 or 800m on foot. Bus 152 from Piazza Garibaldi.*

Take the plunge into the steamy sulphurous crater (752m across), but don't worry as this 4,000-year-old volcano just west of Pozzuoli hasn't erupted since the 12th century. The smell of rotten eggs (that's hydrogen sulphide for all you chemistry fans) did not put off spa goers and Grand Tourists who came to drink,

bathe and admire the pressurised mineral springs and fumaroles (steamy volcanic vents) like Bocca Grande (Big Mouth) – spouting 160-degree water vapour. Children love stamping on the hollow-sounding lunar landscape which is stained here and there with yellow and bright red sulphur and Arsenic deposits. Solfatara's sights, sounds and smells are entertaining if a little disorientating: as well as whistling, hissing geysers there are spluttering, bubbling mud pools, a well serving supposedly medicinal water and ancient *sudutoria* (sweating rooms) – steam grottos – named Purgatory and Hell. A word of warning: the ground is hot (180 degrees Fahrenheit in places!) so wear

20th century. Years of public outcry, Vatican outrage and life-long harassment by the Italian Government ensued – it forced them to annul their first marriage. They married again in 1966 in France after becoming French citizens and stayed, happily and in love, until he died in 2007.

Carlo was sentenced in 1979 in absentia to 6 months jail for suggesting, in his film *Massacre in Rome,* that Pope Pius XII collaborated with the Nazis. Later the government seized his art collection and fined him $24million for taking money out of the country. In 1982 the Italian authorities forced Sophia to serve 19 days in prison for tax evasion. Tax evasion? In Italy? She certainly saw the funny side of it.

But Sophia still loves where she comes from. A massive Napoli FC fan, to spur them on she said she would do a striptease if they were promoted to Serie A. She might have been 73 years old at the time but Napoli's form improved suddenly and they were promoted. Sophia has yet to fulfil her part of the deal... although she did give the Neapolitans a taster when she appeared in the Pirelli Calendar in 2007.

Is there a movie star who has aged so wonderfully and lived her life with such gusto?

thick soles, and the fumes can be uncomfortable to asthma sufferers.

Open 8.30am–7pm daily. Admission 5.50€ (4.40€ with Artecard); 4€ up to 10 years; children under 4 free. Amenities Café. Toilets.

SHOPPING

If you don't want to eat in restaurants all the time, explore the fab foodie shops of Pozzuoli and Bacoli for a lunchtime picnic treat.

Buono ★ (Corso Umberto I, 43. 📞 *081 526 0472*) For a morning *merenda* (snack) or pastry and coffee break in Pozzuoli, this place is hard to beat. The *sfogliatelle, pizzette* (little pizzas) and ice cream taste even more

delicious on the terrace overlooking Pozzuoli's *lungomare* (promenade).

Dolci Qualita (Via Carlo Rosini 45. 📞 *081 526 528*; *www.dolci qualita.com*) sells wonderful local honey and fab wines including Falanghina DOC *vino bianco* and Per è Palummo, a *vino rosso*.

Il Mercato Ittico – the wholesale fish market – next to the Temple of Serapide, Pozzuoli, down by the waterfront is one of the biggest in Italy. For picnics and supplies, Daber (📞 *081 526 7443*. Via Anfiteatro 1, Pozzuoli) is a handily placed supermarket outside the amphitheatre and near the train station.

Monkey Cafe (Via Lucollo, 2. Bacoli. 📞 *081 868 7082*) in Bacoli

Neapolitan Gestures

Animated Neapolitans have quite a few gestures to get their point across. Here are a couple of gestures and what might be said while you are doing it.

Che saporito! Che buono!: How tasty! How delicious!

When you have tasted something especially delicious, plunge your index finger in your cheek and move hand from side to side in a half-twisting motion.

Ma che 'vvuò? Ma che buuò?: What are you saying? What do you want?

Bring thumb and fingers together and move hand up and down. The meaning and tone of this gesture can vary enormously from beseeching to humorous and even darkly menacing.

---

has a youthful vibe and serves sweet and savoury *spuntini* snacks like brioche and roast meats.

FAMILY-FRIENDLY DINING

Pozzuoli and the Campi Flegrei area are renowned for fabulous fish. For a look at the bountiful catch, check out the *pescherie* dotted around town. Most places will rustle up a simple plate of pasta for young and picky eaters.

Garibaldi ★★

Via Spiaggia 36, 80070 Bacoli. ☎ 081 523 4368

Since its humble beginnings as a fisherman's eatery in the early 20th century, the Garibaldi has been a fixture beside the curvy bay of Bacoli. Children will love the views of the beach and pasta *al pomodoro fresco* (with fresh tomatoes) while parents will get a *peperoncino* kick from their spicy version of the classic *spaghetti alle vongole veraci* (spaghetti with mussels). Vegetarians and meat eaters will be

happy with the menu. Sweets include *panna cotta* (like crème brulée) with *frutti del bosco* (forest fruits) and a chocolate mousse.

Open 12–3pm, 7–11pm Tues–Sun. Main Courses 9€–18€ Credit: AmEx, DC, MC, V. Amenities Highchairs. Reservations available.

Il Capitano

Lungomare Cristoforo Colombo 10, 80078 Pozzuoli. ☎ 081 526 2283

Drop into this portside restaurant for some classy family dining – it's smart yet relaxed, which should keep everyone happy. The Captain's coordinates are handy if you have arrived by boat or fancy a superb culinary experience after a day's sightseeing in the Campi Flegrei. As you'd expect from a salty seadog of a name, the Captain does some fine fish dishes including a deliciously crispy *frittura del mare* (fried seafood medley) – all freshly caught and bought from Pozzuoli's famed fleet. They'll also create child-friendly dishes like bucatini pasta with a simple tomato *salsa*, if children prefer ingredients hailing from *terra firma*.

Open 12–3pm, 7–11.30pm Wed–Sun. *Main Courses* 9€–20€. Credit: AmEx, DC, MC, V. *Amenities* Highchairs. Reservations available.

Il Casolare ★ GREEN

Via Pietro Fabris, 12/14, 80070 Bacoli. 📞 081 523 5193; *www.sibilla.net/ilcasolare*

For an agriturismo experience with a slightly boho flavour, try this place between Baia and Bacoli. Children can marvel at the views and imagine volcanic eruptions spewing out of the crater that surrounds the rustic 19th-century *masseria* (land-owner's grand house) – while adults can chat to the friendly chefs about their abundant crops, all farmed here. Produce, artwork and knick-knacks fill the many dining rooms and terraces, giving it an earthy, ramshackle yet endearingly eccentric atmosphere. The enthusiastic foodie owners are happy to prepare tasting dishes for guests, such as *coniglio alla bacolese* (Bacoli-style rabbit), *baccalà* (dried salted cod) and lots of *contorni* (vegetables). For less

Delicious ice-cream

adventurous youngsters ask head-honcho Tobia Costagliola to rustle up something plain. There are themed party evenings and one of their functional rooms can accommodate a family of four for just 70€.

Open 8.30pm daily. *Fixed Price Menu* 25€–35€. *Credit* None. *Amenities* Highchairs. Reservations essential. Book in advance by phone or website.

La Villetta ★★

Via Lungolago 58, 80070 Bacoli. 📞 081 523 2662

A warm family atmosphere makes this old favourite over-looking the Lago di Miseno well worth seeking out. In the summer there's al fresco dining in the leafy courtyard. Traditional Neapolitan fare fills the menu: a bit of meat, lots of tasty vegetables, fish straight from the Mar Tirreno and some devilishly delectable desserts. You'll all be crying "delizioso!" e "buono!" while plunging index-fingers in cheeks: the Neapolitan gesture for "tasty!" (see Neapolitan Gestures box p. 106)

Open 12–3pm, 7–11pm. *Main Courses* 7€–15€. *Credit* AmEx, DC, MC, V. *Amenities* Highchairs. Reservations available.

FAMILY-FRIENDLY ACCOMMODATION

There's a dearth of decent hotels in the Campi Flegrei but the good quality ones you do find here offer excellent value.

Remember most of the sights are not too difficult to reach from Naples, so you can travel here from your hotel in Naples.

Averno Damiani Camping, Hotel & Apartments VALUE

Via Montenuovo Licola Patria 85, 80078 Pozzuoli. ☎ *081 804 2666; www.averno.it*

There's a decent choice of great-value accommodation suitable for active families in this quiet spot near Lake Averno. It's hardly a luxury complex but nevertheless it's perfect for families seeking a sociable and active holiday. The Phlegrean Fields archaeological sites as well as a couple of okay beaches at Cuma and Miseno are nearby. As well as camping pitches and simply furnished cabins within the grounds, there are a few hotel rooms and decent apartments (with kitchenettes for those seeking the flexible self-catering option). Sporty children will go mad for the facilities, which include swimming pools, a go-kart track and a *campo di calcetto* (five-a-side football pitch)/basketball court. For teens there is a disco – not quite as hip as the Nabilah Beach Club at Bacoli (see p. 99). Mums and dads can use the spa, sauna, hydromassage treatments and the well-equipped gym.

*Rooms 10. **Rates** 85€–105€ double; 100€–140€ bungalows for 2–5 people; 130€–260€ apartments (with kitchenettes). **Credit** AmEx, DC, MC, V. **Amenities** Bar. Disabled access. Gym. Launderette. Outdoor thermal pools. Restaurant. Sauna. Spa. Sports facilities. **In room** Cots. Extra bed (10€). Non-smoking rooms. Safe. Shower/bath. TV. WiFi.*

Cala Moresca ★★

Via Faro 44, 80070 Bacoli. ☎ *081 523 5557. www.calamoresca.it*

High above Miseno (p. 99) amid lush gardens, this hotel has lots of facilities for families. Many of the simply furnished rooms have balconies and stunning views of the Bay of Naples towards Procida and Ischia. There are plenty of room options and nine mini-apartments suitable for families of various sizes. Children enjoy the large pool and access to a private beach – a word of warning though: it's rocky and not suitable for toddlers. Young children can use the small playground and for those who like a run around there are tennis, basketball and volleyball courts. Staff can arrange excursions and fishing, golf, rowing, canoeing, windsurfing, sailing, scuba diving, aerobics and yoga. The management also provides Easy Napoli cards (see p. 92) at weekends for families wanting to do some sightseeing.

*Rooms 36. **Rates** 110€–210€ double; 120€–230€ family apartments (with kitchenettes). **Credit** AmEx, DC, MC, V. **Amenities** Bar. Cots (15€). Disabled access. Dry cleaning service. Extra bed (15€). Gym. Laundry services. Non-smoking rooms. Outdoor pool. Restaurant. Sports facilities. Sun deck. WiFi. **In room** A/C. Fridge. Internet. Safe. Shower/bath. TV.*

Hotel Miseno VALUE

Via della Shoah, 21, Porticciolo Casevecchie 80070 Bacoli. 📞 *081 523 5000; www.hotelmiseno.it*

Sitting on the *Case Vecchie* harbour-side seats at the Hotel Miseno, children can watch the comings and goings of fishermen at close hand. Parents will appreciate the great value offered, although those who demand lots of facilities and immaculate rooms may not be so mad about the Miseno. However, we like its fabulous setting, relaxed family-run atmosphere and the bar-restaurant Miseno a 'Mmmare, which combines top nosh from the sea with the occasional samba band. The amiable owners are happy to arrange boat trips and airport transfers.

Rooms *12.* **Rates** *60–85€ double.* **Credit** *AmEx, MC, V.* **Amenities** *Bar. Boat trips. Under-3s in cots free. Extra bed (10€). Non-smoking rooms. Parking. Restaurant.* **In room** *A/C. Fridge. Shower/bath. TV.*

Hotel Relais Villa Oteri

Via Lungo Lago 174, 80070 Bacoli. 📞 *081 523 4985; www.villaoteri.it*

This elegant hotel in Bacoli provides comfortable accommodation and great services for families – indeed it feels more like a four-star than a three star. It's in a great location for the Bacoli beach, which may not be the prettiest but has a lively atmosphere – especially in the summer months. The restaurant staff serve inventive Neapolitan specialities like squid salad with almonds and are happy to rustle up simple pasta dishes for children. Guests are able to get discounted use of the nearby Stufe di Nerone spa facilities and a gym. They can also arrange cheaper rates for the use of a pool and the beach at Bacoli.

Rooms *9.* **Rates** *70€–110€ double; 95€–130€ triple.* **Credit** *AmEx, DC, MC, V.* **Amenities** *Bar. Cots (20€). Dry cleaning service. Extra bed (20€). Gym (for additional fee) access.*

Averno Damiani Camping, Hotel & Apartments

Villa Giulia, Pozzuoli

Laundry services. Library. Non-smoking rooms. Restaurant. Spa access (for additional fee). *In room* A/C. Fridge. Safe. Shower/bath. TV.

Villa Giulia ★

Via Cuma Licola 178, Pozzuoli. ☎ 081 854 0163; www.villagiulia.info

The neighbourhood is a little drab but you will find this haven sitting in lush gardens hidden behind high walls. Leafy, tranquil gardens containing citrus trees, a Neapolitan summer kitchen (with a pizza oven) and a fab pool make this historic townhouse turned B&B near Cuma a real gem for families. As well as five comfy doubles there are five apartments of various sizes – there's bound to be one to suit each family's needs. If you don't fancy cooking every night, the owner can provide meals if requested well in advance. The owner speaks excellent English and is keen to share her local recommendations. Sporty children can try some of the activities available in the area including tennis, golf and horse riding.

Rooms 10. Rates 90€–140€ double; 95€–130€ triple. Credit AmEx, DC, MC, V. Amenities Bar. Cots (20€). Dry cleaning service. Extra bed (20€). Gym (for additional fee) access. Laundry services. Non-smoking rooms. In room Shower/bath. TV.

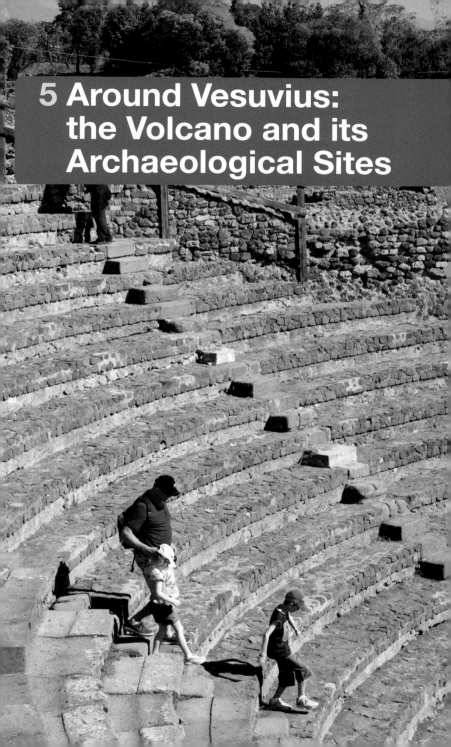

5 Around Vesuvius: the Volcano and its Archaeological Sites

Vesuvius – mainland Europe's only active volcano – is probably the most ubiquitous natural sweep of cooled magma of them all, adorning the walls of Italian restaurants from Alaska to Zetland. Living under the volcano gives Neapolitans their gusto, playful sense of humour and a dark, superstitious nature. It's well worth dipping into the *Zona Rossa* (Red Zone) where some 600,000 Napoletani dice with danger by living in an area greatest at risk from any pyroclastic flows. You can walk around the crater and gaze into its depths, imagining what lies deep below the steamy, sulphurous vapours.

Being in Vesuvio's presence and visiting its ancient victims buried in the infamous eruption of AD79 is both a humbling and inspiring experience; one that will ignite imaginations and flicker the tickers of children and grown-ups alike. Exploring these awe-inspiring ruins gives you fleeting glimpses and fascinating insights into Roman life in the first century AD. The untold treasures and revelations trapped in a 1,700-year-old gaseous volcanic bubble at Pompeii and Herculaneum, the lost towns, are overwhelming. Dip into the area for a few days – you'll need a day at least for sprawling Pompeii and another to ascend Vesuvius and explore Herculaneum. For families keen on Roman archaeology there is the opportunity of visiting all five of the major archaeological sites around Vesuvius (Herculaneum, Pompeii, Oplontis, Stabiae and Boscoreale).

Don't expect wonderful resorts and fab family-orientated hotels along this stretch of coast – over-development and industry have obliterated much of the natural beauty that drew Roman epicureans and Neapolitan aristocrats to build lavish villas at the fruitful foot of the volcano.

On the other hand do expect the tastiest produce on restaurant menus and at *frutta e verdure* (fruit and veg) stalls: the tomatoes (*pomodorini del piennolo* and *san marzano*) are like nothing else on Earth while the bulbous oranges and lemons are squeezed into a thirst-quenching, icy *granita*. So while the children are refreshed with a rustic slush, older noses can enjoy the fruits of Vesuvio – Christ's Tears and Tail of the Fox (Lacryma Christi and Coda di Volpe) wine.

VESUVIUS

16km (10 miles) E of Naples, 8km (5 miles) NE of Herculaneum

From every corner of the Bay of Naples you can see its pleasingly curvy outline – the magma and debris Vesuvius spewed into the bay for millennia has wrecked cities yet continues to renew the Campanian soil with minerals and fecundity. Mainland Europe's only active volcano is the symbol of the Bay of Naples – its power and presence has created a city that feels more like Rio de Janeiro than Ravenna. Grand Tourists flocked to its rim by foot, on a sedan chair and then aboard a

VESUVIUS

Attractions ●
Agriturismo Il Cavaliere **1**
Bel Vesuvio Inn **2**
Boscoreale – National Antiquarium of Man and
  Environment in the Territory of Vesuvius **3**
Osservatorio Vesuviano **4**
Parco Nazionale del Vesuvio Crater **5**
Scavi di Ercolano (Herculaneum) **6**
Scavi di Pompeii (Pompeii Excavations) **7**
Scavi di Stabia (Roman Stabiae) **8**
Villa Oplontis **9**

celebrated funicular railway. Nowadays a cramped minibus ride and a walk make it a less stylish ascent. A visit to "hell's-chimney pot" (as it was known in the Middle Ages) and a walk around its rocky rim makes for a memorable adventure. As well as peering into the snoozing cauldron and taking in the views near its zenith at 1,200m (4,000ft), families can hire a vulcanologist guide to take them on one of the walks around the Vesuvius

National Park. And just in case you're worried that the pot might blow with you on top of it, remember that the volcano is probably the most carefully monitored in the world. According to the official Emergency Plan, Vesuvius will signal its violent intent weeks in advance (see box p. 116).

Essentials

Getting There

The route to Vesuvius necessitates the use of motor transport (car or bus) to reach the car park below the summit. You still have to walk the final leg to the summit over lava fields and volcanic rocks – to reach the summit, at 1,281m (4,202ft), from the car park you climb around 250m (over 800ft).

By Car All vehicles, except the Presidio Vulcano Vesuvio four-wheel drive vehicles driven by official guides, must stop at the entrance to the park at 1,017m (3,336ft) in altitude.

By Train From Naples or Sorrento, take the Ferrovia Circumvesuviana Railway (800 053 939; *www.vesuviana.it*), which departs regularly from the Stazione Vesuviana (Corso Garibaldi; Metro: Garibaldi) and along the coast from the Sorrento station to Ercolano.

By Bus Hidden away outside Ercolano (Herculaneum) station is the small Compagnia Trasporti Vesuviani office selling bus tickets and combined tickets to the national park – the operation is typically shambolic and the small minibuses depart from just outside the station (straight up the hill from Ercolano Scavi itself) to the car park. The combined ticket is 15€.

INSIDER TIP

The minibuses are often oversubscribed and very overcrowded so prepare to sit on knees and don't bring much baggage with you!

Fast Facts

Banks There are branches of Banco di Napoli at Via Plinio 45, San Sebastiano al Vesuvio 081 574 8995 and in Ercolano at Via IV Novembre 3 081 777 3466. In Pompei there's a branch of Banca Monte Dei Paschi Di Siena at Piazza Longo B. 40 081 863 6511.

Chemist Farmacia Pompeiana is at Via Roma 12, Pompei. 081 850 7264.

Hospital & First Aid Medical assistance can be sought at Via Colle San Bartolomeo, 50, 081 535 9111 or Croce del Sud, Via Nolana, 165 081 850 5746.

Maps & Leaflets Decent maps of the Vesuvius area including walking maps are available from the Vesuvius National Park centre.

Post There's a post office in Pompeii at Piazza Esedra 3. 081 536 5200.

Believe it or not, Vesuvius (at present) has a lower altitude than Britain's highest mountain Ben Nevis. How many feet/metres lower is it though? The person with the closest answer gets carried to the top of Vesuvius on a sedan chair like a 19th-century Grand Tourist.

Answer: 210ft – Ben Nevis is 4,406ft above sea level, while Vesuvius is 4,196ft above sea level (or 1,279 metres according to the latest records).

Toilets There are makeshift festival-style public toilets at the Vesuvius Centro Visite car park. The toilets near the Herculaneum entrance and the ones at Pompeii at the Forum are adequate. Otherwise your best bet is to buy a coffee and use the *bagno* in a café outside the attractions.

Visitor Information

The Vesuvius National Park (Piazza Municipio 8, 80040 San Sebastiano al Vesuvio. ☎ 081 771 0939; *www.parconazionaledel vesuvio.it*) has information about the park and guided walks in the area.

What to See & Do

Children's Top Attractions

❶ Roaming the Roman ruins at Pompeii and discovering its captivating treasures, p. 129.

❷ Hot-footing it up Vesuvius and peering into the steamy crater, p. 116.

❸ Confronting the nine-headed hydra, a mythological monster at Herculaneum, p. 128.

❹ Checking the shaky needle on the seismic scales and learning about Vesuvio at the observatory, p. 115.

❺ Trekking the lava trails around Vesuvius and looking for rare species including magma-loving lichen, p. 119.

❻ Popping into Poppaea Sabina's old pad and being wowed by its dreamy pastoral scenes, p. 144.

❼ Feeding the animals and feasting on fabulous farm produce at an agriturismo, p. 145.

Down on the Farm on the Slopes of Vesuvius

Il Cavaliere, Via Gramsci 109, 80040 Massa di Somma, ☎ *081 574 3637; www.agrodelcavaliere.altervista. org/ Bel Vesuvio Inn, Via Panoramica 40, 80040 San Sebastiano al Vesuvio* ☎ *081 771 1243; www.agakituris mobelvesuvioinn.it*

Take a few hours out of the archaeological explorations by visiting one of the fabulously fertile agriturismi on the slopes of Vesuvius. Both Il Cavaliere (see p. 145) and Bel Vesuvio Inn (see p. 146) welcome families and children to meet their farmyard

Vesuvius Blows Again

Unlike those unsuspecting Romans going about their business on that August day in AD79, who were unaware that the fertile hump covered in vines above them would explode with such cataclysmic force, we know it's going to blow its top again. Nine out of 10 vulcanologists reckon that the next eruption could happen any time soon. Vesuvius has been dozing since 1944 so those magma chambers below the quietly steaming cone are filling up. The pressure will give and the most disturbing statistic is that more than half a million people live within the red (for danger) zone; a further 1.1 million in a yellow zone would be threatened by the vast debris of an eruption.

animals, including goats and chickens, and sample their bountiful and tasty produce – including cheeses, hams, wine, veg, apricots and the tastiest piennolo tomatoes – in a relaxed ranch setting. Both organise excursions in the surrounding Vesuvius National Park and child-friendly activities like horseriding, mountain biking, playground fun, footie and swimming in the pool.

Amenities Baby changing. Café. Disabled access. Picnic area. Shop. Toilets.

Osservatorio Vesuviano ★
AGES 4 AND UP

☎ 081 610 8483; www.ov.ingv.it Bus from Ercolano Scavi station.

For families and children with an avid interest in vulcanology, the Vesuvian Observatory is a must-see. The exhibition explains the different types of volcano on planet Earth using video, scientific instruments and displays of volcanic rocks. You can even monitor the seismic and geochemical activity recorded by the Vesuvius Observatory surveillance team – fingers crossed the needle doesn't go haywire in the near future!

Open 9am–2pm Sat and Sun. *Admission* free. *Amenities* Baby changing. Disabled access. Toilets.

Parco Nazionale del Vesuvio Crater ★ ★ ★ AGES 7 AND UP

Centro Visite (Visitor Centre) ☎ 081 777 5720/081 739 1123)

The Vesuvius National Park Authority looks after the protected area around the volcano. Once you reach the Centro Visite (Visitor Centre) take Nature Trail no. 5 incorporating part of the walk to the summit and halfway around the Vesuvius crater.

The walk up to the crater itself is along a steep, wide path covered in volcanic rocks and takes about 30 minutes. Sturdy shoes, a warm layer and refreshments are essential. This can be hard work, especially under an unforgiving *mezzogiorno* sun, and can be tough-going for the children. The views along the path and around the crater (600m or 1,970ft in diameter) are incredible. Bring a camera and record the views across the Bay of Naples, the Mar Tirreno and beyond into the Campania countryside. Even the most nonchalant child will be dumbfounded on seeing, smelling and hearing the jets of steam rising from the luridly coloured rock crystals among the silver-grey pumice. It's a scene that seems to belong to another planet. The 200m (656ft) chasm to the crater floor adds to the dizzying, disquieting spectacle.

Special guided tours also start from the Visitor Centre, run by top *Guida Vulcanologica* personnel such as amiable Roberto Addeo, who will show you the steaming fumaroles within the crater – these are beyond the perimeter fence and are out of bounds to the general public. Do not attempt to go into the crater on your own as there have been many fatalities. Although the staff are responsible, well briefed on safety and experts in their field, there is an element of danger to this short scramble down to the fumaroles.

A rickety rusty sign with scribbled handwriting points the way to Pompeii, way down below. You can stock up on postcards, refreshments, snacks and Lacryma Christi wine, produced on the slopes of Vesuvius, at the shop near the summit.

Open from 9am daily; closing times vary throughout the year – last admission is about 90 min before sunset. *Admission* 7€ adults; 5€ under-18s and students; free for under-8s accompanied by an adult.

The Smoking Cone of Vesuvio-Monte Somma

When the African and Eurasian tectonic plates met, the earth's crust became superheated and magma escaped violently into the Bay of Naples, forming the Campanian Volcanic Arc and the volcanoes of Sicily. Vesuvius's *Gran Cono* (large cone) and surrounding steep slopes sit within the caldera of Monte Somma: the remains of a larger and taller (1,149m: 3,770ft) crater that formed some 18,000 years ago and subsequently collapsed. Between the Gran Cono and Monte Somma is the *Valle del Gigante* (Valley of the Giant), in turn divided between the *Atrio del Cavallo* (Hall of the Horse) in the west and the *Valle del Inferno* (Valley of Hell) to the east.

Over the past 25,000 years there have been many "effusive" eruptions (these spew lava), including the last eruption in 1944.

More violent are Vesuvius's "explosive" or "Plinian" eruptions, which propel smoke and ash high into the atmosphere – and include the infamous event of AD79 and the last such explosion in 1631. Vesuvius has been dormant for more than 60 years now, its longest period of inactivity in nearly 500 years. Chances are the next eruption will be a big one, perhaps similar to the massive one in 1631 which killed some 4,000 people...

Fumaroles, Vesuvio

ERCOLANO (HERCULANEUM)

9.5km (6 miles) SE of Naples, 8km (5 miles) SW of Vesuvius

Herculaneum was a more illustrious victim of the AD79 eruption of Vesuvius. A smaller and richer town than Pompeii, its elegant resort villas, many built on the seashore, were buried by huge pyroclastic flows that sealed it for nearly two millennia.

During the eruption, the resort was buried under a torrent of mud, gas, lava, ash and rock up to a depth of more than 15m (50ft). This mixture of volcanic debris hardened, making excavations tricky. On the upside, the nature of the inundation helped preserve extraordinary architectural detail and remarkably few of

the roofs collapsed. The searing heat of the pyroclastic flow carbonised organic materials and, coupled with the deep burial, helped seal the site for 1,700 years. In 1709 the first excavations were instigated by Emmanuel de Lorraine, Prince d'Elbeuf, who stumbled across the back of the theatre while digging a well.

What is so exciting about Herculaneum is that so many new discoveries are made intermittently and so many more are waiting to be unearthed. In the 1980s, 250 skeletons were found huddled together in boathouses along with some exquisite jewellery. Unfortunately there are large areas that the archaeologists cannot access as they are buried under the ugly modern town. Experts reckon we have

Walking in the National Park `AGES 8 AND UP`

Ente Parco Nazionale del Vesuvio, Piazza Municipio 880040 San Sebastiano al Vesuvio, ☏ 081 771 0911; *www.vesuviopark.it*

Active families keen on thrilling treks may be interested in exploring the Vesuvius National Park (see also p. 116). There are nine colour-coded trails varying in difficulty from low to high. One of the easier routes is Trail 9 (Grey route): *Il Fiume di Lava* (The Lava Flow): this ½-mile circular trail starts and ends at Via Osservatorio. The estimated time of the walk is 90 minutes and covers the area of lava that spewed from the mountain during the eruption in 1944. Look out for rare plants along the way such as the yellow lichen – *Stereocaulon vesuvianum* – that thrives on mineral-rich cooled magma – the mere mention of it makes botanists quiver with excitement. The more colourful Trail 4 (Orange Route) crosses the Tirone Alto Forestry Nature Reserve, established in 1972. The complete trail is a seven-hour round trip and covers more than five miles of wonderful landscapes containing pines, *macchia mediterrenea* (maquis – or Mediterranean scrub) and holly. If you have small children, you can also choose small sections of the longer walks. Keep your wits about you and you may see or hear cuckoos, foxes, martens, hares and lizards. *Contact the park wardens for more information about guided walks. Roberto Addeo is an experienced guide and vulcanologist who can be contacted on his mobile* ☏ *+39 347 351 6815 or by email* **E: vesuviotrek@libero.it**

only brushed the charred surface of the so-called **Villa dei Papiri** (see p. 128) and its important library of Greco-Roman scrolls. There's nothing like talk of lost treasures to excite children, so a couple of hours' exploration of ancient Herculaneum is a fascinating journey into the past for *tutta la famiglia*.

The lavish villas on the promontory and the lack of artisans' houses suggest Herculaneum was a resort for the idle rich. Perhaps 5,000 residents lived here at the time of Vesuvius's devastating eruption. Unlike Pompeii, the streets are not deeply rutted by the constant traffic of mercantile carts. The earth along the main thoroughfare, the Decumanus Maximus, was not paved over but compacted and closed to vehicles using small stone columns – Roman traffic-calming measures!

> **INSIDER TIP** ≫
>
> For families keen on Roman archaeology, you can visit all five of the major archaeological sites around Vesuvius (Herculaneum, Pompeii, Oplontis, Stabiae, Boscoreale) within three days by buying a special cumulative ticket (adults 20€). These are available from the sites' ticket offices. Children under 18 get in free.

Who the Devil were the Plinys?

At the time of the AD79 eruption Pliny the Elder was head honcho of the Roman Fleet at Misenum over the bay in the Campi Flegrei. The ever-curious Pliny, a prolific writer and scientist, threw down his quill and summoned a small fleet of galleys to cross the bay by boat in order to save some friends at Stabiae. His nephew, Pliny the Younger, remained at his uncle's Misenum villa documenting the events, leaving us a valuable account. Pliny the Elder perished at the foot of the volcano, probably through inhalation of poisonous gases. Pliny the Younger writes:

".... his body was found intact and unharmed, and still fully clothed in a tunic. He looked more like that of a sleeping – rather than a dead – man."(Book of Letters, VI-16.)

Essentials

Getting There

By Rail Public transport links to Herculaneum – or Ercolano as the locals call it – are pretty quick and easy. Take the Ferrovia Circumvesuviana Railway (📞 *800 053 939* (*numero verde* – freephone number within Italy); *www.vesuviana.it*) from the **Stazione Circumvesuviana** on Corso Garibaldi; Metro: Garibaldi) to Ercolano Scavi (on either the Sorrento or Poggiomarino lines); the 20-minute journey costs 2€. A shuttlebus outside the station takes passengers to the excavations, which are only a 10-minute walk away.

By Taxi If you're in a large group with lots of luggage, the best way is to take a taxi from Naples for around 35€.

By Car Driving is an option but may prove to be a nightmare.

Herculaneum

HERCULANEUM

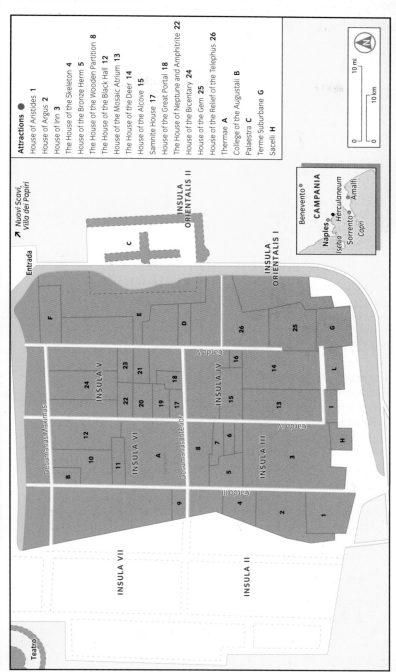

Attractions ●

House of Aristides **1**
House of Argus **2**
House of Inn **3**
The House of the Skeleton **4**
House of the Bronze Herm **5**
The House of the Wooden Partition **8**
The House of the Black Hall **12**
House of the Mosaic Atrium **13**
The House of the Deer **14**
House of the Alcove **15**
Samnite House **17**
House of the Great Portal **18**
The House of Neptune and Amphitrite **22**
House of the Bicentary **24**
House of the Gem **25**
House of the Relief of the Telephus **26**
Thermae **A**
College of the Augustalii **B**
Palaestra **C**
Terme Suburbane **G**
Sacelli **H**

Nuovi Scavi, Villa dei Papiri

Entrada

INSULA ORIENTALIS II

INSULA ORIENTALIS I

INSULA V

INSULA VI

INSULA IV

INSULA III

INSULA VII

INSULA II

Decumanus Maximus

Decumanus Inferior

Cardo III

Cardo IV

Cardo V

Teatro

Benevento
CAMPANIA
Naples
Ischia · Herculaneum
Sorrento · Amalfi
Capri

10 mi
10 km

Parking in Ercolano is nigh on impossible and petty car crime is a constant worry. You can get to Ercolano on the A3 Autostrada (Exiting at Ercolano-Portici) or the SS18 road along the coast.

INSIDER TIP >

If you have awkward luggage use your charm on one of the Herculaneum *guardaroba* (cloakroom) staff and deposit it in the store room – you may get a dour shrug in response but the service is free. If you're travelling with babies and small children, the uneven ground is not ideal for buggies – use a papoose.

Planning a Trip

For those braving the roads take the A3 Autostrada and exit at Pompeii Ovest. Follow signs for Pompeii Scavi to Porta Marina where you can park your vehicle. Circumvesuviana railway to Ercolano–Scavi.

The archaeological site at Herculaneum may not be extensive, but be warned: there are quite a few steps, ramps and slopes to negotiate. The lack of shade means that a good sun hat is essential in spring and summer. Plan a route before you go so you don't miss the places that interest your family. Children may get bored as well so it's best to enliven the visit with some spine-tingling tales about Roman life, their myths and gods, and the terrifying days of AD79.

As there are no cafés within the site, bring refreshments and snacks to keep energy levels up – there's lots of walking and many mind-blowing things to see and take in. Unfortunately, some of the buildings have been sealed due to erosion and damage caused by rainwater and pigeons.

Unfortunately **Herculaneum** is not a place to linger in and eat food – after you've seen the excavations it's best to head out of the rather shabby modern town which has been particularly blighted by the recent problems with refuse collection.

If your group is fairly fit, combine a trip to Herculaneum with a journey to Vesuvius (p. 112) – but this is not advisable on a sweltering summer's day!

INSIDER TIP >

If you really need a quick pastry, coffee or cool drink fix head to Italia Caffè e Pasticceria on Corso Italia 17.

What to See & Do

Ercolano Scavi: Herculaneum Excavations ★★★
AGES 5 AND UP

Corso Resina, Ercolano. Information ☎ 081 857 5347/ ticket office ☎ 081 777 7008; *www.pompeiisites.org*

After surviving the *biglietteria* (ticket office) and negotiating the typically disorganised Neapolitan bureaucracy, you'll be faced by a long walkway that descends into the excavations. This broad path allows an overview of the grid-layout: the road intersections (those orientated north–south are the *cardi* while the east–west routes are called *decumani*) define six rectangular *caseggiati* (blocks or sections) of the city, the *insulae*. Below, we've split up the site into these ancient urban blocks. Take advantage of the audio-guide and booklet at the ticket office to find your way around.

> **INSIDER TIP**
>
> Be warned some youngsters may get bored and tired so try and include a visit to the gory and mythological **highlights:** the House of the Skeleton (see p. 125), House of the Relief of the Telephus (see p. 127), and the monster Hydra in the Palaestra (see p. 128). Don't miss the sheer beauty of the House of the Mosaic Atrium (see p. 125), The House of the Deer (see p. 125), Thermae (see p. 126), House of the Great Portal (see p. 125), The House of Neptune and Amphitrite (see p. 125), and The House of the Black Hall (see p. 127).

Open 8.30am–7.30pm daily Apr–Oct; 10am–5pm daily Nov–Mar. Last entrance 90 min before closing time. Closed 1st Jan, 1st May and 25th Dec. **Admission** 11€; 5.50€ 18–25 years; free for under-18s and over-65s. Audioguide 7€ adults, children 4€. Cumulative ticket for all Vesuvian sites (Herculaneum, Pompeii, Oplontis, Stabiae and Boscoreale) valid for three days: 20€ adults, 10€ 18–25s, free for under-18s. **Amenities** Baby changing. Café. Disabled access. Picnic area. Toilets.

Insula II & III

Walking along the Cardo III Inferiore you first come across the **House of Aristides** (Casa di Aristide) (Ins. II, building 1), where many skeletons of victims trying to escape the eruption were found. Next door is the **House of Argus** (Casa del Argo) ★ (Ins. II, building 2), one of Herculaneum's finest villas, named after a small painting depicting the myth of Argus, that mysteriously went

Ercolano Scavi

FUN FACT **The Eruption of AD79**

The towns around Vesuvius, including wealthy Herculaneum and bustling
Pompeii, did not heed the warnings of an earthquake in AD62 and its various
aftershocks. Vesuvius had been bearing juicy grapes for centuries without any
hint of blowing its top. Pliny the Younger's account of what he witnessed at
Misenum in Campi Flegrei has helped vulcanologists piece together what happened on those fateful two days. He was 17 years old at the time and wrote the
account in letters to the historian Tacitus 25 years after the eruption.

A number of small earthquakes in mid-August preceded the eruption, which
occurred in two phases: a Plinian eruption (so called after Pliny the Younger's
account) jettisoned ash, pumice stone and gas 20 miles into the atmosphere in a
pine-tree shape blown by a strong wind in a south-westerly direction. The atmospheric dust blocked out the sun's rays and created an eerie, suffocating atmosphere. The debris rained down for much of the night of the 24th for between eight
and 20 hours, building up a layer of debris three metres thick at Pompeii. Here
roofs heaved and eventually gave way, killing or trapping many people. Lying west
of Vesuvius, Herculaneum avoided the worst of these ash showers.

On the morning of the 25th August, a violent discharge of a superheated
(400°C or 750°F) mixture of gases and ash (a *nuée ardente* – a type of pyroclastic flow) devastated Pompeii; more than 2,000 people were suffocated or burned
to death and many bodies were discovered huddled together. Another huge
pyroclastic flow then finished off the stragglers and the town was completely
buried. The coastal settlements Oplontis (see p. 142), near Torre Annunziata and
Herculaneum (see p. 118) received the brunt of the pyroclastic flows.

At Misenum, Pliny the Younger wrote:

"... A black and dreadful cloud bursting out in gusts of igneous serpentine vapour
now and again yawned open to reveal long fantastic flames, resembling flashes
of lightning but much larger... Soon afterwards the cloud began to descend upon
the earth, and cover the sea... Ashes now fall upon us, though as yet in no great
quantity. I looked behind me; gross darkness pressed upon our rear, and came
rolling over the land after us like a torrent... We had scarce sat down, when darkness overspread us, not like that of a moonless or cloudy night, but of a room
when it is shut up, and the lamp put out. You could hear the shrieks of women,
the crying of children, and the shouts of men...' (Book of Letters, VI-16.)

missing. Discovered in 1828,
this was the first house at
Herculaneum where the upper
floor was revealed – imagine coming across its cupboards and
shelves filled with kitchenware
and carbonised figs and flour.

Just over the Cardo III road is
the back entrance to the **House**

of Inn (Casa dell'Albergo) (Ins.
III, building 3), not an inn at all,
but a sprawling villa that was
undergoing refurbishment at the
time of the eruption. It is home to
the only private *thermae* (thermal
baths) found at Herculaneum; a
carbonised pear tree trunk was
found in the garden.

The House of the Skeleton (Casa dello Scheletro) (Ins. III, building 5) takes its chilling name from the skeleton found on the second floor. Check out the two *nymphaea* (an ornamental alcove/grotto) with its inlaid decorative panel, exquisite floral motifs and a man with a sacrificial lamb. Behind this palatial pad on Cardo IV Inferiore is the modest **House of the Bronze Herm** (Casa dell'Erma di Bronzo) (Ins. III, building 6), with a Tuscan-style atrium, central pool and a bronze sculpture of the homeowner.

The House of the Wooden Partition (Casa del Tramezzo di Legno) (Ins. III, building 8) overlooks Cardo IV and is noteworthy for its corniced façade, open gallery, mosaic paving and wooden partition with bronze handles. A number of side rooms were used as shops, including one used by a *lanarius* (fabric maker) known as the Store with a Clothes Press – you can see the instrument inside.

Insula IV & V

Don't miss the fab views from the **House of the Mosaic Atrium** (Casa dell'Atrio a Mosaico) ★★ (Ins. IV, Building 13) and check out the geometric and chequerboard mosaic flooring that were left wonderfully wavy after the eruption. This sight is bound to get "wows" all round. Next door, the **House of the Alcove** (Casa dell'Alcova) ★ (Ins. IV, building 15) has a ground floor split into two dwellings – the most lavishly decorated contains beautifully painted walls.

The House of the Deer (Casa dei Cervi) ★ (Ins. IV, building 14) was a sumptuous waterfront residence named after two marble groups of deer being attacked by dogs in the garden – the originals are in the Museo Archeologico in Naples (see p. 72). Children will chuckle at seeing the nearby statue of a drunken Hercules relieving himself. The terrace would have had direct views of the sea and the bay's islands and coastlines beyond.

The first dwelling on the Cardo IV Superiore is the **Samnite House** (Casa Sannitica) (Ins. V, building 17), dating from the 2nd century BC, with the layout of a pre-Roman dwelling. Beyond the imposing portal of Corinthian capitals is an elegant open gallery with Ionic columns and fabulous frescoes with architectural reliefs. Neighbouring **House of the Great Portal** (Casa del Gran Portale) ★★ (Ins. V, building 18) has an elegant frontage of two pilasters, demi-columns and exquisitely carved capitals with winged Greek-style Victories – experts reckon this was rebuilt after the AD62 earthquake. Who can spot the panel depicting birds pecking at cherries?

The best-preserved shop in Herculaneum is below **The House of Neptune and Amphitrite** (Casa di Nettuno ed Anfitrite) ★★★ (Ins. V, building 22), a wine store with intact wooden fittings, shelves for

Neptune Mosaic

amphorae and a counter. The vivid colours of the famous Neptune and Amphitrite glass wall mosaic that adorns the east wall will impress arty children especially. Take a close look at the recessed *nymphaeum* with its ornate decoration depicting hunting scenes and attractive motifs, all topped with a head of Silenus (the faithful pal of Dionysus, the god of wine) and some marble theatrical masks. Around the corner on the Decumanus Maximus is the entrance to the **House of the Bicentenary** (Casa del Bicentenario) (Ins. V, building 24), discovered by celebrated archaeologist Amadeo Maiuri in 1938, 200 years after Charles III began the excavations.

Insula VI

On a sweltering day walking around Herculaneum it would be great to have a cool dip – unfortunately we can only pour water over our heads and imagine what it was like to bathe in the **Thermae** (Terme Urbane) ★★★ (Ins VI, building A) built at the beginning of the 1st century AD, in the reign of Augustus. There are separate baths and entrances for men and women, on Cardi III and IV respectively.

On entering the men's baths you first come to the *apodyterium* (dressing-room) which contains niches for storing garments and basins for washing. A circular *frigidarium* (for a bracing cool dip) is on the left, with a blue vaulted ceiling decorated with fish and punctuated with a skylight. On the right are the *tepidarium* and *caldarium* (which must have been hot, hot, hot) – check out the exposed pipes and smoke vents which give an indication of the Romans' plumbing sophistication.

You enter the **Women's Baths** on Cardo IV Superiore. After the waiting room, have a look at the beautifully decorated *apodyterium* (dressing room) with mosaic floors representing Triton swimming with dolphins, an octopus, cuttlefish and a cherub with a whip – very interesting. The *tepidarium* has a mesmerising mosaic floor with a labyrinthine design, while the *caldarium* has sumptuous white-and-red marble benches. The vaulted ceiling was designed with grooves for channelling condensation. A large *praefurnium* (furnace/boiler room) heated the complex and water was drawn by an 8m-deep well.

Imagine coming out of the baths and relaxing in the porticoed garden, exercising in the central outdoor *palaestra* (gym) or playing *pila* (a ball game) in the *sphaeristerium*, a covered hall.

Many wooden objects were found in **The House of the Black Hall** (Casa del Salone Nero) ★★ (Ins. VI, building 12). Beguiling paintings fill the vaulted rooms and the dark interiors of the large room will especially please Goth youngsters. The **College of the Augustali** (Sacello degli Augusti) (Ins. VI, public building B) was the seat of the cult of the emperor

Augustus – two large panels depicting Hercules, Jupiter, Juno, Minerva and the Etruscan god Acheloo are well worth seeking out. The caretaker's skeleton was found on a bed in an adjoining room.

Insulae Orientalis I & II

The **House of the Gem** (Casa della Gemma) ★ (Ins. Orientalis I, building 25), named after an engraved stone found on the site, has an unusual atrium with huge frescoed panels and sturdy pilasters as well as a terrace garden. Don't miss the rather civilised graffiti in the toilets (there are ruder examples in Pompeii (see p. 133)) that record the visit of a famous doctor.

Next door is the largest Herculaneum villa: the **House of the Relief of the Telephus** (Casa del Rilievo di Telefo) ★★ (Ins. Orientalis I, building 26) whose atrium opens onto a *peristyle* with colonnades and a garden. This three-storey mansion is named after a bas-relief depicting the myth of Telephus – the son of the god Hercules – founder of the city. Don't miss the circular plastercast copies of the original marble *oscilla* (discs depicting satyrs to ward off evil) hung between the red-hue plastered columns.

The partially excavated **Palaestra** ★★ (Ins. Orientalis II, building C), the public sports centre has a monumental vestibule with two columns on Cardo V and a lower terrace with porticos. All eyes are drawn to the long pool – believed to have been used for breeding fish – and part of a cruciform swimming pool where a mythical five-headed serpent is entwined around a tree truck. It may be a copy of the original statue found here, but this mythical monster, Hydra, is sure to be a spine-tingling sight for littl'uns.

Check out the 18th-century AD Bourbon excavation tunnels that run beneath the avenue, which give you not only an idea of the scale of the *palaestra* but also the huge undertaking needed to uncover Herculaneum's treasures.

The Suburban District or South Terrace

There are a few more buildings down by the waterfront area accessed via a couple of paths on Cardo IV and Cardo V. The **Terme Suburbane** ★★, the Suburban Baths, include a *frigidarium* with white marble flooring and a *tepidarium* whose stuccoed wall depicts warriors. Check out the impression made by a *labrum* (washing tub) on the volcanic material that inundated the *caldarium*. There's a photo opportunity at the statue of the celebrated senator M. Nonius Balbus, an ally of Octavian (who became Augustus).

Alas, a visit to the buried **Theatre** nearby and its 18th-century tunnels dug by Prince d'Elbeuf's speculative excavators is not always possible (ask at the box office). On the western fringes of the South Terrace are the **Sacelli** and the **Sacred Area**, containing two temples – one dedicated to Venus with a fresco of a garden and the other to four gods: Neptune, Minerva, Mercury and most aptly Vulcan. Vaulted warehouses and boat storehouses line the old shore in this district (in AD79 it was right on the beach) where 300 human skeletons and their valuables were found in 1980. A 9m-long Roman boat was unearthed in 1982, containing a rower, soldier, swords and a pouch of coins among other things.

Villa dei Papiri and I Nuovi Scavi (New Excavations) ★★★

Historians believe that this grandiose villa – named after the miraculously preserved rolls of papyrus containing Greek writings found here – belonged to Lucius Calpurnius Piso Caesoninus, the father-in-law of Julius Caesar. 18th-century engineers stumbled across the villa when excavating a well. It is built on several levels with a colossal 820ft (250m) frontage along the ancient shoreline.

A large collection of bronze and marble busts of Greek figures found here are housed in the Museo Archeologico Nazionale in Naples (see p. 72). Around 1,800 papyrus rolls were unearthed in the library, believed to have been collected by the Epicurean scholar and philosopher Philodemus of Gàdara. Many of the carbonised scrolls were clumped together and badly damaged by well-meaning conservators attempting to separate the leaves. In the 1990s multispectral imaging techniques developed by NASA were used to decipher the text on the opened scrolls. Most of the scrolls are kept at the Palazzo Reale library in Naples.

Astounding discoveries are still being unearthed – in 2007 a throne was found with exquisite ivory bas-reliefs depicting Greek mythological figures. For a guided visit to the villa and the Nuovi Scavi, ask at the information point or contact Arethusa ℂ *081 739 0963*; *www.arethusa.net*.

POMPEII

27km (17 miles) SE of Naples

Covered by a deluge of ash, pelted by pumice and then obliterated by a wave of searing gas, magma, mud and volcanic debris, the Roman city of Pompeii was buried and forgotten about for nearly 2,000 years.

Walking around Pompeii is the closest the human race can get to time travel. You'll be spellbound by the scale and sophistication of the city. Children will be captured by the almighty nature of one cataclysmic event.

Some 20,000 inhabitants lived in flourishing Pompeii. Many fled during the first deluge of volcanic debris but thousands stayed behind – some would not have been able to move home while others remained to protect their homes from looting. Many perished when roofs collapsed under the weight of ash and pumice before the almighty pyroclastic surge engulfed them and buried everything in its wake. Youngsters will be spooked by the plastercasts of victims, created by archaeologist Giuseppe Fiorelli. By pouring plaster into cavities left by bodies in the ash you can see the final positions of the instantly incinerated victims: men, women, children and dogs frozen in time. These poignant glimpses of a horrific fate are a tad unsettling.

On a lighter note, the burial of Pompeii and its inhabitants gives us the most valuable insight into Roman life and kicked off a boom in archaeology. Children can wander down Via dell'Abbondanza and play the bartender at a *thermopolium*; bleach some clothes in the fullers' vats (they held a brew of urine and potash – groo!) or practise their oratory in the Forum. They will enjoy imagining the lives of the people here. The tangible objects – the tools, statues, amphorae – and the architecture – the spas, villas, gardens, shops and temples, theatres and sports grounds – reveal the occupations, aspirations, attitudes and actions of the ancient *Pompeiani*.

Essentials

Getting There

By Rail Pompeii is easily reached from Naples and Sorrento by way of the Ferrovia Circumvesuviana railway (ℂ *800 053 939* Numero Verde – a Freephone number within Italy; *www.vesuviana.it*) from the **Stazione**

POMPEII

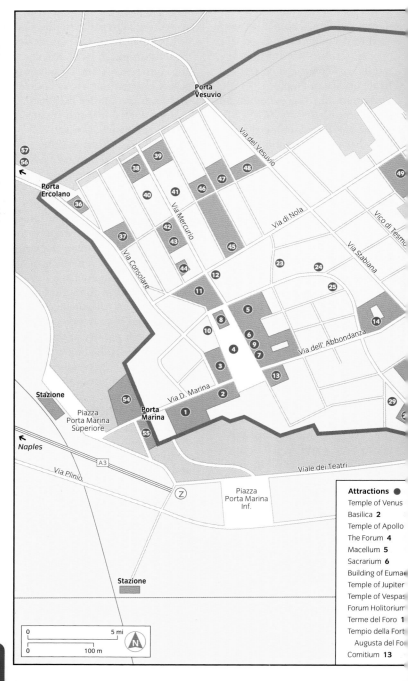

Porta Vesuvio

Via del Vesuvio

Porta Ercolano

Via Mercurio

Via Consolare

Via di Nola

Vico di Tesm

Via Stabiana

Via dell' Abbondanza

Via D. Marina

Porta Marina

Stazione

Piazza Porta Marina Superiore

← Naples

A3

Via Plinio

Z

Piazza Porta Marina Inf.

Viale dei Teatri

Stazione

0   5 mi
0   100 m

N

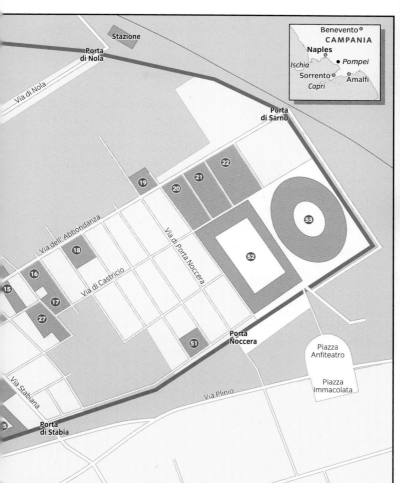

Circumvesuviana on Corso Garibaldi; Metro: Garibaldi to Pompeii Scavi – *Villa dei Misteri* on the Sorrento line or on the Poggiomarino lines to Pompeii Santuario; the 40-minute journey costs 3€. The Pompeii Scavi station is more convenient for the classic visit to the ruins beginning at the Porta Marina entrance near the Villa dei Misteri, whereas the Pompeii Santuario station is handy for staring at the Anfiteatro entrance which is nearer the town centre, cathedral and many of the hotels. You may decide to take the Poggiomarino line and the Pompeii Santuario stop if you have lots of luggage and would like to check into one of the hotels nearby. Another alternative is the FS (Ferrovie dello Stato: State Railway) station on Piazza XXVIII Marzo, which is on the southern margins of the town centre.

By Car Take the Autostrada A3 and exit at Pompei Ovest, then follow signs to Pompei Scavi. There are car parks by the main entrance, including the one at Camping Zeus (☎ *081 861 5320*) next to the Villa dei Misteri.

Planning a Trip & Getting Around

Pompeii is so huge, you'll need to come prepared for a mighty long walk on uneven ground. Children under 10 will probably only manage a couple of hours so get yourself a map and plan your route.

Wheeling buggies across pitted lava slabs is no fun. A papoose is more practical. Heat and lack of shade and facilities are the main concerns so bring hats, lots of water (in a cool bag), sun cream and snacks. There's a severe lack of toilets and food outlets – and the main ones at the Forum are not always well-maintained or well-stocked! There are left luggage stores at the Piazza Anfiteatro and Porta Marina entrances.

> **INSIDER TIP** ≫
>
> If you have older children who are really keen on seeing Pompeii's restricted areas, which are protected under lock and key, contact the Ufficio Scavi (☎ *081 857 5347*; *www.pompeiisites.org*) who run guided tours and themed adventures. Arethusa also run similar tours (☎ *081 861 6405*; *www.arethusa.net*) at Pompeii and Herculaneum.

Some hotels provide a semi-decent map. Otherwise there are plenty available outside the entrances – as a bit of sport, remember to haggle, otherwise you'll get ripped off!

The city covers 158 acres and its walls are punctuated by seven gates (porta): Marina, Ercolano, Vesuvio, Nola, Sarno, Nocera and Stabia. In the **Foro Triangolare** (Triangular Forum) area, with its Doric temple dating to Greek times, many of the city's older houses lie within a 6th-century BC irregular street plan. The later grid layout, with rectangular *insulae* (urban blocks) set within

TIP ❯❯ Titter Ye Not! ❮❮

Erotic frescos and blush-making fertility symbols abound: you can bet your bottom euro that these will be spotted and questions asked! Thankfully, the saucy 1,700-year-old graffiti will go over young heads unless they have PhDs in vulgar Latin. Here's one of the tamer scribbles: Long live lovers. Death to those who know not how to love. Double death to those who hinder love.

the *decumani* (east–west streets) and *cardi* (running north–south), dates from the 4th century BC onwards. The description of the sites in this book starts at the western flank of the city at the Porta Marina.

INSIDER TIP ❯

To avoid the worst of the crowds don't visit during the early afternoon rush hour. It's often far too hot to traipse around – especially for children – at this time anyway.

Open 8.30am–7.30 pm daily Apr–Oct (last admission 6pm); 8.30am–5pm daily Nov–Mar (last admission 3.30 pm). Admission 11€. A cumulative ticket for all five archaeological sites around Vesuvius 20 €; free under-18s; half-price 18–25s, over-65s and EU school teachers. Amenities Baby changing. Café. Picnic area. Shop. Toilets.

What to See & Do ★★★
AGES 5 AND UP

Porta Marina & Around the Forum

Through the Porta Marina and its small tunnel – often full of the echoes of excited young voices – is the **Temple of Venus** (Tempio di Venere), built in honour of the city's guardian deity. Next to the temple on the

same side is the **Basilica**, the seat of the law courts. Hop on the raised tribunal opposite the entrance and pretend to be one of the judges. To the north is the **Temple of Apollo** (Tempio d'Apollo), built by the Samnites (a southern Italian people who ruled this area from 425BC for two centuries) on the remains of an earlier 6th-century BC sacred building. The bronze statue against the west portico is of Artemis shooting arrows (the bow is missing).

The **Forum** (Foro) ★★ itself is a 58,000 sq. ft (17,400 sq. metres) rectangular public area with plenty of space for youngsters to play. The dozy resident dogs slouching around the ruins and the multilingual chatter of passing tour groups means there's never much decorum in the forum. This was the centre of the city's public life and a natural meeting place, so if you're thinking of splitting up, pick a plinth to return to – there are quite a few empty ones east of the Forum, around the **Macellum** (the market), the **Sacrarium** (where the town's deities were venerated) and the **Building of Eumachia** (Edificio d'Eumachia): home of the wool fullers, who cleaned and thickened woollen cloth. At the north end, the **Temple of Jupiter** (Tempio di Giove), flanked by two triumphal arches, became the Roman Capitolium – it has a raised podium where statues of Jupiter, Juno and Minerva once stood. Nearby, the doorway decoration at the Building of Eumachia has birds and insects amid acanthus leaves while the bas-reliefs on the **Temple of Vespasian** (Tempio di Vespasiano) depict the sacrifice of a bull on the central marble altar.

At the north-western corner of the Forum are the public latrines and **Forum Holitorium** (Granai del Foro) ★★ (grain-store) where you can see some of the fascinating archaeological finds and poignant plastercasts of some victims of the AD79 eruption.

On to the Forum Baths (**Terme del Foro**) ★, built around 80BC. Seek out the rich architectural details including terracotta telamones (male figures supporting the ceiling) and a stuccoed *tepidarium*. At the junction with Via della Fortuna and Via di Nola is the **Temple of Fortuna Augusta** (Tempio della Fortuna Augusta), whose once-magnificent Corinthian columns, double staircase and towering marble-faced entrance were built in honour of Fortuna Redux, the imperial cult. Marcus Tullius, a military officer, imperial knight and pal of Augustus, paid for it.

Along Via dell'Abbondanza

Pompeii's busiest street is filled with shops, workshops and many fascinating insights into Roman life, from inscriptions advertising commercial wares, to lovers' graffiti and political sloganeering. It's fun to look out for them as you make your way along this broad road, with Vesuvius on your left, gradually

Temple of Apollo, Pompeii

Pick up a Pompeiian Picnic & Foodie Treats to Take Home

Beware of tourist traps when you're hungry in Pompeii. The streets near the entrances to the excavations are chocker with nondescript cafes and restaurants – it's best to avoid them if you can keep thirst and hunger at bay. The *bar-ristorante* at the Forum, at the heart of the Pompeii Scavi, is overpriced, overrun and often under-stocked. Instead head along Via Roma into modern Pompeii to pick up great-value picnic ingredients. A decent supermarket is **Mirto** (Via Lepanto 142). On the same road at Via Lepanto 156 is the wonderful **Melius**, a deli with a difference: pop in for ready-made meals as well as cheeses and salami to fill your *panini* bought from the *paneficio* (bakery) next door. This is the best shop for stocking up on foodie treats to take home as presents for friends and family, or better still for your own fridge and larder: fill your bags with wine, oil, parmigiano reggiano and cheeses from Campania (although better to do so after your visit round the ruins).

descending down to the Porta di Sarno. At each junction there are the stepping stones used by the original locals in bad weather. Look out for the ruts in the road made by carts and imagine the noise of this busy high street – horses neighing, wooden carts heaving with produce rattling on stone slabs, people chatting while collecting water from the fountains and the lively bartering of wily tradesmen and punters.

Starting at the main Forum you come to the **Comitium** where the municipal elections were held. Don't miss the wonderful restored **Botanic Garden** ★ filled with fruit trees and herbs, manned by botanical researchers the *Antica Erboristeria Pompeiana* and a horticultural company.

The **Thermae Stabiae** (Terme Stabiane) ★★, in Via Stabiana, are often mobbed by long tour groups snaking around and

gawping at the intricate stucco work in the *tepidarium*. Raiders emptied these atmospheric chambers of their statues and furnishings following the eruption. After visiting the various bathing rooms, the Pompeians would walk, talk and sip drinks under the porticoes surrounding the *paleastra*. Female bathers entered their similarly elegant bathing chambers on Vicolo del Lupanare, but paid nearly double the price for the privilege, according to some scholars.

Take time for a breather at the **Holiconius Crossroads** (Quadrivio di Holiconio), one of the main nerve centres of Pompeii. Traffic was only allowed north, east and south of here; a towering stone barrier made of tufa blocks barred vehicular access eastwards to the Forum. While you're swigging a

The Forum

cool drink, look up the Via dell'Abbondanza and imagine a grandiose archway heralding the road's ascent to the Forum.

If you ever wondered how the Romans laundered their clothes, visit the **Fullonica di Stefano** ★★, with scrubbing tubs and laundry equipment in situ. Children can play barman and punter at the Thermopolium (inn serving hot drinks) along here. This area is part of the *nuovi scavi* (the new excavations) begun in 1911. Many buildings along the south-side stretch of Via dell'Abbondanza have faithfully reconstructed balconies, roofs and windows. In contrast, the sunnier side of the street awaits excavation and restoration work.

The **House of P. Paquius Proculus** (Casa di Paquio Proculo) ★ and **House of Ephebus** (Casa dell'Efebo) ★ are among the best-preserved examples of middle-class dwellings. Drop into the **Shop of Felix the Fruit Merchant** (Bottega del Fruttivendolo Felix) ★ on the corner for a gander at its many humorous Bacchic scenes. At the **House of Successus** (Casa di Successus), you'll see an endearing painting of a boy being chased by a duck and a small statue of a boy. The nearby **House of the Fruit Orchard** (Casa del Frutteto) ★★ has fine paintings of fruit trees.

Just over the Via di Porta Nocera junction stands the **House of the Moralist** (Casa del Moralista) ★ with a cute loggia overlooking a lush garden. The **House of Octavius Quartius** (Casa di Octavius Quartio) ★ has paintings portraying Venus fishing, scenes from *The Iliad* and pergola-covered avenues shading a long marble pool. Next door the **House of Venus** (Casa di Venere) has a stucco relief above the door – a crown and laurels – which is the imperial insignia. A pearl of a fresco depicting Venus lounging in a shell, flanked by cupids was found here. An even grander pile is the **Villa of Julia**

Handy Architectural Terms

The starting point is the three Grecian orders of columns

Doric – The first and most uncomplicated of the orders, its straight up and down plainness is meant to symbolise man.

Ionic – Characterised by two large scrolls – or volutes. They are said to symbolise women.

Corinthian – The most decorative of the orders, this has a bell-shaped top adorned with acanthus leaves and volutes. Apparently, it symbolises virgins.

The Romans created two more styles: the **Tuscan** order, which is without any decoration at all; and the **Composite** order – a mish-mash of the three Grecian orders.

Balustrade – An upright pillar or column that supports a handrail, perhaps of a stairway.

Caryatids – Sculptures of females used as columns.

Cornice – A horizontal moulding – or ledge. Inside, it's purely decorative; outside, it acts as a gutter, draining water away from the building.

Cupola – A dome on a roof.

Frieze – The centre of an entablature and often decorated.

Loggia – An open gallery or corridor on the facade of the building: like a portico but recessed.

Nymphaeum – a shrine with fountains and statues dedicated to nymphs and pleasure.

Pediment – The gable end or front of a Grecian-style structure. The bit supported by the columns and above the frieze and cornice.

Plinth – The lower part or base of a column.

Portico – The classical version of a porch!

Stucco – Plaster made of a mixture of sand, crushed stone, lime and water and applied to walls for a smooth or highly decorative finish, creating reliefs.

Temples – The type of temple depends on the numbers of columns. A distyle: two columns. A tetrastyle: four columns. An octastyle: eight columns...

Felix (Casa di Giulia Felice) ★★) near the Sarno Gate (Porta di Sarno), which has a house, peristyle, large gardens and baths to explore.

Around Via Stabiana

The **Pistrinum of N. Popdius Priscus** is the best-preserved bakery in town. A poignant photo can be taken at the **House of the Bear** (Casa dell'Orso), of a long-snouted mosaic bear suffering the slings and arrows of outrageous fortune. You may want to avert the eyes of youngsters at the **Lupanare**, a brothel with a secret staircase and eye-bulging diagrams advertising the services on offer.

To the west of the southern section of Via Stabiana is the **House of the Lyre Player** (Casa di Citarista) ★★ where you'll find copies of lively bronze statues, including a wild boar and some snarling dogs. In the nearby **House of the Menander** (Casa del Menandro) ★★★ some unfortunate souls were trapped under a collapsed section of the *peristyle*, where they perished. Rich paintings – one of the poet Menander – and some alluring mosaics in the private *thermae* (baths) make this villa, allegedly belonging to a magistrate and friend of the Empress Poppaea, Nero's second wife, a must-see.

The Theatre District

This district shows the influence of Greek culture upon Pompeii's population and its city planners. The **Triangular Forum** (Foro Triangolare), with its monumental scale, Ionic portico leading to a Doric colonnade and temple, and its use as a venue for athletics and religious festivals, demonstrates the importance of the Hellenistic model between the 6th and 2nd centuries BC – these people were aping the Greeks. In the north-eastern corner of the Forum is the **Palestra Sannitica** where athletes trained and where the statue of Doryphorous (see Museo Nazionale Archeologico in Naples p. 72) was discovered. Small bones were found on the main altar of the **Temple of Isis** (Tempio del Iside), adding to the mystery surrounding the Egyptian cult of Isis – imagine shaven-headed priests in black robes and men with dog-faced masks performing strange rituals here. The **Temple of Jupiter**

Meilichios (Tempio di Giove Meilichio or Tempio di Asclepio) was dedicated to a Greek cult and other gods – Jupiter, Juno and Minerva – whose terracotta statues can be seen in the Museo Nazionale Archeologico di Napoli (see p. 72).

Children can play the thespian at the **Teatro Grande**. In its heyday, a two-storey Greek-style *scaenae frons* at the back of the stage, had entrances for the thesps and niches with honorary statues, each framed with imposing entablatures and columns. Be careful on the steps as many a Roman and 21st-century child has taken a tumble. Next to the Large Theatre is the **Odeum**, the small covered theatre built around 80BC, which was mainly used for concerts. South of the **Doric Temple** and the theatres is the **Gladiatorial Barracks** (Caserma dei Gladiatori aka the Quadriporticus, a huge piazza surrounded by an arcade.

Between Via Consolare/Via del Farmacista & Via del Vesuvio/Via Stabiana

Up in the north-west corner of Pompeii, near the Porta Ercolano, is the **House of the Surgeon** (Casa del Chirurgo) ★, a colossal building where some gruesome-looking surgical instruments were found. Nearby is the **House of the Sallust** (Casa di Sallustio), one of the city's oldest villas (dating from the 3rd century BC), which was damaged by a 1943 American bomb.

FUN FACT ▷ **Leave your Toga** ◁

Upon entering the antechamber with its *clipei* (shields) decorated with nymphs, cupids and floral patterns, male bathers, perhaps Octavius Quartius or Ludicrus Sextus, would undress and enter the *tepidarium*. Next stop was the circular *frigidarium* with its large cold-water plunge pool, bucolic decorative flourishes and starry, lapis lazuli coloured dome. They would then linger awhile, perhaps having a dip in a lukewarm bath before leaving a cloth towel and any ointment jars in one of the niches. The temperature rose considerably in the *calidarium's* 40 degree C steam and adjoining hot baths. A sauna was followed by some ointment rubbing and a massage back in the *tepidarium*.

Along Via del Mercurio, the **House of Apollo** (Casa di Apollo) ★★★ has a wonderful mosaic (Achilles at Skyros) while over the road, the **House of Meleager** (Casa di Meleagro) contains a fish pond, fountain and a basic fridge. A large painting of a wounded Adonis tended by Venus and some cupids, amid landscape frescos, is the main attraction at the **House of the Adonis** (Casa di Adone).

A number of dwellings make up the huge **House of Castor and Pollux** (Casa di Castore e Polluce) ★★, which has an impressive colonnade and mythological paintings of Apollo and Daphne, Adonis and Scylla. Paintings of the Dioscuri, the Divine twins Castor and Pollux, which decorated the entrance, and of Perseus and Andromeda, are in the Archaeological Museum (Museo Archeologico Nazionale) in Naples (see p. 72). It's worth popping into the **Osteria** at the junction with Vicolo del Mercurio, which has some paintings depicting everyday tavern life.

In the **House of the Little Fountain** (Casa della Fontana Piccola) ★★★, trompe l'oeil effects and painted panels adorn walls while in the *peristyle* there are mosaics, with a comedy mask and a cute cherub holding a goose. The **House of the Large Fountain** (Casa della Fontana Grande) ★★ has a mosaic fountain and tragic-comedy masks. A number of noteworthy mosaics and paintings found in the **House of the Tragic Poet** (Casa del Poeta Tragica) ★★ – including a theatrical scene involving actors – are worth tracking down in the Archaeological Museum in Naples. Children will recognise the chained dog with the warning 'Cave Canem' (Beware of the Dog – much reproduced and available from all good (and not-so-good) stalls and shops around Campania.

There's often a large crowd around the copy of the statuette of a dancing faun at the **House of the Faun** (Casa del Fauno) OVERRATED. It is one of Pompeii's largest private houses, covering more than 3,000 sq m and one

Goddess of Abundance

Ere`, why is it called Via dell'Abbondanza? Pompeii's busiest street is named after a stone relief on the fountain near the Forum – it depicts the Goddess of Abundance with a water spout coming from her mouth and a cornucopia on her left shoulder. Unfortunately someone or something spiteful cut off her nose. Perhaps Vulcan and Vesuvius…

of the most popular sites. Intricate mosaics composed of tiny, finely worked *tesserae* were found here, including an epic piece showing Alexander the Great confronting Darius at the Battle of Issus – all in the Archaeological Museum in Naples (see p. 72).

To the north on the Vicolo del Labrinto, a mysterious mosaic maze depicting Theseus slaying the Minotaur was discovered at the **House of the Labyrinth** (Casa del Labirinto) ★. Nearby, the magnificent **House of the Vettii** (Casa dei Vettii) ★★ is packed with sophisticated paintings, mythological scenes, cheeky cherubs and salacious figures. A

House of the Faun

fresco of a well-endowed Priapus was uncovered on the vestibule wall and is now under lock and key. This popular and weighty subject was meant to ward off bad luck. Children and adults alike will be tickled by the playful winged cherubs and psyches, one of whom is riding a crab and cracking the whip. Alas, this much-visited house has been damaged by the hordes descending upon its dreamy interiors, something that the Italian government is finally talking about dealing with.

It's believed that the influential Poppaei family owned the lavish **House of Gilded Cherubs** (Casa degli Amorini Dorati) ★★ on Via del Vesuvio, famed for its marble reliefs depicting bacchanalian scenes, a sacred altar to Egyptian gods, duplicated floral motifs and those flying gold cupids behind antique glass.

Via dele Terme, Via della Fortuna & Via di Nola

On the south side of the Via di Nola is the **House of the Centenary** (Casa del Centenario) ★★ which was excavated in 1879, 18 centuries after the AD79 eruption. This large property, owned by one

Graffiti

Ahhhh, AD79. Those were the golden days of graffiti. While you'll need an honours degree in Latin to decipher them, you can still appreciate the witticisms of the Romans with an amusing turn of phrase. Look out for the cheeky scribbles on walls all over Pompeii.

- Epaphra is not good at ball games.
- Whoever loves, go to hell. I want to break Venus's ribs with a club and deform her hips. If she can break my tender heart why can't I hit her over the head?
- Postpone your tiresome quarrels if you can, or leave and take them home with you (outside the House of the Moralist)
- Hectice, baby, Mercator says hello to you
- If anyone does not believe in Venus, they should gaze at my girl-friend
- Chie, I hope your haemorrhoids rub together so much that they hurt worse than they have ever before!

"Walls, you have held up so much tedious graffiti that I am amazed that you have not already collapsed in ruin".

A. Rustius Verus consists of three houses joined together. A fabulous fountain portraying a young satyr pouring wine was found at the rectangular pool in the garden. The sprawling villa includes baths with Egyptian features and a *nymphaeum* with fountains and exotic paintings. Top of the bill goes to the famous painting found in the atrium of the servants' quarters (now in The Archaeological Museum in Naples (see p. 72)), depicting Bacchus wearing a cape of grapes amid a panther, birds, snakes and the vineyard-covered mountain of Vesuvius.

Further up the Via di Nola is the **House of the Gladiators** (Casa dei Gladiatori) ★, which has a *porticus* surrounding a large peristyle and graffiti relating to gladiatorial contests.

Around the Amphitheatre & Porta Nocera

In 1961, 13 victims of the eruption were discovered near the Porta Nocera, at the **Garden of the Fugitives** (Orto dei Fuggiaschi).

The **Great Palaestra** ★★ has a sloping pool in its grassy centre and is enclosed on three sides by a handsome portico – this was the place to exercise and where sporty competitions took place. Double rows of plane trees have recently been planted to recreate the supposed layout of AD79.

Dominating the area is the imposing **Amphitheatre (Anfiteatro)**, an elliptical structure that captures the imagination of all the family. Its construction began in around 80BC and it was completed around the turn of the new millennium, making it the oldest structure of its kind that has been so well preserved. Head to the centre of the ellipse and imagine gladiatorial battles in front of 12,000 baying spectators. The *cavea* (sections for different social classes) is composed of three tiers, with the upper section occupied by women and children. Alas, of late, the authorities have discouraged people from using the staircases to the upper tiers, hanging orange ribbon and signs barring entry.

Outside Porta Marina & Porta Ercolano: the Suburban Villas & Baths

A collection of erotic artwork was recently exposed in the 1st century BC-built **Terme Suburbane** (the Suburban Baths) ★★, just outside the Porta Marina. Some of the lewd images may not be for youngsters' eyes, but the multi-storey complex is worth visiting for its mosaics, stuccoed cherubs and intriguing layout – experts reckon this was the only unisex baths in Pompeii and may have incorporated a brothel.

The nearby **Villa Imperiale** ★ has grand frescoed rooms splashed in that rich Pompeian Red.

Outside the Porta Ercolano, is the Via dei Sepolchi, lined with tombs, which leads to two lavish villas. The first, the **Villa of Diomedes** (Villa di Diomede) ★, excavated in the late 1700s, had the largest garden in Pompeii.

Tragedy struck below the elegant garden-colonnade – and its discovery caused quite a stir in the late 18th century; 18 skeletons of adults and children who had tried to escape Vesuvius's spewing were found in the vaulted cellar. The nearby **Villa of Mysteries** (Villa dei Misteri) ★★★ was an opulent pile that had been transformed into a large winery by the time of the eruption, complete with wine press and huge cellar. What makes the trek here worthwhile is the famous **Dionysian Cycle fresco** in the so-called Hall of Mysteries – nine scenes from a ritual dedicated to the Greek god of wine and having a good time, Dionysus – which was outlawed by Rome at the time.

Around Vesuvius: Villa Oplontis, Boscoreale & Stabiae

Villa Oplontis, the largest suburban Roman villa in decent condition, is 20 miles south-east of Naples near the small port of Torre Annunziata. Its lavish interiors dazzle. Higher up on the slopes of Vesuvius some 19 miles from Naples is **Boscoreale**, once a rural hamlet and suburb of Pompeii, now a visitor attraction with an archaeological museum and some excavated Roman villas. Busy **Castellammare di Stabia**, famed for its spas and warships, has the remains of four Roman villas (two have been excavated) and an antiquarium (museum), which is being restored.

Boscoreale – Antiquarium Nazionale Uomo e Ambiente nel Territorio Vesuviano (National Antiquarium of Man and Environment in the Territory of Vesuvius) ★
AGES 3 AND UP

Via Settetermini 15, Località Villaregina. ☎ *081 857 5347;* **www.pompeiisites.org** *Circumvesuviana railway – Napoli–Poggiomarino line – to Boscotrecase and the shuttle bus to Villa Regina.*

Opened in the early 90s, this captivating collection of archaeological finds is from the area's working farm: children will enjoy imagining life on a Roman farm and especially the visit to Villa Regina replete with replanted vineyards, a *torcularium* (grape press) and huge wine cellar. A hoard of silver and many beautiful frescoes were discovered in the 1800s at two nearby villas, the Villa di Pisanella and Villa di Publius Fannius Synistor. The treasures now adorn the salons of the Louvre in Paris, the Metropolitan Museum of Art in New York and the Museo Archeologico Nazionale in Naples.

Open *8.30am–7.30pm (last admission 6pm). daily Apr–Oct; 8.30am–5pm (last admission 3.30pm) daily Nov–Mar.* **Admission** *6€ including entry to Oplontis and Stabia; free under-18s.* **Amenities** *Baby changing. Café. Disabled access. Picnic area. Shop. Toilets.*

Scavi di Stabia (Stabia Excavations) ★ AGES 5 AND UP
Via Passegiata Archeologica. 80053 Castellmare di Stabia ☎ *081 871 4541; www.pompeiisites.org.*

Circumvesuviana railway (Napoli–Sorrento line) to Via Nocera and then bus 1 Rosso (red).

The archaeological digs at Roman Stabiae kicked off in the 18th century and new excavations using more sophisticated methods have brought more treasures to light since the 1950s. Just outside of town on the slope at Varano is the **Villa di Ariana** (Via Piana di Varano ☎ *081 274 200*) named after a painting of the mythological Ariadne, found snoozing by Dionysus. It's a bit of a hike to reach but there are some wonderful views from the villa. Nearby is the **Villa di San Marco** (Via Passegiata Archeologica ☎ *081 871 4541*), a residence of a wealthy family replete with fabulous frescoes and stuccowork. Despite being built in the 1st century AD and damaged by the 1980 earthquake, you can still imagine toga-garbed Romans prancing around the beautifully proportioned spaces.

Open *8.30am–5pm (last admission 3.30pm) daily Nov–Mar; 8.30am–7.30pm (last admission 6pm) daily Apr–Oct.* **Admission** *6€ including entry to Oplontis and Boscoreale; free under-18s.* **Amenities** *Baby changing. Café. Shop. Toilets.*

> **INSIDER TIP** ≫
>
> For those visiting the Roman Stabiae at Castellammare di Stabia, don't miss Liberty-style Caffè Spagnuolo (Via Giuseppe Mazzini 45 ☎ 081 871 1272) which serves quality coffee, delicious pastries, focaccia-bread snacks and ice cream.

Madonna of the Rosary

After visiting the ancient city of Pompeii, if time and energy levels allow, head into the modern town along Via Roma to take a look at the magnificent **Santuario della Madonna del Rosario ★** (Piazza B. Longo 1, 80045 Pompeii. ✆ *081 857 7111; www.santuario.it*, Open 9am–1pm and 3:30–6:30pm May–Oct; 9am–1pm weekdays plus 3–5pm Sat–Sun Nov–Apr. Admission free). This major pilgrimage shrine dedicated to the Madonna of the Rosary, built in the late 19th century has a flamboyance that will impress young and old alike.

Villa Oplontis ★ ★ AGES 4 AND UP

Via Sepolcri, Torre Annunziata ✆ *081 862 1755; www.pompeiisites.org. Circumvesuviana railway (Napoli–Sorrento or Napoli, Poggiomarino or Napoli – Torre Annunziata lines) to Torre Annunziata.*

The intimate scale of the villa, believed to have once belonged to Nero's second wife Poppaea Sabina, makes it easy to get around in a short space of time. The real draw here is the delicate decorative flourishes – especially the trompe l'oeil architectural details in the atrium and the cornucopia of lively scenes depicting birds, theatrical scenes, landscapes and bowls of fruit. Unlike at Pompeii and Herculaneum the interiors have not been tampered with and the paintings have been left as they were at the time of the AD79 eruption. It's believed that the villa was being restored at the time – bodies were found as well as gold jewellery, coins and a cache of statues in the storeroom. The spa baths and gardens must have created the atmosphere of a kind of Eden; these magical spaces were filled with

plants and flowers, pools and fountains and a backdrop of paintings teeming with creatures including blue birds, peacocks, lizards, frogs and a butterfly. After the visit children will be asking for their Girls Aloud posters to be painted over with some Roman frescoes!

Open 8.30am–5pm (last admission 3.30pm) daily Nov–Mar; 8.30am–7.30pm (last admission 6pm) daily Apr–Oct. Admission 6€ including entry to Boscoreale and Stabiae; free under-18s. Amenities Baby changing. Café. Shop. Toilets.

FAMILY-FRIENDLY DINING

Addu' u Mimi

Via Roma 61, 80045 Pompeii ✆ *081 863 5451*

Don't be put off by the sometimes surly service at this relaxed trattoria on busy Via Roma. The interiors are pleasant enough, and the food is pretty good value for families, although the portions are not particularly bountiful. Their *insalatoni* (large salads) are hardly heaped but will go down well with veggies or any-one after a healthy change. The pizzas will fill children's stomachs and the seafood pasta dishes should satisfy hungry adults after a day pounding the lava slabs of Pompeii.

Open *noon–3pm and 7.30–11pm Sat–Thurs.* **Main Courses** *6€–10 €.* **Credit** *AmEx, DC, MC, V.* **Amenities** *Highchairs. Reservations accepted.*

Carlo Alberto VALUE

Via Carlo Alberto 15, 80045 Pompeii
☎ 081 863 3231

Healthy portions, good value and a relaxed atmosphere make this long-established *ristorante-pizzeria* a sound family choice. It's near the Santuario in the new town, so far away from the *scavi* (excavations) and the captive market that stumbles out of the ancient city to get promptly ripped off. The pizzas are very good – you can't go wrong with their pizza Margherita – and they have a children's menu for fussy little eaters.

Open *noon–3pm and 7.30–11pm daily.* **Main Courses** *7€–15 €.* **Credit** *AmEx, DC, MC, V.* **Amenities** *Highchairs. Reservations accepted.*

Il Cavaliere GREEN FIND

Via Gramisci 109, 80040 Massa di Somma, ☎ 081 574 3637; agrodel-cavaliere.altervista.org

Families can combine a visit to this agriturismo farmyard, where children can see goats, horses and chickens, with laidback dining on the terrace or one of the cosy rooms inside. The Children's Menu includes *penne al sugo*

(pasta with tasty sauce), *cottoletta* (breaded meat) and good-ol' fashioned *patatine* (chips!). Adults can enjoy the Cavaliere antipasto selection of meats, cheeses and Vesuvian veg followed by a pasta dish and barbecued meat, all washed down with the local white wine made with an old variety of Catalan grape. They also have accommodation and a children's pool. Stunning views of the bay and the looming presence of Vesuvius add to the special atmosphere.

Open *noon–3pm and 7.30–11pm Sat–Thurs.* **Main Fixed Menu** *25 € and children's menu 12€.* **Credit** *AmEx, DC, MC, V.* **Amenities** *Highchairs. Reservations recommended.*

President ★

Piazza Schettino 12, 80045 Pompeii
☎ 081 850 7245; www.ristorante president.com

For a posh family dining experience, stop by Il President's. Eating in these elegant *saloni* is a bit of an event, especially if you sign up for one of their imaginatively themed evenings that transport you back in time. Ever fancied food that the ancient Pompeiani scoffed? A family banquet that may have been eaten in the Villa di Giulia Felice along the Via dell'Abbondanza? Or perhaps the simple strong flavours of la *cucina povera napoletana*: including the tiny pizzas eaten by Neapolitans on the streets of 17th-century Naples and the classic plump sponge – *il Babà*? You can combine a meal here with a candlelit walk around the ancient city – see the website for the latest gastronomic events.

Open noon–3pm and 7.30–11.30pm Tues–Sun. *Main Courses* 13€–27€. *Credit* AmEx, DC, MC, V. *Amenities* Highchairs. Reservations recommended.

FAMILY-FRIENDLY ACCOMMODATION

This is an area to dip into for a day or two. Herculaneum is not the place to stay in as it's grimy and unattractive – besides there are no decent hotels. The reason you come to Pompeii is to see the ancient city and while the modern town does have its charms, it's not somewhere children will enjoy for more than a day or two. Your best bet is to travel here from your hotel base along the Amalfi Coast.

Bel Vesuvio Inn FIND GREEN

Via Panoramica 40, 80040 San Sebastiano al Vesuvio ℓ *081 771 1243; www.agriturismobel vesuvioinn.it*

Imagine an 18th-century farmhouse with some modern touches set amid vineyards and the fertile countryside on the slopes of Vesuvius. Children love the space to play – youngsters have a playground – and they can pet the farmyard animals while adults lap up the tranquil setting and the three local DOC wines or Dad can try his luck at *bocce* (Italian boules). Herculaneum and the Vesuvius National Park are nearby and

horsey families can go trotting around the old lava flows. Breakfasts and meals feature their own products including piennolo tomatoes, chicken, cheeses, salamis and apricot jam.

Rooms 11. *Rates* 120€–210€ double; 150€–240€ rooms and suites suitable for families. Breakfast included. *Credit* AmEx, DC, MC, V. *Amenities* Bar. Cots. Disabled access. Extra bed (30€). Internet. Laundry service. Non-smoking rooms. Restaurant. *In room* A/C. Fridge. Safe. Satellite TV. Shower/bath.

Crowne Plaza Hotel Stabiae

SS145 Sorrentina, Localita' Pozzano, 80053 Castellammare di Stabia ℓ *081 394 6700; www.ichotels group.com*

Housed in a striking former factory building at the start of the Sorrento peninsula and close to the archaeological sites, this newish hotel has stylish family accommodation. Children can splash around in the fabulous indoor and outdoor pools, and in the sea at the private beach. Rooms have clean contemporary lines and many have terraces with breathtaking views of the bay and Vesuvius. The hotel restaurant is a little pricey but there are lots of places to eat in nearby Vico Equense, including the home of *pizza al metro* – pizza by the metre! (L'università della Pizza, Via Nicotera, 10, ℓ *081 879 8426*). As the hotel is isolated it's not ideal for families without a car, although there is a free shuttle bus to Vico Equense and the train station.

Rooms 157. *Rates* 160€–240€ double; 150€–350€ rooms and suites suitable for families. Breakfast included. *Credit* AmEx, DC, MC, V. *Amenities* Babysitting. Bar. Concierge. Cots. Disabled access. Dry cleaning service. Extra bed. Gym. Internet. Laundry service. Non-smoking rooms. Parking. Pools (indoor and outdoor. Private beach. Restaurant. Sauna. Spa. *In room* A/C. Fridge. Safe. Satellite TV. Shower/bath.

Hotel Diana

Vico Sant'Abbondio 10, 80045 Pompeii 081 863 1264; www. pompeihotel.com

Perfectly placed near the Santuario, the Scavi, public transport, shops and restaurants, the modern and welcoming Hotel Diana has a lot to offer families on a budget. Friendly service and well-tended rooms mark out this award-winning three-star (Italian hospitality award winner 2007) from Pompeii's inexpensive and rather irksome hotel pack. The brightly decorated guest rooms come in a range of sizes to suit most family group needs. Bathrooms are on the small size but adequate. After a long day exploring the ancient past, the leafy garden filled with citrus and palm trees is the perfect place for children to play and for adults to relax in.

Rooms 13. *Rates* 70€–110€ double; 95€–150€ rooms and suites suitable for families. Breakfast included. *Credit* AmEx, DC, MC, V. *Amenities* Babysitting. Bar. Cots. Dry cleaning service. Disabled access. Extra bed (25€). Internet. Laundry service. Non-smoking rooms. *In room* A/C. Safe. Satellite TV. Shower/bath.

Hotel Forum ★★

Via Roma 99, 80045 Pompeii. www.hotelforum.it

There is a relaxing atmosphere and fabulous service at the Forum, starting in the lobby which is its sociable hub – the girls at the desk are friendly and efficient, going out of their way to help you. Recent renovation has created a creamy contemporary façade and a new wing. Children can play on the Internet here while you pick up some top tips from the staff and their excellent free map of the ancient site. The modern extension offers lots of possibilities for families of various sizes, contemporary interiors and serene bathrooms with Roma-inspired skylights. A word of warning though: some of the rooms in the old part of the hotel have rather thin walls – which can be very annoying when your neighbours are deaf but very talkative. The large buffet breakfast area looks a little tired but is pleasant enough – the leafy garden is a wonderful setting to make your best-laid family plans for the day.

Rooms 36. *Rates* 120€–210€ double; 150€–240€ rooms and suites suitable for families. Breakfast included. *Credit* AmEx, DC, MC, V. *Amenities* Babysitting. Bar. Cots. Disabled access. Extra bed (30€). Internet. Laundry service. Non-smoking rooms. Restaurant. *In room* A/C. Fridge. Safe. Satellite TV. Shower/bath.

Hotel Diana, Pompeii

Hotel Santa Caterina ★

Via Vittorio Emanuele 4, 80100 Pompeii 📞 *081 856 7494; **www.hotel santacaterinapompei.com***

Saint Cath's friendly English-speaking staff and a good location on Via Roma opposite the Pompei Scavi entrance and near the train station means hassle minimus for those travelling with children. There are lots of room options for families of all sizes including a spacious suite. Warm Pompeian red hues and Roman-style paintings abound, and everything is generally spick and span. For dramatic views ask for a room facing Vesuvius or the amphitheatre. Two rooms are designed for disabled access.

***Rooms** 20. **Rates** 100€ double; 130€ triple; 150€ suite. Breakfast included. **Credit** AmEx, DC, MC, V. **Amenities** Babysitting. Bar. Cots. Disabled access. Extra bed 25€. Internet. Non-smoking rooms. Parking. Restaurant.*

***In room** A/C. Fridge. Safe. Satellite TV. Shower/bath.*

La Murena B & B

Via Osservatorio 10, 80056 Ercolano. 📞 *081 777 9819*

For families wanting to climb Vesuvius, visit the observatory, explore Herculaneum and have a tranquil base to boot, this well-maintained place on volcanic slopes is a good punt. There's a beguiling garden perfect for both adult relaxation and children's play, as well as lots of accommodation options including suites and an apartment, replete with kitchen and terrace for al fresco dining. Oh and it'll be cool on the slopes, unless Vesuvius blows!

***Rooms** 3. **Rates** 80€–100€ double; 140€ suite; 250€ entire house. Breakfast included. **Credit** AmEx, DC, MC, V. **Amenities** Cots. Non-smoking rooms. **In room** A/C. Shower/bath. TV.*

SORRENTO & THE AMALFI COAST

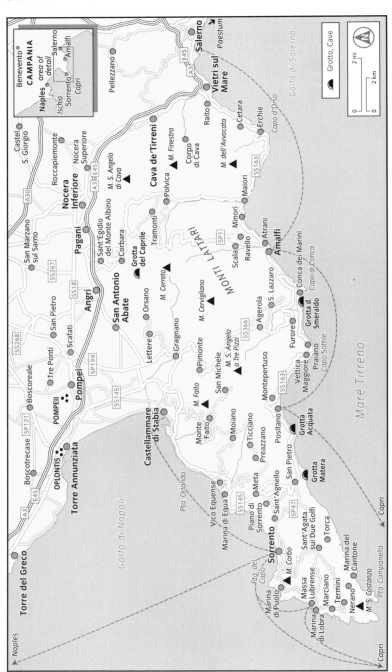

Castel S. Giorgio · Roccapiemonte · Nocera Superiore · Nocera Inferiore · San Marzano sul Sarno · Pagani · Sant'Egidio del Monte Albino · Corbara · M. S. Angelo di Cava · Tramonti · Cava de'Tirreni · M. Finestra · Corpo di Cava · M. dell'Avvocata · Polvica · Maiori · Erchie · Cetara · Raito · Vietri sul Mare · Salerno · Paestum

Benevento · CAMPANIA · area of detail · Naples · Ischia · Sorrento · Capri · Amalfi · Salerno

San Pietro · SS268 · Tre Ponti · Scafati · Angri · San Antonio Abate · Grotta del Caprile · M. Cerreto · Orsano · Lettere · Gragnano · Pimonte · M. Faito · San Michele · MONTI LATTARI · M. Cervigliano · Scala · Ravello · Minori · Atrani · Amalfi · Conca dei Marini · S. Lazzaro · Agerola · Furore · Grotta d. Smeraldo · Capo di Conca

Boscoreale · Boscotrecase · Pompei · POMPEII · OPLONTIS · Torre Annunziata · Torre del Greco · Castellammare di Stabia · Monte Faito · Moiano · Ticciano · Preazzano · M. S. Angelo a Tre Pizzi · Montepertuso · Positano · Vettica Maggiore · Praiano · Capo Sottile · Grotta Acquata · Mare Tirreno

Vico Equense · Marina di Equa · Piano di Sorrento · Meta · Sant'Agnello · San Pietro · Grotta Matera · Golfo di Napoli · Pta. Orlando

Sorrento · M. Corbo · Sant'Agata sui Due Golfi · Torca · Marina del Cantone · Pta. del Capo · Massa Lubrense · Marciano · Termini · Nerano · M.S. Costanzo · Marina di Lobra · Marina di Puolo · Pta. Campanella · Capri

Naples · Capri

Golfo di Salerno · Capo d'Orso · Mare Tirreno · Capri

Grotto, Cave · 2 mi · 2 km

Cute pastel-coloured villages stacked on verdant hillsides; terraced olive and lemon groves between dramatic cliffs and a deep blue sea; hidden coves and dazzling marine grottoes where emperors and epicureans plunged the depths and Saracen pirates lay in wait to storm the watchtowers; a maritime republic, Greco-Roman civilisations and canoodling celebrity couples on yachts. The beauty of the Sorrentine Peninsula and Amalfi Coast has bewitched visitors ever since tectonic forces lifted its limestone rock from the ocean floor. Despite the negatives – traffic on its curvy roads and lack of long sandy beaches – there is so much here to see and do for families, from watery adventures in secluded bays, historic sights and walks amongst the gods to music festivals and mouth-watering treats aplenty.

The Sorrentine Peninsula extends from the ancient spa town of Castellamare di Stabia to wild Punta Campanella, which juts out into the Tyrrhenian Sea, almost touching the island of Capri. Children will love the sweeping drive along the famous SS163 coastal road with its soaring crags above and heart-in-the-mouth chasms to azure blue waters way below. First stops Vico Equense and Sorrento retain some of their ancient elegance and have some allure for families, but the real magic is elsewhere.

Once you've lost the roads clogged with coach tours, there are charming villages and fishing harbours to seek out. The Amalfi Coast starts around Positano, after Sant'Agata sui Due Golfi, where the Amalfi Drive curves around towering limestone cliffs mottled with *macchia mediterranea* scrub.

Nestled along this stretch are picturesque villages and resorts, starting with Positano's *presepe* (nativity scene)–like pile of pastel-hued houses followed by Amalfi itself, still basking in the faded memories of its powerful maritime republic. Sublimely isolated Ravello is way up high: its ethereal gardens and Norman-Saracenic architecture have inspired writers and composers for centuries. Even when it's mobbed by tour buses, Ravello's cloisters and belvederes make for a restful family destination. There may be queues and crowds in the chic spots but at every turn up and down the *costa* there are historic villages, fishing harbours and hidden crannies to find your very own glimpse of beauty. The cathedral city of Salerno has cloisters created in a Moorish dream and a *lungomare* made for a languid family *passeggiata*. Further south you'll come across the magical Greek ruins at Paestum.

VICO EQUENSE

39km (20 miles) SE of Naples

Vico Equense has been through the wars in the past and has invariably come up smelling of lemons – much as it does today. It has a rather rosy complexion with its pastel-coloured buildings set against the azure sea at its feet while craggy cliffs and verdant woods float above leading to the *Sentiero dei Dei*: the Trail of the Gods. It may have survived the eruption of AD79 (see p. 124), but after centuries of prosperity, invading Goths and Saracens brought a period of depopulation and impoverishment. In the 12th century, Carlo I di Angio renamed this former Roman colony Aequa and the town was thereafter known as Vico Equense (vico from the Latin *vicus* meaning village). A period of rebuilding started by the Angevin dynasty was continued by the Spanish Aragonese. The town centre has an elegant air with a smattering of interesting buildings including Catalan courtyards, a Gothic cathedral and some intriguing small museums. If Vico's cultural fixes become too stodgy, sample the myriad toppings at the renowned home of **pizza al metro** – pizza-by-the-metre – at **Da Gigino Università della Pizza** (see p. 185). It will more than measure up to children's expectations!

Essentials

Getting There & Getting Around

By Train Vico Equense is easily reached on the **Ferrovia Circumvesuviana** Railway (☎ *800 053 939*; *www.vesuviana.it*) from stations on the Sorrentine peninsula as far as Sorrento, and from Naples go to the Stazione Circumvesuviana just off Piazza Garibaldi. The journey from Naples takes around 40 minutes and costs 3€.

By Boat There are a number of companies plying the coast including Metro del Mare (☎ *199 600 700*; *www.metrodelmare.com*) which runs the MM1, MM2 and MM3 services from Napoli Beverello (see p. 163) between late April and October, stopping at Seiano-Vico Equense, Sorrento, Positano, Amalfi, Minori and Salerno. From Beverello, a trip to Seiano-Vico Equense takes 40 mins and costs 7€ for adults, 3€ for 4–12-year-olds and free for 0–3-year-olds.

By Bus The daily Sita autobus (☎ *081 552 2176*; *www.sitabus.it*) between Naples and Sorrento stops at Vico Equense. **Unico Costiera** is a series of integrated travel tickets that works with the Circumvesuviana railway – if you are travelling a lot consider the 24-*ore* (hour) and 3-*giorni* (day) tickets, costing 6€ and 15€ respectively. For those arriving by air, a bus service from Capodichino Airport stops at Vico Equense. It's run by **Curreri Viaggi** (☎ *081 801 5420*; *www.curreriviaggi.it*) with 12 services daily (6 there and 6 back) – the last bus departs the airport at 7.30pm.

By Car For anyone travelling from Naples by road, take the A3 Autostrada towards Salerno and exit at Castellamare di Stabia, then take the SS145 coastal road towards Vico Equense.

Taking the Amalfi Drive and hair-pin mountain roads may be exhilarating for children and adults alike, but they present hazards and headaches – and we're not just talking about fearless Neapolitan drivers. The combination of shifting motion around the bends, heat and heart-in-the-mouth vistas is a heady cocktail. Make sure you bring car sickness tablets, a bottle of water and spare plastic bags!

Visitor Information

For up-to-the-minute listings and information, go to the tourist office at Via San Ciro, Vico Equense (📞 *081 879 8826*; *www.vicoturismo.it*)

Family-friendly Events

La Pacchianelle

Locals dress up in costumes to act out a traditional "living" *presepe* (nativity scene). Lots of children and women in peasant garb present the baby Jesus with useful local products for a newborn: fish, cheese, meats and pastries.

6th January

Sagre

There are lots of *sagre* (local festivals) in Vico's surrounding villages to celebrate the harvest and production of various fruits and foods including:

La Sagra di Melone at Bonea (Melon Festival) and La Sagra della Melanzana (Aubergine Festival) at Preazzano. Late August.

What to See & Do

Children's Top Attractions

❶ Soaking up the drama and beauty of the breathtaking Amalfi Drive, see left.

❷ Boating around the coast finding hidden coves and grottoes, p. 156.

❸ Swimming with the mythical sirens around *Li Galli,* rocky islets set in turquoise waters, p. 166.

❹ Munching a metre of pizza in Vico Equense, p. 185.

❺ Discovering the ancient Greek lost city of Paestum, p. 178.

❻ Walking in the Monti Lattari (Milky Mountains), in the Valle dei Mulini and Trail of the Gods, p. 159.

❼ Dreaming up fantastical fables in the enchanting gardens of Ravello, p. 171.

❽ Playing on the beach, eating *gelati* (ice cream) and padding about the leafy lanes of Positano.

Vico has few sights, so after spending a few hours in the morning exploring the town you can easily add on a trip to a beach at **Marina d'Equa** or **Seiano**. Just outside Seiano is the excellent Bar De Simone at Piazza Seiano 6 📞 *081 802 9153,* which does fab pastries including *pasticiotti all'amarena*. In the centre of Vico Equense is Piazza Umberto I, where youngsters will enjoy a gander at the wonderful white-marble fountain with its cheeky, curly-tailed dolphins. Take a stroll down Via Monsignor Natale towards Largo dei Tigli to enjoy stunning views of the coastline.

Chiesa di Santissima Annunziata AGES 5 AND UP

Via Cattedrale. Vico Equense

The 14th-century Gothic church and ex-cathedral may sit dramatically over cliffs but it's not as creepy and foreboding as it sounds – indeed its newer exterior displays a peachy complexion to the azure sea and looks a tad like a tempting but rather sickly sweet iced cake. The approach to its imposing campanile passes through narrow atmospheric streets lined with Catalan-style buildings from the Aragonese era. Children will adore the arch cutting through the belltower which beckons you into a viewing area with jaw-dropping panoramas. Don't forget your camera!

Open *8am–12.30pm and 3.30–7pm daily.* **Admission** *free.* **Amenities** *none.*

Museo Antiquarium Equano

Casa Municipale, Via Filangieri 98, Vico Equense.

Archaeology buffs and children who dig the ancients will enjoy a visit to this museum housed in the town hall. Greek remains from Vico Equense's Necropolis sit alongside bronzes, amphorae and various fascinating fragments left by Etruscans and other Italic tribes.

Open *9am–1pm Mon, Wed and Fri; 3.30–6.30pm Tues and Thurs; 9.30am–12.30pm Sat–Sun.* **Admission** *free.* **Amenities** *none.*

Museo Mineralogico Campano AGES 5 AND UP

Via San Ciro 2. Vico Equense ☎ *081 801 5668; www.museomineralogico campano.it*

A certain Pasquale Discepolo and his passion for rocks led to the establishment of this cracking little museum. Having visited Vesuvius and pondered the force of its vulcanology, it's good to look at the beauty behind the beast – namely the crystalline forms of its geology. The names and the crazy shapes seem from another planet and are sure to capture the imaginations of

Vico's Beaches

From Punto Orlando to Punto Scutulo on the border with the *comune* of Meta di Sorrento, there are a number of beaches and inlets worthy of your fun-seeking attention, including popular Meta, Seiano and the intimate stretch of diminishing pebble beach, Alimuri, backed by dramatic cliffs. Alas, many of the small inlets like Tordigliano are very tricky to get to without a boat. Others are accessible by higgledy-piggledy paths which are far from ideal terrain for families with small children.

Vecchio Macdonald

Children can sing along to the *Old Macdonald had a Farm* tune with new Italian *amici (friends)* at Agriturismo La Ginestra, which welcomes families for a tour around the *fattoria* (farm). Youngsters can say ciao to the chickens and pet the deer and goats – and the whole family can join in a hearty organic meal for 12€. La Ginestra also has decent accommodation (see Family-friendly Accommodation, p. 185) and organises excursions into the Monti Lattari mountains as well as quirky cookery classes. Via Tessa 2, Santa Maria del Castello, 80069 Vico Equense. 📞 *081 802 3211*; *www.laginestra.org*

children. Adults will also appreciate a close look at rocks with evocative names like the lapis lazuli with its dreamy cool blue hues collected from Monte Somma. Among the well-thought-out themed collections are Libyan arrowheads, dinosaur fossils and models as well as sparkling gems in the most vivid colours.

Open Tues–Sat 9am–1pm and 5–8pm Mar–Sep; Tues–Sun 9am–1pm and 4–7pm Oct–Feb; 9am–1pm all year, Sun and Bank Holidays. **Admission** *2€.* **Amenities** *Disabled access. Shop. Toilets.*

INSIDER TIP

Ice cream-bar-gastronomic shop **Gelateria Latteria Gabriele** (Corso Umberto I 5 📞 *081 801 6234*) not only has cool 60s décor, it's filled with fine pastries and yummy gelati, which are served atop brioches, in coppe (cups) or in cones.

SORRENTO

52km (32 miles) SE of Naples

Perched on cliffs 45m (150ft) above the sea, Sorrento's beguiling cobbled streets have a strange mix of genteel attractions and joyous heaps of tourist kitsch. It is bumper-to-bumper on the busy streets and it boasts spindly bathing platforms instead of beaches – you have to travel by road or boat to find stunning coves ideal for splashing around – but Sorrento is fine for a short-term family base from which to explore the area. Ancient Surrentum was a favourite of holidaying Roman big-wigs Agrippa and Augustus well before it gained notoriety in the 19th century when Romantic artists, composers and writers came to paint and ponder its citrus groves and intimate coves. Nowadays it's invaded by British package holidaymakers so be prepared for an eyeful of sunburnt bodies. If you tire of the Piazza Tasso coach crowds, there are plenty of villages and harbours between the lemon and olive groves to explore, where you will hear local dialects spoken and it's less pricey.

Essentials

Getting There & Getting Around

By Train Sorrento is easily reached on the **Ferrovia Circumvesuviana** Railway

Piazza Tasso, Sorrento

(📞 800 053 939; *www.vesuviana.it*) from stations on the Sorrentine Peninsula. In Naples, go to the Stazione Circumvesuviana just off Piazza Garibaldi. The journey takes around 55 minutes and costs 3€.

By Public Transport Unico Costiera is a series of integrated travel tickets that works with the Circumvesuviana – if you are travelling a lot, consider the 24 *ore* (hour) and 3 *giorni* (day) tickets which cost 6€ and 15€ respectively.

By Boat A stylish and exciting way to arrive, whether it is from Naples, Capri or Ischia, is by ferry or hydrofoil. Quite a few companies provide services to and from Sorrento's Marina Piccola, including: Alilauro (📞 081 497 2211; *www.alilauro.it*); Caremar (📞 081 017 1998; *www.caremar.it*); LMP: Linee Marittime Partenope (📞 081 807 1812/081 878 1430; *www.consorziolmp.it*); Metro

del Mare (📞 199 600 700; *www. metrodelmare.com*); NLG: Navigazione Libera del Golfo (📞 081 552 0763; *www.navlib.it*). Most of the carriers offer child discounts. Check the back pages of the free bimonthly *Qui Napoli* tourist booklet or the local paper, *Il Mattino,* for the seasonal timetables.

If you've got the cash to splash you can hire a fancy boat from one of the many companies based in Sorrento, including Nautica Sic Sic (📞 081 807 2283; *www.nauticasicsic.com*) based at Marina Piccola. Hire a guide as well and the most wonderful coves and beaches will be accessible – ideal for a day's swimming and maritime messing about. **Tony's Beach** (📞 081 878 5606) also hires out boats from its maritime HQ at the Marina Grande.

By Bus There is a daily **Sita autobus** (📞 081 552 2176; *www. sitabus.it*) between Naples and

Sorrento. For those arriving by air, a bus service from Capodichino Airport, run by **Curreri Viaggi** (📞 *081 801 5420*; *www.curreriviaggi.it*), operates 12 daily services (six there and six back) – the last bus departs the airport at 7.30pm. While in Sorrento you can get around using the yellow shuttle buses. Tickets are available from *edicole* (newsstands) and *tabacchi* (tobacconists) and cost 1€ for 90 minutes of travel.

By Car Traffic is a real problem in and around Sorrento, especially during the height of summer – it's not fun. If you have to travel by car from Naples, take the A3 Autostrada towards Salerno and exit at Castellamare di Stabia, then take the SS145 coastal road towards Sorrento.

If you do want to hire a car, there's an Avis office at Via degli Aranci 11D (📞 *081 878 2459*). The best way to get around, especially with a family, is to hire a driver who will act as a guide. The charming Benvenuto family based in Praiano have been in the business for over 60 years and have a fleet of quality Mercedes vehicles for groups of various sizes (Via Roma 54, 84010 Praiano. 📞 *346 684 0226/ 089 874 024*; *www.benvenutolimos.com*). Giovanni and his father Umberto provide a really professional service and know all the best family-friendly restaurants.

By Taxi Taxis are handy and are available from taxi ranks in Piazza Tasso 9 📞 *081878 2204*.

Visitor Information

The **Sorrento Tourist Office** is just off Piazza Tasso (Via Luigi De Maio 35. 📞 *081 807 4033*; *www.sorrentotourism.com*. 9am–6pm Mon–Sat all year; also 9am–12.30pm Sun Jul–Aug) and should be your first port of call to pick up a city map and any additional information needed about the town and area.

Family-friendly Events

Sorrento's Summer International Music Festival
Runs from 23rd July to 7th September.

Festa di Santa Anna
Local fishermen lead a week of feasting, dancing and concerts to celebrate the **Festa di Santa Anna**.
From 25th July to 2nd August.

Teatro Tasso AGES 7 AND UP
Piazza Sant'Antonio 25. 📞 *081 807 5525; www.teatrotasso.com*

Neapolitan folk music pulls in the punters at this recently renovated former 1920s cinema. Expect to hear old favourites including Funiculì funiculà, Marechiaro, O' Sole Mio and Torna a Surriento during a lavishly staged 75-minute show, which may be accompanied by a meal in the upstairs gallery. Il Tasso also stages pop and jazz concerts and the occasional family-friendly performance earlier in the day.

Sporty Sorrento

Fancy a family ten-pin bowling competition? Sorrento's bowling alley is at Via Sant'Antonio (📞 *081 807 1348*).

The two tennis clubs in Sorrento get very popular in the summer. Each has half a dozen clay and concrete courts. Book in advance to play in the cool evenings. Equipment hire also available. Tennis Sorrento: Viale Montariello 4 (📞 *081 878 1246*)/ Tennis Sport Sorrento: Via Califano (📞 *081 807 4181/081 807 1616*). Horsey types can go riding with **Centro Ippico La Selva** (Via Belvedere, Colli Fontanelle, Sant'Agnello 📞 *081 808 3196*).

What to See & Do

Sorrento's town centre is built upon a Greco-Roman layout and at its modern-day heart is the bustling, traffic-ridden **Piazza Tasso**, named after the poet Torquato Tasso. A white marble statue of him was erected in 1870 and stands in the piazza. Check out the often overlooked ruins of an abandoned watermill left to crumble in a deep, dank ravine nearby. The sight of **Il Vallone dei Mulini**, an inaccessible ecosystem filled with lush vegetation (including rare ferns), amid the tourist melee, makes you think of lost worlds and magic kingdoms. Equally out of place and also appealing – amid the coach parties, Disneyland-style "Dotto" trains and hordes spilling out of the cafés – is the **Sedile Dominova**, a 15th-century loggia with *trompe l'oeil* frescoes, where local old *signori* sit at tables playing cards; it's an old working men's social club. The adjoining baroque church, the **Chiesa di Santa Maria del Carmine** has exuberant stuccowork and a vibrant yellow façade. The Via

della Pietà has fine medieval palaces: **Palazzo Veniero** at no.14 is 13th century showing Byzantine and Arabic influences, while **Palazzo Correale** at no. 24 has a handsome portal, windows and tiled courtyard. The more understated **Duomo di San Filippo e San Giacomo** (Corso Italia 1 📞 *081 878 2248*; 8am–noon and 4–8pm daily) has been rebuilt many times and contains some fine 18th-century paintings from the Neapolitan School and eye-catching inlaid wood stalls. Four Roman columns support the cute campanile which has a majolica-tiled clock face.

INSIDER TIP »

For bar refreshments, ice cream and pastries (including *ciambelle* (doughnuts) and sweet *cornetti* (croissants) drop into **Premiata Pasticceria Pollio** at Corso Italia 172 (📞 *081 877 2889*).

Museo Bottega della Tarsia Lignea AGES 7 AND UP

Via San Nicola 28 📞 *081 877 1942.*

As well as the many artisan shops selling traditional inlaid wood products around Sorrento, there is a collection of 19th-century marquetry furniture housed in the grand Palazzo Pomarici Santomasi.

Open *10am–1pm and 3–6pm Tues–Sat; closed on public holidays.* **Admission** *8€.* **Amenities** *Toilets.*

Museo Correale ★ AGES 7 AND UP

Via Correale 50 📞 *081 878 1846; www.museocorreale.com*

Along beguiling Via Correale is the former aristocratic home of the Correale di Terranova family, which offers an insight into the tastes and lavish furnishings of the Neapolitan nobility as well as wonderful views. Their collection of Greek and Roman marbles, and Posillipo School landscapes may not excite youngsters but the detailed porcelain figures might capture their imaginations.

Open *9am–2pm Wed–Mon, closed Tues.* **Admission** *8€.* **Amenities** *Shop. Toilets.*

INSIDER TIP ❯❯

Escape the crowds and bring a picnic to the gardens at **Piazza della Vittoria** where there are lots of benches and fine views of the sea. Look carefully and you'll see the ancient remains of a Roman shrine, and then stop to admire the interlaced arches in the nearby 14th-century cloister of the **Chiesa di San Francesco d'Assisi** (Piazza Francesco Saverio Gargiulo; 8am–1pm and 2–7pm daily).

Shopping

Via San Cesareo is the main trawl of the town and where numerous shops and stalls sell limoncello, garlands of chillies, inlaid wood, cameos and ceramics.

Football Shop Via San Cesareo 95 📞 *081 807 2323* is the place for *calcio*-crazy youngsters who collect Italian football tops.

Wet & Wild Sorrento

For wonderful walks south of Sorrento, wild stretches of coastline in the Monti Lattari, around Agerola and on the Sentiero dei Dei (Trail of the Gods), contact experienced hiking guide Giovanni Visetti (📞 *339 694 2911; www.giovis.com*). His website has detailed maps and descriptions of the itineraries, as well as some gorgeous photos to whet your appetite for adventure. The **Area Marina Protetta di Punta Campanella** has pristine swimming, snorkelling and diving waters with many underwater caves to explore including the Grotta della Cala di Mitigliano and the Grotta dell'Isca. **Diving Sorrento** offers courses for older children and adults as well as snorkelling excursions from its HQ at the Nettuno Holiday Village at Nerano (Via A. Vespucci 39. 📞 *081 808 1051/ 081 808 3980; www.divingsorrento.com*)

Beaches & Harbours

Most of the finest bathing spots are found in secluded coves and are accessed by path, stairway or by boat – check with your hotel about access. Remember most are pebbly beaches so not really sandcastle friendly. Sorrento doesn't have a large beach – the piers that jut out to sea are not ideal for very small children but older ones may enjoy jumping and diving off them. There are steep paths down to **Marina Piccola**, the harbour backed by hotels seemingly growing out of rock faces and where you can catch ferries to Naples. There are sun-bathing jetties here. Despite its name, **Marina Grande** is the more intimate harbour and feels more like a fishing village with its pebbly beach strewn with boats. Around the headland going westwards towards Massa Lubrense is the intimate harbour **Marina di Puolo**, which has a small pebbly beach which becomes chocker at the height of summer. **Sant'Agnello** and the **Marinella** beach is a mile east of Sorrento. Sitting next to an impressive castle by the sea is the much-loved **Marina di Equa**, where you'll find a popular beach harbour and some fabulous restaurants. Unfortunately there have been problems with pollution and sewage on this stretch of coast so ask about the latest water quality before going for a dip.

Gargiulo & Jannuzzi Via Fuori Mura 1 ☎ *081 878 1041* has marquetry boxes, furniture and ceramics galore. Some are quite reasonable but for those who buy big, they can be shipped home very reasonably.

Linea Casa Viale Enrico Caruso, 14B ☎ *081 877 2622* is an interesting design shop with fabulous espresso cups and stylish kitchen kit.

Mercato di Via San Cesareo (Tuesday) If your son's trunks have been washed out to sea or Dad's expanding belly has caused his shorts to split, you can pick up cheap and cheerful replacements here.

Pink Elephant Piazza San Antonino, 8 ☎ *081 877 1011* has an array of limoncello brews and other local specialities.

MASSA LUBRENSE TO PUNTA CAMPANELLA

60km (38 miles) S of Naples

It may be tricky to get to, but the rewards of exploring this rugged corner of the Sorrentine Peninsula outweigh any hassle involved. Come to Massa Lubrense for its natural beauty. It was destroyed by Carlo I

Ice Cream Treats

Treat the family to arguably the yummiest ice cream in Sorrento. The Cioffis have been making gloriously good gelati for over three decades. Choose from over 80 different *sapori* (flavours) for your cone or 350 coppe combinations. Crazy flavours include **spaghetti-ice ai ciocco-latini gelato** (spaghetti ice cream with little iced chocolates) and the delectable rum babá. Adults might want to try the **semifreddo** or **sor-betti.** Handily there is seating available inside and in the flowery gardens.

Open 10.30am–11pm daily.

Corso Italia 16, 80067 Sorrento. 📞 *081 878 1364; www.bougainvillea.it.*

d'Angiò and then by Saracen and Turkish pirates (defensive towers built to curb these raids dot the coastline) but Massa re-emerged in the 16th century, with a newly built cathedral **Santa Maria delle Grazie.** This fine church, rebuilt in the 18th century, has wonderful majolica flooring and superb views of Capri from a nearby *terrazzo.* In old Massa Lubrense you'll find the original cathedral, **Santissima Annunziata,** with its Baroque stucco work and Franciscan Monastery built in

Sorrento Shopping

the 1580s. A steep, winding walk trails between the old houses of the *borgo* and reaches the nearby 14th-century Aragonese castle. Only a cylindrical tower and battlements remain, but the views of Capri and the Bay of Naples blow the mind.

From Massa Lubrense go down to the intimate little port of **Marina della Lobra,** whose marina is filled with boats. Angelo's Bar is a great place to order refreshments, snacks and ice cream, then pull up a seat and soak up the serene maritime scene while the children mess about on the dockside. The small pebbly beach is not sandcastle friendly but it's a wonderful spot to have a nosey around while the locals tinker with their boats. The exuberant green-and-yellow cupola of the sanctuary-cum-monastery campanile of **Santa Maria della Lobra** peaks through the higgledy-piggledy shapes of fishermen's houses and holiday residences. Take a look

inside this 16th-century church to see more majolica flooring and a wood-carved ceiling. Very fit families might enjoy a walk back to Massa Lubrense along a path that hugs the Chiaja shoreline as far as San Montano, where a steep path (Via Siringano) returns to Massa. If you're based in Sorrento and your family is into hiking, venture towards **Punta Campanella** for a taste of the rest of the peninsula. The sights, smells and sounds will generally come as a pleasant surprise after touristy Sorrento, giving the area a more authentic local *Meridionale* atmosphere.

There are several trails in and around Punta Campanella – maps and info are available from the visitor centre in wild, unspoilt Massa Lubrense (see p. 160).

> **INSIDER TIP >>**
> Massa Lubrense and many of the villages near Sorrento are served by the **SITA** bus company (📞 081 552 2176; *www.sita-on-line.it*).

Escape the Crowds at Punta del Capo Beach

This is a trip for families with older children who like a bit of adventure and don't mind negotiating rocky shorelines. Escape the crowds and stroll 3km to the secluded Punta del Capo beach. Take the Via del Capo, which is just off Piazza del Tasso, Sorrento – eventually passing through citrus and lemon groves. Budding history fans can have a nosey at the villa where Maxim Gorky lived between 1924 and 1933, and where Lenin sojourned during his exile (no public entry). The natural wonders increase as the path descends to the sea and the ruins of the once-sumptuous Roman Villa of Pollius Felix come into view. The limpid waters of the regally named Bagno della Regina Giovanna (Queen Giovanna's Bath) look inviting but take care as there are sharp, crumbly rocks around this enclosed pool.

Side Trip: on the Road to the Amalfi Coast: Sant'Agata sui Due Golfi

The *sui Due Golfi* means "on the two Gulfs" – the village pokes its head above the two dramatic coastlines and has commanding views over the two bays: Naples and Salerno. The views of Capri and Li Galli (see p. 166) – a group of rocky islets that were home to the mythical Sirens – complete the spellbinding panorama. Don't miss the wonderful **Chiesa di Santa Maria delle Grazie** in the village: the swirling shapes and vibrant marble work of the 17th-century Florentine altar as well as the majolica clock on its handsome façade will impress even the most jaded, "churched-out" nipper.

POSITANO & THE AMALFI COAST

La Costiera Amalfitana (Amalfi Coast) boasts the impossibly scenic coastal road passing above Positano's steep stairways and beaches – a detour heads up to the Valle dei Mulini: the Valley of Mills, which is a wonderful place for a family walk. Amalfi has maritime marvels and a must-see Duomo. As an antidote to its stories of graft and glory on the high seas, you can climb 300m (1,000ft) to genteel and dreamy Ravello, which has inspired many an artist including Boccaccio and Wagner. At Scala, Atrani, Minori, Cetara and Vietri majolica-tiled domes

embellish the coast's natural wonders of fjord-like valleys, coves and limestone ridges as far as the city of Salerno. Be warned though: the roads along the Amalfi Coast are very narrow in places and often get jammed with coaches from May to October.

Essentials

Getting There & Getting Around

By Boat If you are planning to go direct to the Amalfi Coast, be it Positano, Amalfi or Minori from Naples, by far the most comfortable ride (except when seas are rough) is to take a ferry or hydrofoil. There are a number of companies plying the coast including Metro del Mare (☎ *199 600 700; www.metro delmare.com*) which runs the MM2 and MM3 services (90 mins; one way ticket to Positano: 12€, 0–12 years 3€, 0–3 years free) from Napoli Beverello between late April and October. For Ravello, take the boat to Amalfi and pick up the bus. To avoid the traffic on the roads you can travel by hydrofoil between Positano, Amalfi, Minori, Maiori, Citara and Vietri. For all the latest seasonal timetables check *Qui Napoli* and/or the back pages of Naples's newspaper *Il Mattino*.

By Bus If you brave the bus ride, which can be a nightmare in the summer, you can take a SITA (☎ *081 552 2176; www.sita bus.it*) service from Naples or other major, or minor, places

Magical Marine Adventures

Hire a boat for a magical way to see the rugged coastline and its secluded coves and get all the family access to the best swimming waters and beaches. Unless you're an experienced mariner you are better off hiring the local expertise of a skipper. Try **Coop Marina della Lobra** (**☏** *081 808 9380*; *www.marinalobra.com*) based in small, but wonderful, Marina della Lobra. There are two well-established boat hire outfits based at Marina del Cantone: Cooperativa San Antonio (Via Cantone 47; **☏** *081 808 1638*) and Nautica O Masticello (**☏** *081 808 1443* or **☏** *339 314 791*; *www.masticiello.com*). The latter rents out *Guzzi* – traditional wooden Sorrentine sailing boats – as well as motorised rubber dinghies and flashy yachts.

along the coast. Local buses are also handy to get around: the bus from Positano to Amalfi takes 25 minutes and costs about 1.50€. Cute orange buses do a circuit along Viale Pasitea and up to Via Marconi before returning to Piazza dei Mulini in Positano – it's a good idea if you don't feel up to the steep climb on foot. The SITA bus to Ravello from Amalfi takes about 30 minutes and runs throughout the day at half-hourly intervals from 6.30am to 1am.

By Car The most convenient way of getting around, especially if time is of the essence, is to hire a chauffeur – and it's not as pricey as you might think.

If you are pining to drive the famous Amalfi coastal road (the SS163), try the spring months, avoiding summer and public holidays when the procession of tour buses holds up traffic. Prepare for eccentric Italian driving and wonderful, sweeping turns over sheer drops, which

should get the children whooping in the back.

By Taxi For travelling short distances, taking a taxi is not as pricey as you may think – just make sure you agree a price beforehand or ensure that the driver switches the meter on before setting off. The taxi drivers along the coast are not as fly as some of the chancers in Naples. Taxis are available at Piazza Flavio Gioia in Amalfi (**☏** *089 872 239*), at Positano's Piazza dei Mulini and Ravello's Piazza Duomo (**☏** *089 857 917*). The wonderful Benvenuto family-run company is perfect for short and long outings (**☏** *346 684 0226/ 089 874 024*. See p. 157).

Visitor Information

The tourist office is a homely affair and can be found at Via del Saracino 4 (**☏** *089 875 067*; *www.aziendaturismopositano.it*; open 8.30am–2pm Mon–Sat; plus 3.30–8pm in Jul–Aug.

Fast Facts

Banks Banco di Napoli is at Piazza Duomo 1, Amalfi (☎ 089 871 005.

Chemist Farmacia del Cervo is at Piazza Duomo 42, Amalfi ☎ 089 871 045 and Farmacia Rizzo is at Via Pasitea 22, Positano ☎ 089 812 3175.

First Aid Medical assistance can be sought at Croce Rossa Italiana, Via Nuova Chiunzi 1, Maiori ☎ 089 852 002.

Laundry Granducato D'Amalfi Service is at Via Giovanni d'Amalfi 26, Amalfi.

Post There's a post office at Corso delle Repubbliche Marinare 33, Amalfi ☎ 089 830 4811.

Family-friendly Events

New Year Celebrations
Positano

New Year involves a legendary cacophony of fireworks and feasting on lentils – they are said to resemble coins and bring a run of luck with money in the New Year

La Festa della Madonna di Montepertuso
Montepertuso (above Positano)

The Madonna who created the hole in the mountain (Montepertuso means mountain with a hole) to wrestle control of the village from the devil is celebrated with a colourful procession followed by much feasting and merriment.

2nd July

The Festival of the Assumption (La Festa della Assunta)
Amalfi

Saracen attacks and the heavenly intervention are re-enacted with much in the way of histrionics, costume-wearing and consumption of fine food and drink all thrown in.

14th and 15th August

What to See & Do

Belvedere
SS163

Approaching the turn-off for Positano from the west you come to the popular panoramic terrace, where you can stop to peer over the railings onto citrus trees and verdant plots down to the shore and across the sea towards **Li Galli** and other sparkling visions. Refreshments, snacks and invariably a colourful red, orange and yellow cascade of chilli peppers are on sale – but be warned: you pay an extravagant euro for the privilege of a *peperoncino*.

The direct route down to Positano from the main parking area is along Via dei Mulini. On the way (at no 23) you pass **Palazzo Murat** and its enchanting *cortile* (courtyard), which Joachim Murat, Napoleon's brother-in-law and King of Naples, built as a regal retreat. It's now a swanky hotel. The adventurous should follow the whims of the *scalinatelle,* a route that allows you to have a nosey into the gorgeous gardens and sniff their blossoms. There are lots of small boutiques and interesting shops before you reach Positano's most recognisable sight and its snazzy dome.

> **INSIDER TIP** >>
>
> Skipping in between the pastel-coloured houses with their flowery fronds is fun if a little precarious for littl'uns. Kit out the family in the most comfy and practical shoes before going *giù e su* (up and down) Positano's *scalinatelle* (little stairways) and clambering over the rocks along the coast and up in the hills.

Grotta dello Smeraldo ★
AGES 6 AND UP

If you like your marine grotto to be covered in otherworldly stalactite and stalagmite shapes and for its waters to take on hypnotising blue-green hues, then take a boat trip or the fun lift ride to the **Grotta della Smeraldo** (9am–7pm Mar–Oct and 9am–4pm Nov–Feb weather permitting; admission 6€) The grotto measures 30m (98ft) by 60m (197ft) and is 24m (79ft) deep in places. Peer into the depths and you'll see a ceramic *presepe* (nativity scene) which is the focus of Christmas festivities. For the most intense light effects, arrive between noon and 3pm, and if possible arrive by boat, although the commentary spouted by the onboard guides can veer between irritating and laughable nonsense. You can take a boat from Amalfi or from various other harbours along the coast. The Positano–Amalfi

SITA bus service also stops near the grotto. Access via the staircase is not really suitable for children.

Li Galli

For a really special place to swim, hire a boat and join the mythical Sirens at Le Sirenuse, nowadays called **Li Galli** after "The Cockerels": in Greek Mythology these creatures had bird-like bodies and human heads.

The three rocks that make up the small archipelago – Gallo Lungo, Castelluccio and La Rotonda – harbour limpid waters perfect for swimming and splashing-good fun. There are a number of people hiring out boats on the beach including **Lucibello** (Via del Brigatino 9 ☎ *089 875 032*; *www.lucibello.it*), who offer a number of trips around Capri, exploring the coast, Amalfi and the Grotta dello Smeraldo (see p. 166). They also do free shuttle trips to Praiano (below Monte Sant'Angelo where cute village houses set into the roadside rock have been transformed into nativity scenes) and a ferry service to and from Capri (return tickets: adults 25€ and children 15€). **Gennaro e Salvatore** (Via Trara Genoino 13. ☎ *089 811 613/ 089 875 475*; *www. gennaroesalvatore.it*) run boat trips to Capri, along the coast, and to I Galli and Nerano.

Santa Maria Assunta ★
AGES 5 AND UP

Piazza Flavio Gioia ☎ *089 875 480*

Yellow and green majolica tiles from Vietri cover its dome,

La Spiaggia Grande, Positano

whose bulbous boldness and extra cute cupola with a cross on top can be seen throughout the area. In the early 1700s the existing structure took shape, rising from the remains of a 13th-century Benedictine abbey. The triple-naved interior has lots of ornate white and gold stuccowork, and contains *La Madonna Nera* (the Black Madonna), a Byzantine icon that is the focus of the Festa della Assunta (Feast of the Assumption) every 15th August.

Open 8am–noon and 4–7pm daily. **Amenities** none.

Swimming Beaches

Children will want to get down to the beach just around the corner from the church of Santa Maria Assunta. Entering the main beach (**La Spiaggia Grande**), an array of restaurants, artists with easels and boat operators opens out before you. Lines of parasols, deckchairs and loungers fill the eastern half of the pebbly beach. There is no charge for parking your towels on the public beach, although it can get crowded with bodies and boats. Two defensive towers, Torre Trasita and Torre Sponda, frame this alluring beach scene. La Spiaggia Grande is bordered by a shady prom, **Via Positanesi d'America,** that hugs the cliffs. There are quite a few nearby beaches: **Spiaggia Fornillo** is just to the west beyond Torre Trasita (accessed by path or boat from Positano's Marina). The others are **La Porta, Fiumicello, Arienzo** (where film director Franco Zefferelli had a villa – good for celebrity spotting), **San Pietro** and **Laurito** (backed by restaurants and a hotel) to the east.

Shopping

Positano is famed for its practical yet chic goods: sandals, bags, beachwear and colourful ceramics. Most of Positano's shops line

Viale Pasitea or are on or just off Via dei Mulini, which runs from Piazza dei Mulini (where there is a car park) down to the beach.

La Botteguccia (Via Trara Genoino 13 ☎ 089 811 824) makes hand-made sandals.

Sartoria Maria Lampo (Viale Pasitea 12 ☎ 089 875 021) is one of the original 60s boutiques that brought Positano fashion-fame.

This region is the land of lemons and I Sapori di Positano, Via dei Mulini 6 (☎ 089 812 055) is dedicated to all things lemony: biscuits, sweets, soap, candles and of course, limoncello.

AMALFI

61km (38 miles) SE of Naples

Splendid views, fertile soils, warm waters – it's remarkable that Amalfi was not totally capitalised by the Romans who were famed for nabbing the best spots for carousing and debauchery. But it wasn't until the 6th century that, as part of the Duchy of Naples's Byzantine Empire, Amalfi was transformed into a prosperous port – trading salt and slaves for the gold of the east. It gained its own archbishop – a status symbol if ever there was one – in 987AD and became a maritime republic with its own doges, laws, taxes and vast wealth. Today Amalfi is a World Heritage site and popular with holidaymakers who love its wondrous atmosphere and compact charms. This is a place for enjoying the sun, the food, the sea and the colourful town buildings clinging to cliffs.

Essentials

Getting There & Getting Around

See Positano & the Amalfi Coast Essentials section, p. 163.

Visitor Information

For tourist information go to the Palazzo di Città on Corso delle Repubbliche Marinare ☎ *089 871 107; www.amalfitourist office.it. Open 8.30am–1.30pm and 3–5pm Mon–Fri; 8.30am–1.30pm Sat in the summer (Closed Nov–Apr).*

Family-friendly Events

Regatta Storica (Historic Regatta of the Maritime Republics)

Takes place on the first Sunday of June in Amalfi at four-year intervals. It is shared by the four towns renowned for their once maritime might: Amalfi, Pisa, Genova and Venice – it's Amalfi's turn again in 2009. Children will enjoy this colourful event with its heady mixture of ceremonial pomp, costume drama, musical fanfare and of course the serious matter of boat racing.

First Sunday in June 2009, 2013, etc.

What to See & Do

Amalfi, gorgeous though it may be, has little by way of sights, which means it can all be seen at a leisurely pace in about an hour. More than likely your first port of call will be Amalfi's transport hub, **Piazza Favio Gioia** – hydrofoils, boats and ferries dock at the harbour and SITA buses stop here.

The Duomo ★★★ AGES 4 AND UP

Piazza del Duomo

Dedicated to Sant'Andrea (see box, p. 170), Amalfi's awesome cathedral is sure to hold the attention of even the most blasé of teenagers: its prime position, vibrant façade, Byzantine doors (from Constantinople), Romanesque campanile and huge central staircase dominates the town centre. More than any other church in this area, the oriental (as in not occidental) style reminds you of the influence of those empires Amalfi once traded with. Beyond the atrium is the **Chiostro del Paradiso**, a 13th-century cloister and tomb of choice for the great and good of Amalfi, and now a museum containing some beautiful 12th-century mosaics. To the left of the nave is the **Chapel of the Crucifix** – the oldest part of the church – with some lovely frescos and the entrance to the **Crypt** where the remains of Sant' Andrea lie. Ghoulish children, once they have heard the story of the relics, might enjoy this bit best.

Open *9am–5.30pm daily Mar; 9am–9pm daily Apr–Sept; 10am–1pm Oct–Dec; closed Jan and Feb.* ***Admission*** *3€ adults; 1€ children.* ***Amenities*** *Toilets.*

Museo Civico (Civic Museum) AGES 7 AND UP

Town Hall, Piazza Municipio 📞 089 873 620

The Tavoliere Amalfitane is the maritime code that governed the entire Mediterranean until 1570. You can see the original manuscript here as well as bobbins that belonged to Flavio Gioia, Amalfi's most famous mariner

The Duomo, Amalfi

and inventor of the dry compass. How did he do it? Well, he worked out that a needle suspended over a fleur-de-lys (actually, it could have been any design that had points heading north, south, east and west) would be magnetically sensitive and would automatically point north. You can see a statue of a Flavio Gioia in the piazza named after him down by the waterfront.

Open 8.30am–1.30pm and 4.30–6.30pm Mon–Fri. *Admission* free. *Amenities* Toilets.

Museo della Carta AGES 5 AND UP

Palazzo Pagliara, Via delle Cartiere 23. ✆ *089 830 4561; www.museo dellacarta.it*

Children may enjoy learning about the paper-making process at this small museum set in one of Amalfi's old paper mills. Paper making was imported from the Chinese and Arab worlds by Amalfi's canny merchants who created the European capital of *carta a mano* (hand-made paper). After finding out about the town's paper-making history and seeing the various tools and tricks employed down the ages, you can get your hands on some of the poshest stationery known to man, beast or schoolchild.

Open 10am–6.30pm daily Mar–Oct; 10am–3.30pm Tues–Sun Nov–Feb. *Admission* 4€. *Amenities* Shop. Toilets.

Shopping

Most visitors will be drawn to the buzz and excitement of **Piazza del Duomo**. Most of it is tourist tat but you can pick up some spicy chillies or preserved Amalfitana lemons to take home. If you're looking for pottery beware of cheap imitations of the local Vietri pottery.

Cartiera Amatruda

Via delle Cartiere 100, Amalfi ✆ *089 871 315*

Generations have been making paper at this old paper shop. Buy a fancy quill here to go with the children's new parchments for homework.

FUN FACT ›› St Andrew ‹‹

Amalfi became the final resting place of Sant'Andrea (or St Andrew) – one of the apostles – in 1206 when the Cardinal of Capua nicked his relics from Constantinople and took them to Amalfi. Inside the Duomo you'll find a golden shrine that holds his skull. Not to be outdone by the Neapolitans with San Gennaro's liquefying blood (see p. 61), on certain days the skull seeps a liquid called "Sant'Andrea's manna" which has the power to heal – by some accounts. What happened to the rest of Sant'Andrea? Well, a kneecap, a tooth, an arm bone and some finger bones could once be accounted for. They were taken by St Regulus to St Andrew's in Scotland ("the end of the earth" and the home of golf) but sadly turned to ash when the protestants burned down St Andrew's Cathedral.

Vietri Ceramics

Vietri sul Mare's most famous export – its ceramics – are everywhere on the Amalfi Coast, adorning shop fronts and covering cupolas. Via Madonna degli Angeli in Vietri sul Mare is the place to go for your eye-catching ceramics and the Ceramiche Artistiche Solimne ★★ AGES 4 AND UP at no 7 (℃ 089 212 539) is its most iconic factory with 20,000 pots covering its façade.

D'Antuono

Piazza Duomo 10 ℃ 089 873 6374

Local paper and an intriguing supply of old prints and books fill this alluring outlet.

La Valle dei Mulini

Salita Chiarito 9, Amalfi ℃ 089 873 211

A bottle of limoncello, the traditional sweet lemon liqueur, never tastes quite the same on a patio at home but if you're going to buy it this shop has interesting shaped bottles that can be imaginatively recycled once emptied.

RAVELLO

6km (3.7 miles) NE of Amalfi, 66km (41 miles) SE of Naples

Just round the corner from Amalfi and up a winding road that will make your ears pop is Ravello. Sitting 350m (1,150ft) high, it has always been the place where wealthy families built their most prestigious piles. It might be small but it was an independent principality for most of the second half of the millennium and therefore only answered to the Pope! In the 13th century, wealth garnered from maritime trade led to a flowering of Norman-Saracenic architecture that you can still admire today. For families who love to see things that will take their breath away, it's a great day out. The rarefied air and tranquil atmosphere is truly inspiring and invigorating. Thankfully, much of the town is a no-go for vehicles (you leave your car at a car park hidden away near the Duomo). The charming **Piazza Duomo** has space for children to run around a bit while parents can take in the atmosphere at one of the al fresco café tables – **Bar Klingsor** (4 Via dei Rufolo ℃ 089 857 407) does Neapolitan pastries and refreshments. Among the interesting shops is **Ceramiche Autore** (Piazza Duomo 6 ℃ 089 858 260) owned by the eccentric Pino who sells flamboyantly coloured ceramics.

Essentials

Getting There & Getting Around

See Positano & the Amalfi Coast Essentials section, p. 163.

Visitor Information

For tourist information go to the AAST office at Via Roma 18 ☎ *089 857 096*; ***www.ravellotime.it***. Open 10am–7pm daily (until 8pm in summer).

Family-friendly Festivals

Ravello Festival

For info contact the Festival HQ at Viale Wagner 5 ☎ *089 858 360; **www. ravellofestival.com***

Groan! A load of fusty old Wagner-lovers descending on such a little town sounds like a nightmare but actually this festival is inventively curated and attracts a surprisingly wide age-range of music lovers. Its aim is to bind beauty and music together and create a spiritual experience. If you're in the area on 10th August, don't miss *Concerto all'Alba* (dawn concert) which starts at 4.30am when the whole town rises to watch the sunrise over the bay while a full symphony orchestra, suspended on a clifftop stage, plays along. It makes you feel great to be alive! Even the sleepiest child will be won over.
Late Jun–Oct

What to See & Do

Ravello is a place not to be rushed through, so set aside at least three hours to enjoy its fairytale gardens and serene atmosphere.

The Duomo ★ ★ AGES 4 AND UP

Piazza de Vescovado ☎ *089 858 311*

The simplest of churches are often the most memorable. Dedicated to San Pantaleone – another saint whose blood liquefies (see San Gennaro, p. 61) (the 'miracle' takes place on 27th July) – Ravello's charming Romanesque Duomo was built in 1086 but remodelled in 1786. Protected by a double set of wooden doors are huge 12th-century bronze doors

Duomo, Ravello

which have been undergoing restoration of late; their 54 panels depicting biblical scenes were sculpted by Barisano da Trani and cast in Constantinople. Don't expect heavy, overbearing interiors – on entering, the lightest, freshest church opens before you. The medieval pulpits are spellbinding with their colourful mosaics, bas reliefs and twisting columns. Children will ooh and aah at the six marble lions, imperious eagle and the mosaic of Jonah and the Whale. The latter recalls the frescoed panel of Giotto in the astoundingly beautiful Scrovegni Chapel in Padova. Indeed some of the frescoes here appear to be influenced by Giotto's work. Back down and below the earth, descend into the crypt if you fancy a gander at a collection of pious relics, including a 13th-century sculpture by Bartolomeo de Foggia.

Open *9am-1pm and 5-7pm daily; Museum 9am–1pm and 3–7pm daily Easter–Oct.* **Admission** *free; Museum 2€.* **Amenities** *Toilets.*

INSIDER TIP ≫

Mercato: Ravello's Tuesday market at Piazza Duomo is full of lively banter and the most delicious produce. If your family loves olives then this will be the pit-stop from heaven: pluck the purple-skinned ones from Gaeta and the plumpest vivid green beauties.

Villa Cimbrone ★ ★ ALL AGES

Via Santa Chiara 26 ☎ *089 857 459*

As you enter the mock-Gothic villa you must first walk for 10 minutes or so along a hillside path (perhaps not easy with young ones). But when you get there and past the gatekeepers, wow, is it worth it! Sitting so prettily 450m (1,500ft) above the sea, this castle may have seemed incongruous if not in such fantastic surroundings. Children's imaginations will be spiked by the fairytale turrets and courtyards. Built in 1905 by Ernest William Beckett, Lord Grimthorpe (who built Big Ben), it has lured many an artistic type over the years: E.M. Forster, Lytton Strachey, Henry Moore, Virginia Woolf, D.H. Lawrence, Greta Garbo and Winston Churchill (not just a prime minister but a painter, of course) were some of its famous guests. Wandering amongst the verdant fronds you can read romantic verse by Roman poets and Persian astronomers etched onto plaques. Now a posh hotel, you can still enjoy the terraced grounds which were Lord Grimthorpe's dream, passion and tremendous legacy to lovers of flowers and beauty everywhere. On a clear day, the views of the Gulf of Salerno from the Belvedere Cimbrone are breathtaking and there are plenty of cheesy – yet altogether refined – family photo opportunities by the sculptures perched on the elegant balustrades.

Open *9am–sunset daily.* **Admission** *5€ to the garden. Free for hotel guests.* **Amenities** *Picnic area. Toilets.*

Milling Around

You can escape the tourist trail and absorb the timeless atmosphere of the small hamlets of **Minuta, Campidoglio** and **Santa Caterina**, which made their money from the paper and wool trades. You won't find so many shops selling kitschy gifts and tat – instead you'll find small *alimentari* (food shops), lots of local characters and donkeys laden with packs. The easiest walk is to Minuta (1 hr. approx) where you can visit the **Chiesa della Santissima Annunziata** church and see some fine Byzantine frescos. Even more rewarding is the 6km (4 mile) walk in the *Valle dei Mulini* (Valley of Mills) where you can stroll amid green hills and bathe in fresh streams. Further up there are fabulous ridge walks that require a certain degree of fitness, nerve and navigational skill. Local guide Giovanni Vasetti organises excursions all over the Amalfi Coast and has a page and maps dedicated to the walk on his excellent website: ***www.giovis.com/mulinib.htm***

Villa Rufolo ★ ★ ★ ALL AGES

Piazza Duomo 📞 *089 857 657*

If you have a princess in the family, here is the castle that will be in her dreams for years to come. Built in 1270 by Nicola Rufolo, Villa Rufolo has entertained the great and the good while its Moorish architecture, cool cloisters and breathtaking views from the flower-filled gardens have inspired writers and composers. After gawping at the striking Moorish arcades you can enjoy an amble around the flowery terraces taking in the spectacular views which inspired Richard Wagner's magic garden of Klingsor, in his opera, *Parsifal.*

Open *9am–6pm daily (until 8pm Apr–Sept).* **Admission** *5€ adults; 3€ under-12s and over-65s.* **Amenities** *Toilets.*

SALERNO & PAESTUM

Salerno 5km (3 miles) east of Vietri, 34km (21 miles) E of Amalfi, 55km (34 miles) SE of Naples; Paestum 35km (22 miles) S of Salerno, 100km (62 miles) SE of Naples;

The bustling modern town of Salerno, Campania's second city, is worth a family day out for its historic sights and scenic *lungomare* (seafront prom). Founded in the 6th century BC, Salerno has been ruled by Etruscans, Campanian tribes, Greeks, Romans, Longobards, Normans, Swabians, Angevins and Spanish Bourbons. Despite the frenzied skirmishes of 1943 to 1945 between the Allies, Germans and retreating Fascists, some of the medieval quarter, 19th-century buildings and Liberty-style Art Nouveau *palazzi* were spared destruction. Farther down the

PAESTUM

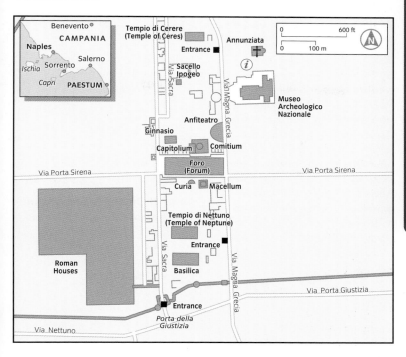

coast from Salerno (half an hour by train) are the magical ancient ruins of Paestum.

Essentials

Getting There & Getting Around

By Train Salerno is a major stop on the coastal line and on services from Naples (the journey takes around 45 mins. and services are very frequent with at least two per hour from Napoli Centrale). The service continues down the coast to Paestum (this takes a further 35 mins).

By Bus SITA (☎ 089 226 604; *www.sitabus.it*) runs buses between Naples and Salerno and SCAT (☎ 0974 838 4150 runs services down the coast to Paestum, Agropoli and beyond from Salerno, as does CSTP (☎ 800 016 659; *www.cstp.it*). Just remember that travelling on Italian buses in the middle of summer is an uncomfortably hot and not very fun business. Within Salerno itself the public bus company CSTP (☎ 800 016 659; *www.cstp.it*) has its main hub at the train station. The bus to Paestum from Salerno leaves from Piazza Concordia (near the station) about every 30 minutes.

By Car From Naples take the A3 Napoli–Salerno autostrada. For Paestum continue on the A3 and exit at Battipaglia. The state coastal road Strada Litiranea is an alternative and also continues to Agropoli and the towns along the Cilento coast.

By Ferry All the major ferry companies offer services between Salerno and Naples – some even stop at harbours along the Amalfi Coast – especially during the summer. Metro del Mare (℡ *199 446 644*; *www.metrodelmare.com*) stops all along the Amalfi Coast. Alicost (℡ *089 234 892*; *www. lauroweb.com*) runs ferries and hydrofoils to and from the islands and Amalfi Coast ports. Molo Manfredi in Salerno is the ferry port.

Visitor Information

The main **Salerno** AACST tourist office is at Via Roma 258 (℡ *089 224 744*; *www.turismoinsalerno.it*) and there's another one at the train station (Piazza Vittorio Veneto; ℡ *089 230 411*). At **Paestum** the AACST tourist office (Via Magna Grecia 151. ℡ *0820 881 1016*; *www.infopaestum.it*) near the archaeological museum is handy and is open from 9am to 3pm Monday to Saturday (until 7pm July–Aug) and from 9am to 1pm on Sundays.

Fast Facts

Bank Banco di Napoli is at Piazza Luciani 1, Salerno ℡ *089 624 852*.

Chemist Farmacia Colucci is at Via Arce 49, Salerno ℡ *089 227 416*.

First Aid Medical assistance can be sought at Croce Rossa Italiana, Via Roma 252, Salerno ℡ *089 222 001*.

Laundry Lavanderia Aurora is at Via Gabriele Giuglielmi 10, Salerno ℡ *089 232 317*.

Post There's a post office at Via Roma 130, Salerno ℡ *089 229 970*.

Family-friendly Festivals

Linea d'Ombra Salerno Film Festival explores the themes of youth and adolescence each spring through both film and other cultural events including gigs and multimedia.
April

Festa della Pizza
www.festadellapizza.it

Music, competitions and much pizza eating will keep children happy. Sporty Spice played in 2007.
September

What to See & Do

Lined with palm trees and gorgeous views of Campania's shimmering seascapes, the *lungomare* (promenade) ★★ is a fab spot for a family stroll. The **Villa Comunale** at its western end has lush gardens and is flanked by historic buildings. The Medieval *centro storico* begins near the Teatro Verdi: beyond the swanky shops on Via di Porta Catena is the Piazza Sedile del Campo, the old market square which contains the handsome, baroque **Palazzo dei Genovesi** (now a university building and occasional venue for exhibitions) and wonderful spouting dolphins of **La Fontana dei Delfini**. Off the piazza is Via dei Mercanti, which turns into Corso Vittorio Emanuele, Salerno's main shopping drag.

Castello di Arechi

Via Benedetto Croce ☎ *089 233 900;* **www.castellodiarechi.it**

For a fab view of the city take a taxi or climb the steep path to this castle and clamber over soaring fortifications built by Byzantines and added to by the Normans, Angevins and Aragonese. Spectacular firework displays and concerts are held here throughout the year. The museum contains collections of historic ceramics, weapons, armoury, glass and coins.

Open *8.30am–7.30pm Mon–Fri and 9am–1.30pm weekends.* ***Admission*** *free.* ***Amenities*** *Baby changing. Shop. Toilets.*

Duomo di San Matteo ★★
AGES 4 AND UP

Piazza Alfano 1, ☎ *089 231 382.*

Salerno's most famous attraction was founded in 845, rebuilt in 1076 and refurbished on numerous occasions since. Through the Romanesque gateway, La Porta dei Leoni, a Moorish-style atrium opens out with some 28 columns pilfered from Paestum. The fine intarsia stonework may even impress the huffiest youngster. A 55m (180ft) campanile from

the 12th century soars above the colonnade. Don't overlook the two bronze doors made in Constantinople (1099) and the exquisitely carved façade. The three-naved interior contains two ambones (medieval raised platforms). Get the children to look out for spine-tingling finely crafted Byzantine depictions of ferocious animals.

The crypt contains the body of San Matteo (Saint Matthew) and – among the Roman and medieval sarcophagi – the tomb of Pope Gregory VII who died in exile in 1085. The adjoining **Museo Diocesano** – the Duomo Museum – contains 11th-century ivory panels.

Open *10am–6pm daily; Museum opens at 9am.* ***Admission*** *free.* ***Amenities*** *Shop. Toilets.*

Museo Archeologico Provinciale **AGES 6 AND UP**

Via San Benedetto 38, ☎ *089 231 135*

Families who dig archaeology should seek out this museum housed in a wing of an 11th-century convent. Its handsome halls are crammed with antiquities organized into themed sections telling the stories of many periods including Roman Salerno and 5th-century burial treasures.

Open *9am–8pm Mon–Sat.* ***Admission*** *free.* ***Amenities*** *Toilets.*

Teatro Verdi

Piazza Luciani, Salerno ☎ *089 662 141;* **www.teatroverdisalerno.it**

Take a peak behind the velvet curtains at this theatre which

Spuntini: Snacks

Fill your family picnic basket or backpack with biscuits, pastries and bread from **Biscottificio Manzoni** (Via de Granito 11, Salerno **℡ 089 227 465**). *Salernitani* flock to Il **Laboratorio di Pasticceria Sabatino Sirica** for their famed *babà* and *sfogliatelle* recipes. For ice cream on the prom go to **Gelateria Bar Nettuno** (Via Lungomare Trieste 136 **℡ 089 228 375**) where you'll find unusual fruity flavours like *anguria* (water melon) and *nocciotella* (praline hazelnut-chocolate) served on brioche.

stages concerts and other performances amid grand baroque surroundings.

Open *9am–2pm and 4–8pm daily.*
Admission *tickets from 12€.*
Amenities *Baby-changing. Shop. Toilets.*

Paestum

Going south of Salerno the flood plains of the river Sele are the site of mainland Italy's most important Greek ruins. Like the 18th-century Grand Tourists, children's imaginations will be swept away by the sense of a lost civilization here.

The train from Salerno takes 35 mins. Double that journey time for the SCAT bus (**℡ 0974 838 4150**) (see p. 175). By car, take the A3 Autostrada and exit at Battipaglia. Alternatively, take the Metro del Mare from Naples or Amalfi to nearby Agropoli.

Exploring the Ruins and Archaeological Museum
★★★ ALL AGES

Looming out of the Sele river plain and nondescript suburbia, the ancient columns will raise some wows from everyone. The huge site is very exposed, so

bring hats and cool water. After exploring the temples you can cool down and delve into the fascinating history and artefacts in the museum over the road. There are three entrances to the temples: one is just over the road from the archaeological museum and tourist office; the others are by the Temple of Neptune and Porta della Giustizia. It makes sense – especially in hot weather – to start at the most southerly entrance and make your way northwards towards the Temple of Ceres and the Museum.

The Basilica or Temple of Hera was built in 550BC. The 18th-century enthusiasts who discovered it mistakenly thought it was used for civic not religious ceremonies – the first name stuck when in fact it's Paestum's oldest religious building. Children who like gruesome tales should look out for the sacrificial altar and a square well where the sacrificial remains were thrown. Budding scholars will notice straight away that the bulging look of the columns and capital make it the most well-preserved example of an early Doric temple in the world.

Youngsters take note: they make a fine backdrop to a photo of Dad's paunch.

The Tempio di Nettuno or Temple of Neptune was built in the 5th century and is covered in travertine marble – it glows a rich hue at sunset making it very photogenic. The stuccowork that once covered the columns has long since gone. It's the largest temple in Paestum (6m longer than the Temple of Hera) and has 36 fluted columns (six at the end and 14 along the sides). The cornices and horizontal lines curve upwards slightly in the middle to create an elegant appearance and less sagging look. Two sacrificial altars can be seen at the front. Historians believe that the temple was dedicated to Hera Argiva, goddess of fertility.

The Roman Forum was surrounded by a Doric portico and is one of the most complete anywhere in the world. On its north side is the 1st century BC amphitheatre, partly covered by the modern road. Look out for the rectangular buildings by the forum which are *taberna* (shops) as well as a *comitium* (court), basilica, *macellum* (covered market) and various other buildings including temples dedicated to Fortuna Virilis (where women venerated Venus) and Asclepius (the god of healing). West of the Forum is the 12km (8-mile) long Via Sacra (Sacred Road) that linked the principal buildings of Poseidonia with the Temple of Hera.

The Temple of Ceres, further north, is known as an Athenaion as it's dedicated to Athena the goddess. It has 34 fluted columns and is the smallest of the three temples. Three Christian tombs were added in the medieval period.

Museo Archeologico Nazionale (National Archaeological Museum)
★★★ AGES 5 AND UP

Via Magna Grecia 917 ☎ *0828 811 023; www.infopaestum.it*

Across the road from the temples, Paestum's archeological museum

The Temple of Ceres, Paestrum

tells the story behind the ruins. Highlights include sculpture from the sanctuary of Hera Argiva depicting various Homeric scenes and the magical **Tomb of the Diver** ★★★ consisting of four frescoed funerary panels showing various activities. The coffin lid image of a youth diving gracefully into blue water – a life-affirming image that is apparently an allegory of death – is sure to capture the imagination.

Open archaeological area: 9am–1hr before sunset daily; Museum 9am–7pm daily (closed on first and third Mon of each month). *Admission* 4.50€ or 7€ combined. Reductions with Artecard. *Amenities* Baby changing. Disabled access. Picnic area. Shop. Toilets.

Museo Narrante del Santuario di Hera Argiva ★
AGES 5 AND UP

Masseria Procuriali ☎ *0828 811 016; www.infopaestum.it*

Families keen to find out more about ancient Greek cults may enjoy a visit to the sanctuary of Hera alla Foce del Sele and the new multimedia museum some 11km (7 miles) north of Paestum. Pliny the Elder (see p. 120) talked about the sanctuary which was legendary throughout Magna Grecia – according to lore Jason and the Argonauts built it. Two archaeologists discovered the site in the 1930s; many of the buildings had already been dismantled. Little remains today of the once-grand complex but it's an evocative place to visit and very popular with grazing buffalo.

Open 9am–4pm Tues–Sat. *Admission* free. *Amenities* Baby changing. Disabled access. Picnic area. Toilets.

CAFES, SNACKS & FAMILY-FRIENDLY DINING

It's not only the stunning dining settings that make eating out on the Costiera such a treat. Rich pickings from the fertile slopes mean families are served the tastiest ingredients including the best *mozzarella di bufala* from Agerola and the Sele plain, Gragnano pasta, fruits including Sorrentine lemons and Punta Campanella peaches, cheeses from the *Monti Lattari* (Milky Mountains) goat and sheep herds and *verdure* (veg: artichokes from Paestum and Controne beans). Fine olive oils and wines should keep adults happy while the pastries and ice creams will tempt the children. The coast's fleet of fishing boats supply the tables with abundant seafood and the basis of some unusual creations like Cetara's famous jars of tuna and anchovies. Oh and if this is all too weird and tasty for youngsters there's always *la pizza*, and the home of *pizza al metro* served at Da Gigino Università della Pizza (see p. 185) in Vico Equense.

Sweet Eats

Pasticceria Sal De Riso ★

Piazza Cantilena 28, Minori ☎ *089 853 618; www.deriso.it*

On the seafront at Minori and down the road from his family's old bar, a talented young pastry chef, Salvatore De Riso, set up shop where he makes exceedingly good cakes. This is the place to come for child-friendly treats like *delizia di limone* – a lemon slice with a natural citrus punch – and *pastiera napoletana*, the classic Neapolitan cake. The *Babà al distillato di Rhum* and *Profitteroles all'amaretto Disaronno* should go down well with the grown-ups! You should also try the artisan ice creams and *granite (*refreshing crushed-ice slushies with natural juice flavouring). For 12€–40€ they'll create a take-away tray of sweet treats.

Amalfi

Da Gemma

Via Frà Gerardo Sasso 9, Amalfi ☎ *089 871 345.*

Founded in 1872, this venerable *ristorante* still manages to combine classy cuisine with an atmosphere that is enjoyable for family groups. Book a table on the blooming terrace and you can enjoy views of the Duomo while tucking into the langoustines in lemon oil – the children might pass on the finger-lickin' good crustacean and go for the oh-so-cheesy ravioli. The *Crostata Amalfitana* (baked tart) for dessert will please young and old alike.

Open *12.30–2.45pm and 7.30–10.30pm daily.* **Main Courses** *15€–27€.* **Credit** *AmEx, DC, MC, V.* **Amenities** *Highchairs. Reservations required.*

Lido Azzurro

Lungo Mare Dei Cavalieri, Amalfi ☎ *089 871 384*

This no-frills trattoria sits on the promenade in Amalfi and delivers great-value pasta dishes and seafood classics – including *tubetti con zucchini* (tube-like pasta with courgettes) and *spaghetti alle vongole* (clams). They serve excellent Furore DOC wines from the unfeasibly steep slopes just up the road.

Open *12.30–3pm and 7.30–10.30pm Tues–Sun.* **Main Courses** *12€–20€.* **Credit** *AmEx, DC, MC, V.* **Amenities** *Highchairs. Reservations recommended.*

Cetara

Acquapazza

Corso Garibaldi 33, Cetara ☎ *089 261 606*

The children will have to like seafood really to fully enjoy Cetara's fishy delights and especially those served here. Simply prepared pasta dishes abound for the youngsters – they'll whip up something yummy for fussy eaters. The adventurous foodies should sample the *colatura di alici* (the famous anchovy sauce that the Romans loved which is synonymous with Cetara) and a dish combining vegetables and seafood, like cuttlefish with beans.

Open *12.30–3pm and 7.30–11pm Tues–Sun.* **Main Courses** *12€–17€.* **Credit** *AmEx, DC, MC, V.* **Amenities** *Highchairs. Reservations recommended.*

Massa Lubrense

Antico Francischiello Da Peppino

Via Partenope, 27, Massa Lubrense 📞 *081 533 9780.*

Vibrant country-cucina interiors and simply prepared food make Francischiello's, on a hillside between Sorrento and Massa, a perennial favourite with locals. Children enjoy eating on the flowery terrace or in the dining rooms crammed with rustic Neapolitan knick-knacks. The menu covers everything a family could wish for from the freshest seafood and grilled meats to veggie-friendly side dishes and

fruity desserts including the famous *delizia di limone*, apparently invented here.

Open *Noon–3pm and 6.30–midnight daily; closed Wed in low season.* **Main Courses** *9€–16€.* **Credit** *AmEx, DC, MC, V.* **Amenities** *Highchairs.*

Paestum

Ristorante Nettuno

Via Nettuno, Paestum 📞 *0828 811 028*

It's right by the ruins overlooking the temples and offers pretty good value given the captive tourist market cramming its rustic yet refined 19th-century dining rooms. Ask for a table with views of the archaeological site and order some of the seafood dishes – including grilled crustaceans – keeping the youngsters satisfied with *crespolini* (large savoury crêpes) stuffed with gooey goodness of local buffalo mozzarella and prosciutto ham.

Open *Noon–3pm and 7.30–11.30pm daily July–Aug; noon–3pm Tues–Sun Sept–June.* **Main Courses** *16€–25€.*

Cetara Beach

*Credit AmEx, DC, MC, V. **Amenities** Highchairs. Reservations recommended.*

Positano

Il Guarracino ★

Via Positanesi d'America 12, near Spiaggia Fornillo, Positano ☎ 089 875 794.

Tucked away behind the chic restaurants down at the Positano waterfront is this great little bar-ristorante-pizzeria overlooking the Fornillo beach. Children will lap up the yummy pizza and parents can enjoy classic Neapolitan dishes – including lots of seafood – while listening to the waves. The relaxed dining takes place amid bamboo-enclosed balconies reminiscent of a Swiss Family Robinson tropical tree house. It's a bit of a walk but well worth the climb to this arboreal kingdom of top-notch nosh.

***Open** Noon–3pm and 7.30–11.30pm daily. **Main Courses** 8€–17€. **Credit** DC, MC, V.*

La Tagliata ★★★ FIND VALUE

Via Tagliata 22, towards Montepertuso, Positano ☎ 089 875 872

It may be up in the hills way above Positano near Montepertuso, but a visit to this friendly trattoria will live in the family memory for years. Enzo, Peppino and pals distil the essence of Amalfitana hospitality – simply prepared food using the tastiest Parthenopean produce washed down with a healthy dose of *buon umore* and vino. Even the view from the bathroom – looking towards Li Galli (see p. 166) – is magical. Ask for a selection of antipasti and share around the table but leave some space for the *dolci* (desserts) which include lots of calorific *semifreddi* creamy cakes. Lunches are special with the large picture windows thrown open while dinners often overflow with music and dancing on tables. Give them a ring and they may pick you up if you are in the Positano area.

***Open** 12.30–3pm and 7.30–late daily. **Main Courses** 9€–15€. **Credit** AmEx, DC, MC, V. **Amenities** Highchairs. Reservations recommended.*

Salerno

Cenacolo ★★

Piazza Alfano I 4, Salerno ☎ 089 238 818

Down by the Duomo, this top restaurant is the best bet in Salerno for a family occasion. The cuisine is based on traditional Cucina Salernitana with an inventive flourish: children will enjoy the *crespelle* (folded and filled savoury crêpes) while the more mature palate might go for one of the seafood or meat creations. They do lots of small antipasti which are great for sharing around the table. It may be dangerous though as children will be demanding *zucca ripieni* in the future, and pumpkin flowers are not common down the supermarket.

***Open** 12.30–3pm Tues-Sun and 7.30–late Tues-Sat **Main Courses** 16€–24€. **Credit** AmEx, DC, MC, V. **Amenities** Highchairs. Reservations recommended.*

Zì Renato

Via Roma 170, Salerno ☎ *089 228 018.*

For a great-value family feast – with pizza and local dishes on the menu – head to the relaxed checked table-clothed interiors of this reliable trattoria. They make their own pasta on the premises – including the Campanian favourite *scialatelli* – often served with a *frutti di mare* (shellfish) sauce.

Open 12.30–3pm and 7.30–10.30pm daily. **Main Courses** *6€–14€.* **Credit** *AmEx, DC, MC, V.* **Amenities** *Highchairs. Reservations recommended.*

Sant'Agata sui Due Golfi

Don Alfonso ★

Corso Sant'Agata 11, Sant'Agata sui Due Golfi ☎ *081 878 0026*

This is one for a real family occasion as this famous restaurant is perhaps the best in Southern Italy and is accordingly *caro* – expensive! Food heroes Alfonso and Livia Iaccarino provide all the organic produce – including meats – from their plot at Punta Campanella and the fish and cheeses come from local producers. As well as their simply prepared dishes like fish casserole and caciotta cheese ravioli they do delectable *dolci* including an aubergine and chocolate combo. The *menu di degustastione* (tasting menu) will set you back 120€ so you may want to share the fabulous tastes around as a culinary treat for the family. Children under 5 are welcome for the lunch sitting but not for dinner.

Open 12.30–2.30pm and 8–11pm Tues–Sun; closed Wed in low season. **Main Courses** *21€–35€.* **Credit** *AmEx, DC, MC, V.* **Amenities** *Highchairs. Reservations recommended.*

Sorrento

Il Delfino ★

Via Marina Grande 216, Sorrento ☎ *081 878 2038*

Large helpings of the freshest seafood and pasta dishes served right down by the water's edge at the Marina Grande make this a fabulous choice for families. If the wonderful creations such as *fettuccine con gamberetti e spinaci* do not float the children's boat (just tell them that the spinach and prawns will put hairs on your chest!), they'll knock up something for weedy youngsters.

Open Noon–3.30pm and 6.30–10.30pm daily. **Main Courses** *8€–18€.* **Credit** *AmEx, DC, MC, V.* **Amenities** *Highchairs.*

Pizzeria Da Franco `VALUE`

Corso Italia 265, Sorrento ☎ *081 877 2066*

Locals flock to this no-frills pizzeria which will keep children happy with its classic margherita served on a tray in wax paper. Drinks may be served in plastic cups, service is swift and friendly and the delicious pizza is made to measure. The only downside is that there are sometimes long queues.

Open Noon–midnight daily. **Pizzas** *from 6.50€.* **Credit** *AmEx, DC, MC, V.* **Amenities** *Highchairs.*

Vico Equense

Da Gigino Università della Pizza ★★

Via Nicotera 10, Vico Equense 📞 *081 879 8426*

Open 24/7, this Neapolitan institution is the home of pizza al metro and claims to be the largest pizzeria in the world. Take a table in this ever-popular eatery (it can hold around 2,000 pizza munchers at a time) and let the fun begin: they reckon that a metre of pizza will feed five people, so create your top-pings and see how your family measures up against the Neapolitan regulars. If you can find room pick up some *antipasti* and *dolci* off the trolley.

Open Always. **Pizzas** from 14 € per metre. **Credit** AmEx, DC, MC, V. **Amenities** Highchairs.

FAMILY-FRIENDLY ACCOMMODATION

Accommodation can be very pricey for families – especially in the summer months – so it's worth investigating the possibility of renting a villa or apartment. There are lots of British and Italian agencies who handle the brokering and some property owners just deal directly with the public. Be careful to ask for everything you need before booking and be warned that rooms are not always as snazzy or clean as they appear in photos. To find apartments from Italians, type "*appartamento*" or "*appartamenti*" and "*amalfitana*" into the search engine.

Another great-value option is to rent a bungalow at a holiday-camping village like Villaggio Nettuno at Nerano in Massa Lubrense:

Villaggio Nettuno at Nerano in Massa Lubrense

Via A. Vespucci 39, 80061 Massa Lubrense. 📞 *081 808 1051; www. villaggionettuno.it*

Bungalows sleeping 2–8 people for 60€–200€, offering lots of facilities (pool, sports and shop), night-time entertainment, watery activities (snorkelling and boat trips to hidden coves) and superb eateries at the enchanting Marina di Cantone beach. The only downside that accompanies the splendid isolation amid the Mediterranean pines is that it's a fair trek via the winding roads to the other Amalfi Coast attractions.

Amalfi

Hotel Marina Riviera ★ [FIND]

Via P. Comite 19, 84011 Amalfi 📞 *089 871 104; www.marinariviera.it*

There are a number of family accommodation options at this spick-and-span hotel including suites and connecting rooms. Colourful tiles and cool hues throughout make it a relaxing place to come back to. All the rooms have sea views and many have small balconies with table and chairs; others have hydro-massage baths. Breakfast can be taken on the terrace which looks over the port and town. The helpful Gargano family and staff are ready with advice and also run the swanky Eolo restaurant nearby which is great for a family dining occasion with older children.

Rooms 20. *Rates* 210€–250€ double; 360€–450€ suite. Breakfast included. *Credit* AmEx, DC, MC, V. *Amenities* Bar. Cots. Extra bed 60€. Garage parking 20€. Internet. Non-smoking rooms. Restaurant nearby. *In room* A/C. Fridge. Safe. Satellite TV Shower/bath.

Hotel Santa Caterina ★★

Via Nazionale 9, 84011 Amalfi; 089 871 012; *www.hotelsantacaterina.it*

Perched atop a cliff face, with terraced gardens filled with citrus fruits and vines Santa Caterina is in a magical setting. The annexe rooms are a short stroll away and have their own terrace where you can eat out – this is an alluring option for families with older children. Youngsters and adults alike will love the lifts that whisk you up and down the cliff to and from the shoreline pool area – very reminiscent of a 60s' Bond movie. You may even see the locals fishing for octopus in the waters nearby. Meals can be taken on the large terrace (a relaxed option for families during the day), down by the beachside restaurant or in the formal dining area, which may be a little stuffy for some. There are interconnecting rooms and suites to suit larger family groups.

Rooms 29. *Rates* 240€–420€ double. Breakfast included. *Credit* AmEx, DC, MC, V. *Amenities* Bar.

Cots. Extra bed 130€. Garage parking 15€. Non-smoking rooms. Pool. Restaurants nearby. Room service. Spa. *In room* A/C. Fridge. Internet. Safe. Satellite TV. Shower/bath.

Paestum

Oleandri Resort Hotel Residence Villaggio Club ★★

Via Laura 240, 84063 Paestum 0828 851 730; *www.residence oleandri.com*

Children will love the palm-fringed pools, gardens and shaded playground at this resort which resembles one of those sprawling resorts on the Red Sea. Families of all sizes are catered for in doubles, triples, suites and villas – which hold up to seven people. You can eat in the stylish poolside restaurant or pick up provisions at the local stores and cook in your mini-apartment. The Mini Club keeps 3–12-year-olds busy with games and shows. Older children and parents may get a kick out of the sports and other activities on offer: from aerobics and dance to ping pong and beach volleyball. The only negative is that after seeing the Paestum archaeological site and eating at the *favoloso* Nonna Sceppa nearby you'll need a car to go adventuring and dining elsewhere, as the resort is a little isolated.

Rooms 53. *Rates* 65€–250€ double; 100€–450€ family-room triple; 320€–1000€ 4-room villa. Breakfast included. *Credit* AmEx, DC, MC, V. *Amenities* Bar. Cots. Garage parking free. Laundry service. Non-smoking rooms. Restaurant. Room service. Spa. *In room* A/C. Fridge. Safe. Satellite TV. Shower/bath.

Positano

Hotel Vittoria

Via Fornillo 19, 84017 Positano 📞 *089 875 049;* ***www.hotelvittoriapositano. com***

Simply furnished and in a superb elevated location – you can take the lift to the beach or stroll into the centre of Positano – the Vittoria has a winning formula for families. Children will love it because it's right above the beach of Spiaggia Fornillo and they make proper pizza in a wood-fired oven. Breakfast and meals are served on a flower-filled terrace which has sea views aplenty. All the rooms have balconies.

Rooms *34.* ***Rates*** *120€–180€ double. Breakfast included.* ***Credit*** *AmEx, DC, MC, V.* ***Amenities*** *Bar. Beach. Cots. Extra bed 20€. Non-smoking rooms. Restaurant.* ***In room:*** *Fridge. Internet access. Safe. Satellite TV. Shower/bath.*

Salerno

Hotel K

Via D. Somma 47 (just off Lungomare Colombo), 84129 Salerno 📞 *089 725 515;* ***www.hotelk.it***

For superb location and value just a short hop south of the centre of Salerno this hotel takes some beating. There may be no sea views or pool facilities but it's perfect for a couple of days of family sightseeing in the city and daytrip adventures further afield. Beyond the cascading greenery of the exterior is a functionally furnished hotel with plenty of rooms suitable for family groups.

Rooms *53.* ***Rates*** *90€–110€ double; 100€–120€ triple; 110€–130€ quad. 30% discount 3–8 years. Breakfast included.* ***Credit*** *AmEx, DC, MC, V.* ***Amenities*** *Bar. Cots. Extra bed 30€. Garage parking free. Laundry service. Non-smoking rooms. Restaurant. Room service. Spa.* ***In room:*** *A/C. Fridge. Safe. Satellite TV. Shower/ bath.*

Sant' Agata sui Due Golfi

Grand Hotel Hermitage & Villa Romita

Corso Sant'Agata 36, 80064 Sant'Agata sui Due Golfi. 📞 *081 878 0025;* ***www.grandhotelhermitage.it***

There are two options for family accommodation here amid the flowery gardens: the modern Grand Hotel offers the value while the posher Villa Romita once belonged to a Neapolitan philosopher and delivers extra style and comfort. There are grandstand views of the coast from the pool area and many of the rooms have balconies.

Rooms *76.* ***Rates*** *150€–200€ double. Breakfast included.* ***Credit*** *AmEx, DC, MC, V.* ***Amenities*** *Bar. Cots. Dry cleaning service. Extra bed 30€. Non-smoking rooms. Pool. Restaurant. Spa.* ***In room*** *A/C. Fridge. Internet access. Safe. Satellite TV. Shower/bath.*

Sorrento

Hotel Michelangelo

Corso Italia 275, 80067 Sorrento. 📞 *081 878 4844;* ***www.michelangelo hotel.it***

In busy and often overpriced Sorrento the Michelangelo is a good-value choice for families.

Although it's close to all the Sorrento sights and restaurants as well as the public transport hub, it lies in a quiet stretch of the busy thoroughfare Corso Italia. Children will enjoy the small pool and parents can hang out with the entertaining bar-man Pepe. It may not have extensive gardens but there is plenty of green space and lemon groves nearby.

Rooms 121. *Rates* 200€–250€ double. Breakfast included. *Credit* AmEx, DC, MC, V. *Amenities* Bar. Cots. Dry cleaning service. Extra bed 20€. Non-smoking rooms. Pool. Restaurant. *In room* A/C. Fridge. Internet access. Safe. Satellite TV. Shower/bath.

Vico Equense

La Ginestra

Via Tessa 2, Santa Maria del Castello, 80069 Vico Equense. ℂ 081 802 3211; *www.laginestra.org*

High up in the hills above Vico Equense (see p. 151) this *agriturismo* is a superb place to relax for parents and fabulous for children who enjoy seeing farm-yard animals. Even if you are not staying here you can bring the youngsters for a few hours so they can find out about and make friends with the geese, deer and goats. There's a decent choice of room options for vari-ously-sized family groups and organic fare, created using La Ginestra's homegrown produce, waits in the restaurant – expect classic Amalfitana dishes like

scialatielli pasta with tomatoes grown on the slopes of Vesuvius. You can catch public buses near the hotel into Vico Equense and along the coast to Sorrento.

Rooms 7. *Rates* 80€–100€ double; 95€–150€ suites. Breakfast included. *Credit* AmEx, DC, MC, V. *Amenities* Bar. Cots 15€. Excursions. Extra bed 20 €. Non-smoking rooms. Play-ground. Restaurant. *In room* A/C (extra charge). Shower/bath. TV.

Vietri Sul Mare

Hotel La Lucertola

Via Cristoforo Colombo 29, 84019 Vietri sul Mare. ℂ 089 210 255; *www.hotellalucertola.it*

Farther down the coast away from the Amalfitana chic-spots you get more for your money and La Lucertola hotel delivers on value and service. There's a chil-dren's playground popular with the odd passing *lucertola* (lizard). Recent refurbishment to the 1970s' structure has transformed the rooms and there are plenty of options to create your very own minimalist family pad with the latest technology. As in many places on the coast, there are lots of hills to negotiate around the hotel so perhaps it's not ideal for families with toddlers.

Rooms 33. *Rates* 90€–115€ double; 125€–160€ triple. 30% discount 3–8 years. Breakfast included. *Credit* AmEx, DC, MC, V. *Amenities* Bar. Cots. Extra bed 30€. Garage parking 15€. Non-smoking rooms. Restaurants. Room service. Spa. *In room* A/C. Fridge. Safe. Satellite TV. Shower/bath. WiFi.

7 The Islands: Capri, Ischia & Procida

The islands of the Bay of Naples all have their own individual allure. Coveted and celebrated by Roman emperors and artists, Capri is the shiniest jewel in the glittering waters of *la baia* – its four square miles are packed with glamour and dramatic scenery. However, sky-high prices, jet-set poseurs and day-tripping crowds go with its natural lustre. The so-called L'Isola Azzurra (The Blue Island) may be the most prized gem but Ischia and Procida are no ersatz rocks; both of these cooled dollops of magma, plopped into the sea by the Campi Flegrei caldera volcano, offer rich pickings for families. As well as providing better value than precious, pricey and precocious Capri, Ischia and Procida also have sandy beaches that the stunning limestone coves of Capri, beloved of Roman emperors and dodgy Russian oligarchs and their yacht-entourage, lack.

Ischia is larger, with thermal spa resorts, historic attractions, the best beaches and fertile volcanic soil, allowing sub-tropical species to thrive – these lush microclimates are sheltered by the extinct volcano Monte Epomeo, which you can reach on foot.

Procida is the most down-to-earth with ragged yet picturesque fishing village buildings stacked like multicoloured dwellings straight out of a Neapolitan nativity scene. Its small scale means that its intimate beaches are close to leafy lanes lined with small villas and market-gardens brimming with produce.

Despite the quayside chaos in Naples, taking a boat and gliding across the Bay of Naples to the islands on hydrofoil, large ferry or small vessel is nearly always a joy. Children are spellbound by the dramatic, gradually shifting views of the bay, the sound and smell of sea spray, the motion of the ocean (hopefully when the waters aren't choppy!), and the serene approach to each island adventure – each island's magic brings out a little bit of the Saracen pirate, Roman emperor and film star in all of us.

Children's Top Attractions

❶ Ascending the slopes of Monte Solaro, Capri, by chairlift, p. 198.

❷ Playing on the beach at Maronti, Ischia, p. 213.

❸ Walking in the footsteps of Tiberius at Villa Jovis, Capri p. 202.

❹ Watching the boats come in at Corricella, Procida p. 218.

❺ Eating pizza and seafood by the Mar Tirreno, p. 221–222.

❻ Bombing and diving in the limpid waters around Capri, p. 200.

❼ Swinging like Tarzan at the Indiana Park Pineta, Ischia, p. 208.

❽ Fishing with Ischia's pescatori, p. 208.

PLANNING YOUR TRIP TO THE ISLANDS

Preparing for the boat trip from Naples is a must: Molo Beverello and the quieter Mergellina handle the bulk of the hydrofoils, while the new **Porta di Massa** (see p. 194) is now the place to catch the ferry. Look out for dodgy characters – mainly beggars and opportunist pickpockets at Beverello and Porta di Massa especially.

For less stress and for a speedier journey take an *aliscafo* (hydrofoil) from Mergellina (see p. 193), along Via Francesco Caracciolo. These services are frequent between May and October. Large ferries can be exciting and fun with older children as you get to go out on deck and experience the splash and spray of the Mar Tirreno.

INSIDER TIP ≫

The wind on the waves during your ferry trip to the islands is a classic scenario for sunburn – so don't forget to batten down the hat and slap on the Factor 30.

If you're foolhardy enough to have a car in Naples you can leave it in one of the port area car parks: Parcheggio La Rondine via Marina Varco Immacolatella. ☎ *081 552 4999*. Capri and Procida especially are not the places to take a car. All the islands are hilly so be prepared for negotiating sometimes tricky terrain – check with your hotel before arriving.

As a foot passenger, a few euros are added for each piece of large luggage, although this often depends on the mood/character of the ticket office attendant on duty.

Most of the carriers offer child discounts (under 5s often go free if they don't take up a seat and under 13s travel for about two-thirds of the adult fare) – ask for a "*sconto per bambini*". Some of the carriers offer discounts for return tickets (*andata e ritorno*). Check the back pages of the free bi-monthly *Qui Napoli* tourist booklet or the local paper, *il Mattino* for the latest seasonal timetables.

CAPRI

21 miles (33km) SW of Naples

Families are sure to love the glamour and stunning beauty of Capri – there may be a lack of long sandy beaches but its pristine, azure waters are made for swimming.

It's a great place for people-watching as its beauty and detachment from everyday life attracts a compelling mix: the bronzed and the beautiful, a hotchpotch of international tourists, wrinkly and sun-damaged dames and veteran socialites, the odd jet-setting poseur and famous face.

Capri is a mere 6km by 3km and it lies 5km from Punta della Campanella on the Sorrentine Peninsula.

Capri town is 142m above sea level and 3km by road from the

CAPRI

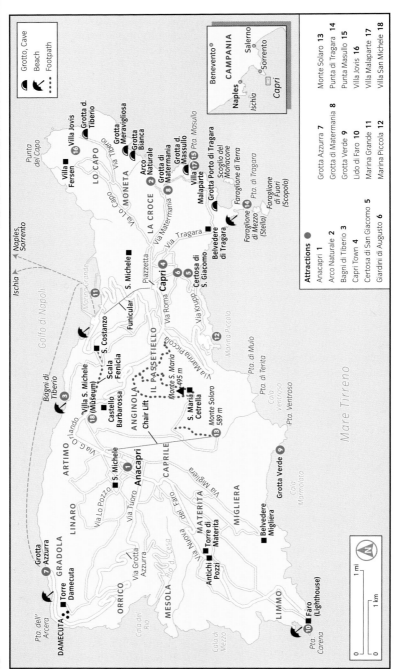

Grotto, Cave
Beach
Footpath

CAMPANIA

Benevento
Naples   Salerno
Ischia   Sorrento
Capri

Attractions

Anacapri **1**	Grotta Azzurra **7**	Monte Solaro **13**
Arco Naturale **2**	Grotta di Matermania **8**	Punta di Tragara **14**
Bagni di Tiberio **3**	Grotta Verde **9**	Punta Masullo **15**
Capri Town **4**	Lido di Faro **10**	Villa Jovis **16**
Certosa di San Giacomo **5**	Marina Grande **11**	Villa Malaparte **17**
Giardini di Augusto **6**	Marina Piccola **12**	Villa San Michele **18**

Capri History

Capri – with the emphasis on the *caa* not the *pree* – has been a legendary island since ancient times. The towering ivory-hued cliffs of limestone broke away from the Sorrentine Peninsula to form an island – a narrow isthmus once connected it to the mainland. Prehistoric tribes and Greeks enjoyed its natural wonders. Emperor Tiberius retired here in AD27, ruling his empire by courier: infamy and rumours of decadence surround his stay and the several villas he built, especially the sprawling Villa Jovis. Since the Middle Ages the island has changed hands frequently as has the whole of Campania – Saracens, Normans, Angevins, Aragonese, French and British have all fought over her towering cliffs and azure bays. In the 19th century many writers, poets, musicians and artists came to stay. When the funicular was built in the 20th century Capri lost some of its mystery due to the steady stream of jet-setters and tourists.

island's main harbour Marina Grande, in a lush bowl between the limestone bulks of Monte Solaro and Punta del Capo. It retains its glossy, chic allure despite the glut of day-trippers who throng its Piazzetta cafés and boutique-lined alleyways. The beating heart of the island is all intimate lanes and glamorous glimpses: it smells sweet, looks celestial and provides quality entertainment. The children will love skipping around the pedestrian lanes stealing the limelight from the *bel gente* (the beautiful people) looking just a tad too vain in their carefully chosen Capri-inspired ensembles.

In contrast **Anacapri**, 3km to the west by road along dizzying hairpins, has a less self-conscious, more village-like and laid back gait. A trip up Monte Solaro on the single-seat chair-lift is a serene and dreamy experience – but you may want to check its suitability for your children first.

There are many off-the-beaten-track family adventures to enjoy all over the island, including wonderful walks to belvederes (panoramic viewpoints) overlooking the Faraglioni rocks and strolls to the ruins of the Emperor Tiberius's notorious palace of pleasure and pain, Villa Jovis. Many of the rocky and pebbly beaches may be crowded so make time for a boat trip around Capri's azure waters; you'll discover hidden coves and bathing pools where de-toga-ed Romans and film stars once made a splash.

Essentials

Getting There

From Naples Lots of companies run services to Capri from Naples. From February 2008 the ferry operators have been using the Porta di Massa dock, leaving Molo Beverello and Mergellina to handle the faster hydrofoils.

The large ferries (*navi*) operating out of Porta di Massa take about 80 minutes to reach the Marina Grande, the main port in Capri. TMVs or Traghetti Veloci (fast ferries) take about 50 minutes, while the *aliscafi* (hydrofoils) take about 35 minutes. During the *Stagione Alta* (high season) adult prices are around 6€ for the ferry, 12 € for the fast ferry and 17€ for the hydrofoil. These are the main carriers: Alilauro ℂ 081 497 2211; *www.alilauro.it*; Caremar ℂ 081 017 1998; *www.caremar.it*; NLG: Navigazione Libera del Golfo ℂ 081 552 0763; *www.navlib.it*; SNAV (ℂ 081 761 2348; *www.snav.it*). Metro del Mare ℂ 199 600 700; *www.metrodelmare.com* operates from late April to late October.

From Sorrento There are hydrofoils and ferries operating out of Marina Piccola. The main operators are: Caremar ℂ 081 017 1998; *www.caremar.it*; LMP: Linee Marittime Partenope ℂ 081 807 1812/ ℂ 081 878 1430; *www.consorziolmp.it*; and NLG: Navigazione Libera del Golfo ℂ 081 552 0763. *www.navlib.it*. Adults pay around 12€ and children between 5 and 12 go for 8€. NLG allows under 5s to travel free as long as they don't take up their own seat.

From Amalfi, Positano or Salerno There are ferries and hydrofoils operating out of Amalfi, Positano and Salerno. The main operators are Alicost ℂ 089 234 892/ ℂ 089 811 986; *www.lauroweb.com*; and Navigazione Libera del Golfo ℂ 081 552 0763;

www.navlib.it. Alicost also operates services from Maiori, Minori and Praiano. A one-way trip to Capri from the Amalfi Coast costs around 17€ for adults, 11€ for 2–10-year-olds.

Getting Around

Traffic on Capri is restricted so you'll have to leave your car on the mainland (see p. 191). Ferries, hydrofoils and other craft arrive at Marina Grande on the north-eastern shoreline of Capri.

By Funicular To reach Capri town, take the three-minute funicular ride (1.30€) from Marina Grande – look out for *Funicolare* lettering above the large arch of the station and ticket booth in front of you as you leave the dockside, amid the T-shirt stalls, café-restaurant seating and gormless day trippers.

By Bus You'll catch your first glimpse of the special mini-orange buses of the SIPPC company ℂ 081 937 0420 here. Staiano Autotrasporti ℂ 081 837 1544; *www.staiano-capri.com* also run services from Anacapri. There are frequent services between the main conurbations and attractions: Marina Grande, Capri, Marina Piccola, Anacapri, Damecuta, Faro, and the Grott'Azzura.

Single bus tickets cost 1.30€ and day tickets are 7€ for travel all over the island. A 60-minute ticket costs 2.10€ and allows one funicular ride and unlimited bus travel within the time frame.

A day pass for 6.70€ allows two funicular rides and unlimited bus travel. Bus trips Caprese-style often entail a cramped and sweaty experience but can be very exhilarating as expert drivers hurtle you and the little orange Iveco bus around hairpin bends. Small children may get a fright and older ones a thrill twisting around the island confronted with sheer cliffs and heart-in-the-mouth chasms! The vintage open-top buses are swanky but pricey.

By Taxi If you're laden with luggage and don't fancy wading through the crowds for Capri's public transport, there are taxis available in Capri (081 837 0543 and Anacapri (081 837 1175. Alas, the taxis on Capri charge exorbitant tariffs.

> **INSIDER TIP** »
> The best bet is to arrange for your hotel to pick you up and drop you off at your destination – the posh ones have handy shuttle services.

Fast Facts

Banks There's a Banca di Roma at Piazza Umberto I 19, Capri (081 837 5942)

Chemist Farmacia Internazionale is at Via Roma 24 in Capri town (081 837 0485.

Hospital & First Aid Medical assistance can be sought at A.S.L. Na 5 Guardia Medica (Piazza Umberto I 1, Capri (081 837 5716.

Laundry Orchidea Lavanderia has branches at Via Caprile 24,

Capri (081 837 2089) and Via Castello 1, Anacapri (081 837 7539).

Post There's a post office at Via Roma 50 (081 837 5829.

Toilets & Baby Changing Use the *bagno* in a café outside the attractions.

Visitor Information

The local tourist body, the ASCT, has offices in Capri town at Piazzetta I Cerio 11 9 (081 837 5308; www.capritourism.com; Marina Grande at Banchina del Porto (081 837 0634; and Anacapri at Via G. Orlandi, 59 (081 837 1524. You can pick up maps and details about the many family-friendly walks on the island from the ASCT staff.

Family-friendly Events

There are a few *feste* (festivals) that take place on the island – each creates a very special spectacle and atmosphere that will excite children:

New Year and La Tarantella

After the shenanigans of the night before, where the streets in and around La Piazzetta are filled with snake-hipped hipsters, the main *piazze* of Capri town and Anacapri shed their disco-partying skin and are reborn in the light of 1st Jan as stages for frenzied tarantella dancing – the sight of twirling, traditional Neapolitan dresses and the shrill sound of jaunty old tunes hammered out by the folksters do wonders for your hangover – allegedly.

1st and 6th January

Procession of San Costanzo

Capri's patron saint and protector – who, according to legend, was washed ashore on the island on his way back to Constantinople – is honoured with a slow procession to Marina Grande. Children love the colour and sense of occasion. Along the route the faithful *Capresi* shower the garlanded statue with rose petals and other *fiori*.

14th May

Procession of Sant' Antonio

Anacapri's saintly protector is celebrated with a sombre and colourful ceremony – with much throwing of fragrant petals – followed by a concert and child-friendly sweet-eating and grown-up *vino*-swigging along flowery lanes.

13th June

Santa Maria del Soccorso

The tiny church up at Villa Jovis (see p. 202) is lit up on the evening of 7th September and the following morning a mass is held in honour of the Virgin Mary. Music, dance and some good-old fashioned feasting ensue.

7th–8th September

Settembrata Anacaprese

The town's four *quartieri* (districts) come together in a fun, themed competition – each district's *cittadini* (citizens) pit their wits against the others in sporting,

gastronomic and other eccentric contests.

First two weeks of September

What to See & Do

Around Capri Town

Piazza Umberto I, known as **La Piazzetta** ★★ (little square), is the social hub of the island. The 17th-century **Church of Santo Stefano** (which contains fragments of Roman flooring from Emperor Tiberius's Villa Jovis) looks down on an intimate square whose pitted flagstones are covered with café seating. It's a wonderful place to take in the relaxed atmosphere, visit the tourist office, consult the map, do some people-watching, sit and sip (cafés are pricey if you sit down though) and view the buildings: **Il Torre dell'Orologio** (clocktower) with its majolica-tiled clock face, the Municipio (town hall), the baroque Chiesa di Santo Stefano and the sprawling **Palazzo Cerio** (☏ 081 837 6218. Tue, Wed, Fri and Sat 10am–1pm and Thurs 3–7pm), which houses a small natural history museum based on the collections of the naturalist and physician Ignazio Cerio.

If arriving in Capri town by **funicular** (see p. 194) you'll arrive at the back of the Piazzetta onto a wide terracotta-tiled terrace, which has a few benches between the island's typical white colonnades and flashes of bougainvillea colour. Grab ice creams from the bar here (Bar Funicolare) and take in the jaw-dropping views.

To avoid paying for the privilege of sitting at a bar's tables, grab a bench. If you want to splurge we recommend **Bar Tiberio** ☎ *081 837 0268* on the Piazzetta.

From the Piazzetta, a labyrinth of medieval, white-washed *vicoli* (alleyways) fans out. The atmospheric arcaded street, **Via Madre Serafina**, has a covered section that follows the town's old ramparts. Children will love the light-wells along here which offer fabulous glimpses of flowery terraces and a jumble of buildings. Legend has it that when Saracen pirates invaded this part of town the *Capresi* would pour hot oil through these small apertures onto the invaders below. From the Piazzetta, Via Lungano and Capri's main drag, Via Vittorio Emanuelle III can be explored. Ambling amid the chic boutiques, bars and independent outlets a sweet whiff of freshly made wafers and ice cream cones will stop the children in their pumps. Order *gelati* from the window or descend into the gastronomic institution **Pasticceria Buonocore** at no 35 ☎ *081 837 6151*.

Continuing on the main mosey you arrive at the grande dame of Caprese hotels and former 19th-century sanatorium (opened by a canny Scots doctor), **Il Quisisana** – meaning "here one heals". To reach the **Certosa di San Giacomo** AGES 3 AND UP ☎ *081 837 6218*; free admission; 9am–2pm Tues–Sun), a 14th-century Carthusian monastery dedicated to the apostle Giacomo (James), take a right after the hotel and follow Via Federico Serena. Although there are no longer any monks, the atmosphere and sombre architecture amid verdant gardens make it a good place for a breather. Two cloisters, a church, belvedere vistas and refectory museum (containing spooky paintings by Wilhelm Diefenbach and Roman statues recovered from the Grott' Azzura) are the visitable parts of this rather run-down complex.

La Piazzetta and Municipio, Capri

Leaving the monastery and following Via Matteotti, you come to the **Giardini di Augusto** ALL AGES ★★ (Gardens of Augustus), a colourful profusion of flowers and vegetation with terraces to explore.

Anacapri

Nestled in the lofty heights below Capri's highest point, **Monte Solaro**, Anacapri has a tranquil feel compared to glitzy Capri town. There's always a buzz in and around **Piazza della Vittoria**, where the bus, taxis, day-trip coaches and crowds converge. Ply the youngsters with ice cream and do some serious people-watching at Bar Bucchetto (see p. 219), overlooking the piazza at the start of Anacapri's main lane Via Orlandi, lined with interesting gift shops, boutiques and restaurants. For a quieter venue head down to Nautilus Caffè ★★ (see p. 219).

Anacapri's whitewashed houses are punctuated with the odd quirky building, including the **Casa Rossa** AGES 4 AND UP on Via Orlandi – a pinky-red hued house with crenulated Moorish flourishes. Its courtyard contains archaeological fragments and classic statues, and there's a small gallery inside displaying Caprese landscape paintings. The baroque beauty of the **church of San Michele**, built in the 18th century, is worth a look inside for its wonderful majolica flooring depicting Adam and Eve in an idealised landscape. The small

square by the church is a meeting place for the locals, including children, who often play beside the restaurants with al fresco seating – this is a wonderful place to linger, have a refreshment or two and for the children to mooch around a bit.

Monte Solaro Chairlift ★★★
AGES: PARENTAL DECISION

Seggiovia Monte Solaro. Via Caposcuro 10 ☎ *081 837 1428*

The must-do Capri outing (if you don't mind heights) is the cable **chairlift** ride up to **Monte Solaro**. Your feet dangle over lush gardens (but never from really dizzying heights) with a metal bar placed across your seat to reassure the sitter (but not the parent, particularly as it can be raised). The journey takes around 12 minutes – the views and slowly becalming atmosphere as you rise to nearly 600m are truly magical. At the top is a strange yet beguilingly scruffy terrace. The lone bar offers ice creams, drinks and snacks. There are deckchairs, parasols and swing chairs to lounge around in. The real draw here is the 360-degree views. However, keep an eye on the children to make sure that they don't go wandering off as there is rough terrain and sheer drops around the summit. Walkers with older children may want to find out about the many walks that pass nearby. Local guide Luigi Esposito (☎ *081 837 5933/* ☎ *347 368 1699; www.capritrails.com*) can organise family hikes.

Grotta Azzura (Blue Grotto) OVERRATED

Capri's legendary marine cavern, in the north-west of the Blue Island near Anacapri, is its most popular excursion. It can leave adults feeling dissatisfied although younger children will be entranced by this oh-so-brief mini-adventure into a magical natural realm. It was once filled with *nympaneum* statues, being part of Tiberius's Gradola villa, but was not "rediscovered" until 1826. It was promptly put on the Grand Tour map and wealthy Europeans thereupon flocked here to view the almost luminous lighting effects caused by the refraction of the sun's rays in the limpid waters. The Blue Grotto can be approached by land (via a footpath – there are buses from Anacapri) or by boat: combine a trip to the grotto with an excursion around the island from Marina Grande (Motoscafisti di Capri, Via Provinciale, Marina Grande, 282 ☎ *081 837 7714*) or about 11€ per head. You then pay 10€ to board one of a posse of small rowing boats that take you through the narrow entrance (it's just 2m wide by 1m (6½ ft x 3½ ft) high so you need to duck down low) into a cavern measuring 57m long, 30m wide and 15m high. The oarsmen exchange banter, shout excitedly while pointing to various rock formations in the cave and occasionally burst into Neapolitan song. Most of them bug you for a tip. The ethereal light effects are only experienced briefly – you get about five minutes inside the cave – amid much chaos and bobbing around. It's also very pricey for a large family. It's open from 9am to 1 hour before sunset and the best lighting effects are said to be around lunchtime between 11am–1pm.

Open *9.30am–sunset Mar–Oct; 10.30am–3pm Nov–Feb.* ***Admission*** *Adult return 8€; adult single 6€; under-8s travel for free – see below.* ***Amenities*** *None.*

> **INSIDER TIP**
> The chairlift operator's policy is that children under a metre must be accompanied by an adult – by sitting on their lap. We'd recommend that you see the set-up for yourself and then make a decision based on what you and your children are comfortable with.

Villa San Michele ★ ALL AGES

Viale Axel Munthe 34, 80071 Anacapri. ☎ *081 837 1401; www.sanmichele. org*

Amid the boutiques, gift shops and posh *pensioni* on Viale Axel Munthe is this villa, built by the Swedish doctor and writer Axel Munthe (1857–1949). The lucky Swede came to Naples to help out with the cholera epidemic relief effort in the 1880s. So smitten was he with Capri that he built this idyllic villa with its beguiling mixture of styles, emphasising – in his words – "light, light everywhere". The dreamy pile has luxuriant gardens, temple-like interiors and the remains of a Roman imperial villa he dug up by chance. Older children will appreciate the loggias and flowery pergolas. Adults can admire the classic statuary and artworks.

Open *9am–4.30pm Mar; 9am–5pm Apr; 9am–6pm May–Sept; 9am–5pm Oct; 9am–3.30pm Nov–Feb.* **Admission** *5€.* **Amenities** *Baby changing. Disabled access. Picnic area. Toilets.*

Beaches, Bathing & Boat Trips

Capri is not for sandcastle makers; there are no fine sandy beaches but lots of bathing spots with patches of shingle and rocky shores jutting into limpid pools. So it's not ideal for toddlers but great for children who like diving, bombing and snorkelling; the waters are exceptionally clean and enticing.

Bathing establishments (*stabilimenti balneari* or *bagni*) offer all the facilities (changing hut, deckchairs, sun loungers, parasols, towels and even refreshments) at a price. Most are open from mid-March to mid-October.

Marina Grande & Bagni di Tiberio

There's a large public beach at Marina Grande, on the north side of the island, and farther west is the more intimate cove, the Bagni di Tiberio ★★★ AGES 5 AND UP , with the remains of one of Tiberius's villas and a Roman theatre. You can reach the shore via a winding path (not really suitable for buggies or toddlers) that starts five minutes' walk up the main road from Marina Grande above the JK Place Hotel. It passes lots of flowery gardens, neighbourhood cats and the Da Paolino restaurant (Via Palazzo a Mare 11, 📞 *081 837 6102*), famed for its meaty squid (*il totano*) served with potatoes. More convenient, however, is to take the shuttle boat service from Marina Grande to the Bagni di Tiberio, which costs around 7€ return. There are beach huts, a small beach and a relaxed seafood restaurant/bar Bagni di Tiberio (Via Palazzo a Mare 41. Main

Public beach near Marina Grande

Faraglioni Rocks, Capri

courses 10€–30€; open mid-May–mid-Sep) where they serve the freshest catch – and you pay by weight. It is run by Carlo di Mattino and his family who I met on an early October morning while he was mending his nets – he explained that after 31st July, the cliffs of Anacapri block out much of the sun.

Marina Piccola ★ ★ ★   ALL AGES

Capri's most famous bathing spot, on the south side of the island, overlooks the Faraglioni Rocks and the Scoglio delle Sirene (Sirens' Rock). It's a wonderful place with some fabulous shoreline seafood restaurants, but there's hardly room to hit a swing-ball in the height of summer. The public beach extends over rocks, which is fine for families with older children. There are a number of bathing establishments here: Bagni Internazionali ☎ 081 837 0264; *www.bagni-internazionali.com*; Da Gioia ☎ 081 837 7702; *www.dagioiacapri.com* and the more secluded Torre Saracena ☎ 081 837 0646; *www.torresaracenacapri.com*.

Near Anacapri and the Grotta Azzurra

The two main bathing spots here (you can get a bus to either from Anacapri) are the Bagni Nettuno (☎ 081 837 1362) and, at the southwest extremities of the island, at Punta Carena, the **Lido di Faro** (☎ 081 837 1798; *www.lidofaro.com*) with a snack bar (Da Antonio's) and sun terrace built onto jagged rocks (not suitable for small children) below the lighthouse and the 292m (958ft) Migliara cliffs. The sea here is particularly good for snorkelling with lots of deep pools.

Capri Walks ★ ★
AGES 6 AND UP

Here are a few suggestions for walks on Capri. Ask at the tourist office (p. 195) for maps and details, although they are all well signposted and frequented. These walks are not suitable for families with toddlers. The ground can be uneven so holding hands is a good idea in

Boat Hire ★★★

For a magical bathing experience in more secluded locations, **hire a boat** to take you to one of the island's many **hidden coves**. Many companies operating out of the Marina Grande and Marina Piccola run four-hour boat excursions around the island passing countless caves, rocks, cliffs and ancient ruins teeming with myths. Most pass through the hole in the Fariglione di Mezzo and visit the **Grotta Verde**, famed for its spooky green light effects. A well-established outfit is **Gruppo Motoscafisti**, Via Provinciale Marina Grande 282, Capri ☎ *081 837 7714/☎ 081 837 5646*; *www.motoscafisticapri.com*.

places. Pack refreshments and snacks.

Belvedere Cannone has wonderful views of the Faraglioni rocks, the Charterhouse, the Grotta delle Felci (where Bronze Age artefacts were found) and down towards the Marina Piccola. From the Piazzetta in Capri town, scale the steps beside the church of Santo Stefano and follow the Via Madre Serafina beyond the Santa Teresa church where a path climbs to the sprawling Castiglione, where a lavish villa courted by billionaires stands. Steps lead to the belvedere. (Approx. 1 hr.)

Arco Naturale & Grotta di Matermania, Punta Masullo & Punta di Tragara

This is a much, much longer walk but can be split up into easier forays. There are steep sections. Follow Via Le Botteghe off the Piazzetta in Capri town, then Via Croce until you reach Via Matromania – follow the signs to a set of steps that descends to the impressive natural archway,

L'Arco Naturale. A path then goes down to the **Grotta di Matermania** – a cave with remnants of a Roman *nymphaeum* (a shrine and pleasure palace) Check out the opus reticulum – diamond-shaped bricks you will have seen at Pompeii and other Roman sites. At the rocky outcrop of the **Punta Masullo** you'll see the trapezoidal staircase and red-hued angular shapes of the **Villa Malaparte**, a celebrated example of Italian rationalist architecture named after its colourful owner, the writer Curzio Malaparte. Spectacular views of the Il Monacone and Fariglioni rocks jutting out of turquoise waters accompany your climb up to the **Punta Tragara**, where more gasps and shutter-clicks can be heard. (Approx. 3 hrs.)

Villa Jovis, Emperor Tiberius's notorious palace of pleasure and pain in the north-eastern corner of the island, can be reached in about an hour from la Piazzetta. Take Via Le Botteghe, Via Fuorolado and then Via Croce and continue through luxuriant lanes passing colonnaded gardens (look out for Villa La Moneta at Via Tiberio 32), exotic plants and scampering lizards. Before reaching the villa you come to the Salto di Tiberio, a 300m (975ft) drop down a cliff face that many of Emperor Tiberius's unfortunate victims experienced whizzing past their eyes. Exploring the 7,000 sq. metres of crumbling walls gives you only a hint of its former glory. Child-like imagination will be needed to fill the imperial apartments, servants' quarters, state rooms and baths with lavish furnishings and the Roman dramas. Don't miss the views from the Loggia, the Emperor's fave stomping ground, and the Specularium, where astrologers predicted Tiberius's fate. At the summit of Monte Tiberio stands a cute rustic church, Santa Maria del Soccorso, from where you can survey the bay. Although arduous in hot weather, this family walk – with a couple of breaks and treats to cajole children – should be memorable. (Approx. 2 hrs.)

Shopping

Only a fool – and a rich fool at that – would go to Capri to do some serious shopping.

Everything is so much more expensive than in Naples. However, there are some lovely little artisan shops and some quirky little boutiques that might just help relieve you of some of that cash burning in your pocket.

100% Capri
Via Fuorlovado 27,29,42,44, Capri 📞 *081 837 7561*

This is a so-very-Italian lifestyle shop with high quality luxuries such as fine cotton beach robes and scented candles. Not too ridiculously priced.

Capri Cosi
If you like Italian design, **Capri Così** ★★ Via G. Orlandi in Anacapri 135 📞 *081 838 2176* has all sorts of funky things from scrumptious-smelling fruit candles to weird and wonderful soap dispensers and bottle openers via crazy wellies and flip flops.

Carthusia
You can now buy **Carthusia** Profumi (Via Camerelle 10 📞 *081 837 0368* and Via Capodimonte 26, Anacapri 📞 *081 837 3668*) at home but it's worth walking into the shop and breathing in the aromas that will forever evoke memories of Capri. The packaging is so trad it's hip while what's

---

FUN FACT ▶ **Salto di Tiberio** ◀

Tiberius's Leap near Villa Jovis is an almost vertical 300m (1,000ft) cliff from where the emperor is said to have jettisoned his victims – this probably came as a relief for them, having experienced a long and arduous torture session. According to the Roman historian and biographer Gaius Suetonius Tranquillus, a group of sailors would wait in the sea below to finish off the unfortunate souls – just in case they hadn't kicked the bucket already.

ISCHIA

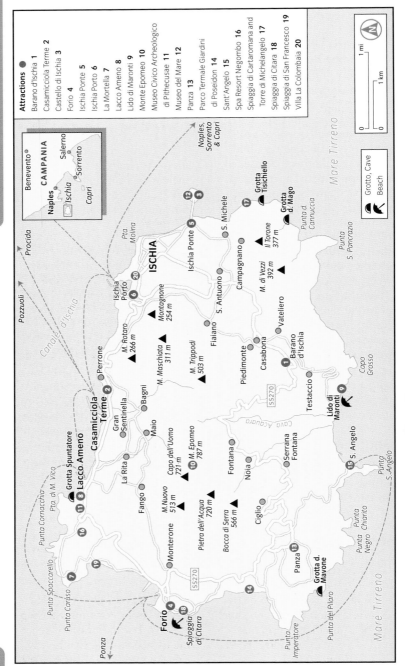

Attractions ●
Barano d'Ischia **1**
Casamicciola Terme **2**
Castello di Ischia **3**
Forio **4**
Ischia Ponte **5**
Ischia Porto **6**
La Mortella **7**
Lacco Ameno **8**
Lido di Maronti **9**
Monte Epomeo **10**
Museo Civico Archeologico
di Pithecusae **11**
Museo del Mare **12**
Panza **13**
Parco Termale Giardini
di Poseidon **14**
Sant'Angelo **15**
Spa Resort Negombo **16**
Spiaggia di Cartaromana and
Torre di Michelangelo **17**
Spiaggia di Citara **18**
Spiaggia di San Francesco **19**
Villa La Colombaia **20**

● Grotto, Cave
⚓ Beach

in it is from age-old monk's recipes, all using the fruit and flora of Capri.

L'Arte del Sandalo Caprese

Via G. Orlandi 75, Anacapri ☎ 081 837 3583

This is ye olde shoe shoppe that you just don't see in the high street any more. Pick the colour, style and heel of your ideal sandal and within an hour they'll be cobbled together. Canfora in Capri Via Camerelle 3 ☎ 081 837 0487 also make classy, cute and colourful leather sandali.

Limoncello di Capri ★

Via Roma, 79, Capri ☎ 081 837 5561 and Via Capodimonte 27 ☎ 081 837 2927

Limoncello di Capri in Anacapri claims to be the founding grandmother of this sweet lemony throat burner. When it was first brewed in the 1900s it aided the digestion of guests at the pensione, Casa Mariantonia.

ISCHIA

13 miles (21 km) NW of Naples and 7 miles (11 km) W of Pozzuoli

Ischia's steamy thermal vents, extinct volcanoes and curvy craters composed of tufa rock attest to its Campi Flegrei caldera origins (see p. 91). Children will be flabbergasted knowing there is fire heating the mineral rich waters deep below their feet – and there is no shortage of steamy jets of gaseous water as evidence. Indeed there are 67 fumaroles (volcanic vents)

and over a hundred thermal springs across the island – families can splash and sojourn in Ischia's spa resorts, with their therapeutic powers once treasured by Greeks and Romans, or choose from many beaches, including the fabulous Spiaggia dei Maronti with its volcanic vents and views of the beguiling hump that is the Punta Sant' Angelo.

Essentials

Getting There

By Boat

From Naples Lots of companies run services to Ischia from Naples – many stop at Procida. The large ferries (Navi) and TMVs or Traghetti Veloci (fast ferries) that, from February 2008, operate out of Calata Porta di Massa take about 90 minutes to reach Ischia Porto, the main port on Ischia and a little longer to reach Forio, the resort port on the west coast of the island. The Molo Beverello now handles all the faster vessels: they take about 1 hour, while the aliscafi (hydrofoils) take about 50 minutes. During the *Stagione Alta* (High Season) adult prices are around 6€ for the ferry, 9€ for the fast ferry and 11€ for the hydrofoil. A shuttle service connects Calata Porta di Massa and Molo Beverello.

From Pozzuoli There are also services from Pozzuoli that stop at Ischia Porto, Forio and at the island's north-coast resort, Casamicciola Terme which cost about two thirds of the prices above.

Generally, fares are slightly cheaper at less busy times of year. These are the main carriers: Alilauro ☎ *081 497 2211*; *www. alilauro.it*; Caremar ☎ *081 017 1998*; *www.caremar.it*; Medmar ☎ *081 551 3352*; *www.medmarnavi. it*; SNAV ☎ *081 761 2348*; *www.snav.it*.

From Sorrento you can reach Ischia by hydrofoil with the operators: Alilauro (☎ *081 497 2211*; *www.alilauro.it*; LMP: Linee Marittime Partenope ☎ *081 807 1812* /☎ *081 878 1430*; *www.consorziolmp.it*; NLG: Navigazione Libera del Golfo ☎ *081 552 0763*; *www.navlib.it*. NLG also operates a summer service to and from Amalfi.

Getting Around

By Bus Ischia's public transport consists of some 19 bus routes – *gli autobus* (buses) are run by SEPSA (☎ *081 991 1808*/☎ *081 991 828*; *www.orari.sepsa.it*) and include two handy routes which circle the island in clockwise and anti clockwise directions: the CD (Circolare Destra) goes clockwise and the CS (Circolare Sinistra) goes anticlockwise. Unico Ischia tickets allow 90 minutes of travel from the moment they are stamped and cost 1.20€ flat rate. Remember to validate the ticket using the onboard machines. Although the services are very cheap and pretty reliable they can get notoriously crowded

during the summer; some of the locals get rightfully irked that there are not enough buses scheduled to handle the influx.

By Car Ischia is a larger island than Capri and Procida, and if you're here for a while you might consider hiring a car. Some of the well-established car hire companies include: Mazzella (☎ *081 991 141*; *www.mazzellarent.it*), Di Meglio (☎ *081 995 222*; *www. ischia-rentacar.it*); Noleggio del Franco (☎ *081 991 334*; *www. noleggiodelfranco.it*).

> **INSIDER TIP** ›
>
> A great way to see the island's sights in comfort is to hire a driver. Giuseppe Lauro ☎ *081 992 651*/ ☎ *339 405 2691*; *www. ischiataxi.it* provides a very professional service for families wanting a tour of the island (from 100€). As well as taking you to out-of-the-way places, he knows some fab places to eat. His Mercedes people carrier is ideal for all sizes of families, is spotless and has excellent air conditioning.

> **INSIDER TIP** ›
>
> For an entertaining ride that children will love, take a **Microtaxi**, a cute three-wheel Apecar taxi, which is no more than a moped with a driver up front and canopied passenger seating with luggage space to the rear. This is not the ideal means of transport for a large family with lots of luggage as space is tight in the back and the engine would struggle up Ischia's rolling terrain with the excessive weight.

Visitor Information

The AACST Ischia tourist office Via Sogliuzzo72; ☏ *081 507 4211/* ☏ *081 507 4231*; *www.infoischia procida.it* dispenses handy leaflets and information. There's another information point along Ischia Porto's main shopping street, Corso Vittoria Colanna at 116 (☏ *081 507 4231*). Both offices are open 9.30am–1pm and 3.30–7pm Mon–Sat May–Sep (mornings only Oct–Apr).

Fast Facts

Banks Banca Monte Dei Paschi Di Siena is at Via Sogliuzzo 44, ☏ *081 982 310* near Ischia Porto.

Chemist Farmacia Internazionale is at Via de Luca Alfredo 117 near Ischia Porto ☏ *081 333 1275.*

Hospital & First Aid For medical assistance phone Guardia Medica ☏ *081 983 499/* Croce Rosa ☏ *081 999 531.*

Laundry Lavanderia Anna is at Via de Luca Alfredo 44 ☏ *081 993 165.*

Post There's a post office at Via de Luca Antonio 42 ☏ *081 507 461.*

Family-friendly Events

Ischia Film Festival

www.ischiafilmfestival.it

Each June the island bustles with cinematographers and film buffs. *Last 2 weeks in June.*

Festa di Sant' Anna

At the Castello Aragonese, www. festadisantanna.it

Centred around the Aragonese Castle, this *festival* celebrates the island's patron with an exuberant procession of boats, spectacular fireworks and feasting each 26th July. Thousands of spectators line the shoreline and cram into boats to watch fantastical shows performed by costumed squads aboard imaginatively themed floating stage-sets. Check out the Festa di Sant'Anna website to get a flavour of the festivities. *26th July.*

What to See & Do

Ischia Porto & Ischia Ponte

Your first port of call is likely to be the busy harbour Ischia Porto and its atmospheric medieval neighbour and island-promontory, Ischia Ponte. A few sandy beaches, Spiaggia dei Pescatori (accessed by steps), Lido d'Ischia (perfect for families) and Spiaggia San Pietro lie between Ischia Ponte and the modern harbour, a volcanic crater that was transformed into a beautifully round natural harbour by Bourbon king Ferdinand II in 1854. Ischia's main shopping street and venue for *passeggiata* posing is known as *il corso* by the locals; near Ischia Ponte, Via Pontano turns into Corso Vittoria Colonna and then Via Roma just before you arrive at Ischia Porto. To the right is the Riva Destra, with its

Active Family Days

Family Fishing Trips ★★ AGES 6 AND UP

Pasquale Saurino ✆ *333 918 309/ Nicola Curci* ✆ *347 036 2411/Antonio Pezzella* ✆ *338 584 5515*

Pescaturismo (Fishing Tourism) is the new thing in Campania and Ischia's amiable fishermen are only too happy to take families out for a boat trip. Early worms should try the Outing at Dawn organised by Pasquale Saurino which departs from Ischia Porto, Sant'Angelo, Forio or Lacco Ameno at 5.30am and returns around 9.30am. Other trips can be arranged for other times and involve fishing with traditional wicker-work traps, squid fishing at night and fishing with a tour of the island. You never know you may catch bream, tuna, octopus, conger eel, bass or Scorpion fish for your *cena* (dinner).

Ischia Trekking

✆ *368 335 0074; www.ischiatrekking.it*

Various organised walks around the island, including an easy trek suitable for children in the Piano Liguori (3 hours), as well as slightly more taxing treks up Mont Epomeo (4 hours) and amid the otherworldly rocks and caves of Pizzi Bianchi (2 hours). Walks cost 15€ per person.

Indiana Park Pineta ★★ AGES 7 AND UP

Loc. Fiaiano, Barano ✆ *077 347 4473*

If your older children are wannabe Tarzans and Indiana Joneses, swing on down to this centre in the woods. The arboreal assault courses bring out the ape in everyone. Six colour-coded routes test the nerve and agility of children and adults (children must be over 1.1 metres tall).

Open *Apr–Oct.* **Admission** *from 10€.* **Amenities** *Baby changing. Picnic area. Toilets.*

yachts and fishing boats on one side and a line of bars, shops and restaurants on the other separated by those typically Neapolitan pitted and sticky, granite flagstones.

Ischia Ponte's fortifications have been around since the 5th century BC. Today's structure was built by the House of Aragon, hence the name Castello Aragonese. Take a walk along the 228m long causeway and then either follow the steep track (not suitable for toddlers) or take a lift to the historic attractions.

Castello di Ischia ★★

AGES 5 AND UP

Piazzale Aragonese, 80070 Ischia Ponte ✆ *081 992 834; www.castello dischia.it*

Alfonso of Aragon built an imposing castle and a bridge in the 1440s. The imposing citadel was once the home of Vittoria

Colonna, the platonic sweetheart of Michelangelo. You can enjoy its changing art exhibitions and a couple of creepy spaces. **Il Convento delle Ciarisse** has a cemetery with a rather macabre resting place for its nuns – a ring of stone seating in a dark room – and a museum of torture instruments.

Open *9.30am–5pm daily; closed Nov–Feb.* **Admission** *8€; children's discounts.* **Amenities** *Toilets.*

Museo del Mare ★★
AGES 5 AND UP

Palazzo dell'Orologio, 80070 Ischia Ponte. ☎ 081 981 124; www.museo delmareischia.it

Housed in the handsome Palazzo dell'Orologio, the Museum of the Sea contains nautical instruments, maritime curios, Marconi's radio equipment, old fishermen's tackle, marine creatures and archaeological finds.

Open *10.30am–12.30pm and 3–7pm daily Apr–Jun; 10.30am–12.30pm and 6.30–10.30pm Jul–Aug; 10.30am–12.30pm Nov–Mar; Closed Feb.*

Admission *3€.* **Amenities** *Shop. Toilets.*

> **INSIDER TIP** ⟩⟩
>
> For relaxation and play in lush gardens head to the pine-wooded parks of Villa Nenzi Bozzi (Piazzetta San Girolamo) or La Pineta dei Bambini (Via Antonio Sogliuzzo) both between Ischia Porto and Ischia Ponte.

Spiaggia di Cartaromana and Torre di Michelangelo
AGES 7 AND UP

Torre di Guevara, Via Nuova Cartaromana. ☎ 081 333 1146.

Near the fine sands of this beautiful beach with its thermal spring waters is a mysterious rectangular tower, la Torre di Guevara, also called Michelangelo's Tower as legend has it that the great artist Michelangelo Buonorotti stayed here. The Renaissance maestro's much talked about relationship with the poetess Vittoria Collana, who resided in the Castello Aragonese over the water, has spawned many a romantic myth – local fishermen

Castello Aragonese, Ischia

still speculate about the existence of a secret tunnel connecting the two castles.

Open *Tues–Sun times vary.*
Admission *free.*

Casamícciola Terme

6.5km (4 miles) northwest of Ischia Porto.

Casamícciola Terme is a busy spa resort famed for its 85 degree C iodine-rich springs. Iron Age inhabitants used the volcanic heat of the area for cooking and pottery. An earthquake destroyed the village in 1883.

Splashing the Cash at the Spas

Piazza Bagni is home to some of Ischia's most venerable spas, which were the popular choice of the European aristocracy in the 18th and 19th centuries. All the spas have been spruced up and fitted with luxurious spaces and state-of-the-art treatments; Parco Termale Castiglione. Castiglione Road 62 ℂ *081 982 551; www.termecastiglione.it* has several outdoor pools including two for children and mud baths, while the glitzy Terme Manzi Piazza Bagni;ℂ *081 994 722; www. termemanzihotel.com* mixes the chic and contemporary with epic history in its lavish interiors – alongside the mood lighting and technology is the bath Garibaldi sat in to cure his war wounds in 1862. The Terme Castiglione with its outdoor spaces and 10 pools is more child-friendly. Spa treatments are very pricey but

use of the pools can be affordable if you phone in advance. A day ticket costs 25€ for an adult and children under 2 enter for free. To get a wee taster, give them a ring to ask about family rates and/or to arrange to come an hour before closing at a knock-down rate of a few euros. Casamiccciola Terme's beaches, dell'Eliporto, del Convento and the main stretch **Marina** with its fine sand can get very busy in the summer. The marina may boast lots of facilities but it's hardly the island's most picturesque.

Lacco Ameno

5 miles (8km) west of Ischia Porto

Lacco Ameno is a more relaxed resort with the most radioactive (naturally that is) waters in Italy – renowned for their curative powers apparently. The Greeks set up the first colony in the Bay of Naples here at Monte Vico but didn't hang around for long, moving on to Cumae and Megaride, probably after the then earthquake-ravaged ground shook them one too many times. They called it Pithikoussai – which could mean one of two things according to etymologists: Island of Monkeys or Island of Terracotta Vases – we like the cheekier moniker. It remained a sleepy fishing village until the 1950s when major investment transformed it into an exclusive spa resort. Along the pleasant promenade you can see a bronze foot that some *calcio* fans reckon to be dedicated to the *piede del*

Il Fungo, Lacco Ameno

dio ("the foot of God"): Napoli's living deity Diego Maradona – but perhaps it's not his most lethal one. Off the shore is *il fungo*, a mushroom-shaped rock while in the town's main square, Piazza Santa Restituta, are its other historical attractions: the grand old dame of spas turned slightly garish, in a Scarface-style, the Hotel Regina Elisabetta and...

Museo Civico Archeologico di Pithecusae AGES 5 AND UP

Corso Angelo Rizzoli 📞 *081 900 356*; housed in the 18th-century Villa Arbusto contains geological exhibits, Roman tombs and archaeological finds left by early Greek settlers, including the Coppa di Nestore. Lush gardens filled with exotic plants can be explored around the back of the villa.

***Open** 9.30am–1pm and 4–8pm Tues–Sun. **Admission** 5€ 25–65 years; 2.50€ 18–25s; free for under-18s; free with Artecard;. **Amenities** None.*

Sanctuary & Church of Santa Restituta AGES 4 AND UP

Piazza Santa Restituta 1 📞 *081 980 706*

The pretty-in-pink church has an adjoining museum and underground Greco-Roman relics. The ancient temple decorations and archaeological finds, including huge amphorae and Egyptian amulets in the form of beetles, will fascinate the family.

***Amenities** None.*

Spa Resort Negombo ★
ALL AGES

Baia San Montano 📞 *081 986 152; www.negombo.it*

A mile to the west of Lacco Ameno is the beautiful Baia di San Montano (Bay of San Montano) – its pristine sands and limpid waters are backed by verdant Mediterranean scrub and this tranquil spa. Its 12 thermal pools are a favourite of Italian big wigs like Silvio Berlusconi so expect the prices for some of the treatments to be in the loose-change range – for a media mogul. The secluded bay and beautiful beach is sheltered from the worst winds and waves, making it ideal for children.

***Open/Admission** phone for details and various packages.*

Forio

Less touristy and traditionally geared to wine-making and fishing, the port and town of Forio has been an enclave of creative types down the years including poet Pablo Neruda and writer-directors Pier Paolo Pasolini and Luchino Visconti. Nowadays it's very popular with Germans. A walk amid the historic centre's ramparts and towers is full of magical encounters.

On Via del Soccorso is **Il Santuario della Madonna del Soccorso** ★★ **ALL AGES** . You'll swoon at the sight of this cute whitewashed church with majolica-tiled flourishes and elegant outline. The best time to admire its simplicity – so full of Eastern delight – is at sunset on the ample terrace.

Dominating the skyline of Forio is the rotund watchtower, **Il Torrione** – home of this **Civic Museum** **AGES 5 AND UP** . (Museo Civico, Via del Torrione ℂ *081 333 2934; www.iltorrione.org*). Inside, there are temporary exhibitions, a collection of artworks (including lots by local hero Giovanni Maltese) and a curious museum dedicated to the Neapolitan song.

Forio Beaches

To the north is the picturesque **Spiaggia di San Francesco**, with coarse sand, and farther north the rocky shoreline of a spectacular promontory, Punta Caruso. To the south, the long **Spiaggia di Citara** is a little scruffy but offers lots of activities and facilities for families including the **Parco Termale Giardini di Poseidon** (via Giovanni Mazzella Citara; ℂ *081 907 122*; **open:** 9am–7pm daily Apr–Oct; **admission:** all day 30€, 3–12 years 15€, under-4s free; 5€ for

1 hr. before closing), a park-cum-spa with over 20 pools with temperatures ranging from 20–40 degrees C and a private beach.

La Mortella ★★★ GREEN
ALL AGES

Località Zaro ℂ *081 986 220; www. lamortella.it*

For a garden experience with dreamlike intensity visit La Mortella, to the west of Lacco Ameno – created by Susan Walton the Argentinian widow of English composer William Walton, with the help of garden architect Russell Page. This must-see sight is located between Lacco Ameno and Forio. Exotic species, fountains, lily ponds, playful water features, pavilions, a sun temple and a tea room make for a very civilised and stimulating visit to a unique micro climate sheltered beneath the lava flows of Monte Zaro. Classical concerts are staged here – check the website or local press for latest listings.

Open *9am–7pm Tues, Thurs, Sat and Sun Apr–Nov.* ***Admission*** *10€ adults; 8€ 8–12 years; 6€ 5–8 years; under-5s free*

Sant'Angelo, Panza & Barano d'Ischia

Sant'Angelo, Ischia's most picturesque village overlooks a small harbour with a mound-like islet connected by a sandy isthmus. Above the town near the busy but beguiling village of Panza are some fab restaurants (like Neptunus see p. 222) overlooking the spectacularly stratified

Sant'Angelo

rocky shoreline. Sant'Angelo is a place for gift shopping, hanging out on the outdoor portside café tables and playing on the beach nearby. Better still, take one of the water taxis to the nearby **Lido di Maronti** ★ ★ ★ **ALL AGES**, a 2km (1¼ mile) stretch of sandy beach replete with steaming fumaroles and bar-restaurants. Near to this so-called "spiaggia calda" (hot beach) is the impressive spa resort of Cava Scura, where the Romans used to let it

all hang out. You can easily spend a day here but remember to bring all your sun protection as it's very exposed – otherwise you'll go back to the hotel looking like a family of – as the Italians put it: *gamberi rossi* (pink crustacea).

Monte Epomeo ★ ★
AGES 7 AND UP
Serrara and the neighbouring village of Fontana lie in the foothills of Ischia's extinct

---

FUN FACT » **The Leopard in Forio** «

Cinema legend Luchino Visconti, director of *Il Gattopardo* (The Leopard) – a great film and novel for older teens – stayed in the fairytale-like **Villa La Colombaia** **AGES 9 AND UP** set in dense woods just out of town. Its Moorish towers and stained glass elevator are sadly in disrepair although there are plans to renovate the building, which nowadays hosts occasional cultural events. The friendly *costodia* who looks after the building sometimes lets passers by have a look around. Be careful though as the roof terraces and stairs are in a bad state and not suitable for young children to walk on.

Monte Epomeo Facts

- It's 788m (2,585ft) high!
- It's the north side of an extinct volcano that erupted 55,000 years ago. Other craters adjoin it: Monte Rotaro and Monte Montagnone to the northeast, Monte Trippiti to the east and Monte Imperatore to the west. The last eruption happened in 1301.
- The mountain covers a surface area of 16 sq. km (34.5%) of the entire island.
- Epomeo derives from an ancient Greek word meaning "look around". Wing your way to the top to see the most awesome views of Naples, Capri and Procida and the entire Campania coastline. On a crystal clear day you can even see the smoking cone of the volcanic Aeolian island Stromboli, off the Sicilian coast.
- Get to the top and you'll also see the hermitage and chapel of San Nicola (Saint Nicholas) cut out of the rocks. This dates from 1459.

volcano Epomeo. The hike to its rocky summit makes for a memorable outing and is suitable for families with older children. First stop is Serrara, which has a pretty square containing the cheery-looking **Church of Santa Maria del Carmine** with its pastel-hued *campanile* and 18th-century stuccowork. The nearby belvedere has spellbinding views of Sant'Angelo and as far as the Pontine islands, off the Lazio coast. Further up the road is Fontana with its medieval buildings including the **Church of Santa Maria della Sacca** built in 1374. The path up to Monte Epomeo, Ischia's highest point at 788m (2,585ft.) starts nearby. It takes about 45 minutes of uphill effort to reach the summit and it's steep and rocky in sections. However, it's very rewarding for adventurous families who'll relish a clamber over weird tufa

rock formations pitted with volcanic bubbles. Clear days bring breathtaking vistas while cloudy ones evoke an eerie, primeval-like atmosphere. Take care though as it's not well fenced and there is a scramble to the top which is a little tricky, especially in wet conditions. A restaurant housed in a former convent building serves simple dishes including a tasty *bruschetta* – you can enjoy snacks and serene views from its fabulous terrace. The remarkable 15th-century **San Nicola Church** cum hermitage hewn out of the volcanic rock of the old volcano is also worth a visit.

INSIDER TIP ≫

You can often find men by the church in Fontana offering their services and their mules to take you to the top. We've never tried it – it looks a tad uncomfortable for all involved.

Shopping

Ischia's main shopping street, *il corso* (Via Pontano, Corso Vittoria Colonna and then Via Roma) links Ischia Ponte and Ischia Porto and is a great place to explore during an evening *passegiatta*. Its mix of shops includes ones selling ceramics, food and specialities, fashion and the odd quirky outlet.

Di Meglio ★ at Via Roma 42 (📞 *081 991 176*; *http://www.ischia ceramiche.it*) is a large outlet selling colourful ceramic plates and tiles.

Further up *il corso* is Napoli Mania ★ (*www.napolimania.com*), the place to go to pick up witty and not so witty tee-shirts in the Neapolitan dialect. They also have innocent slogans on baby bibs, lucky charms for the superstitious and Diego Maradona-related souvenirs and garb for gauglioni (boys).

Ischia Sapori (Via R. Gianturco 2. 📞 *081 984 482*) has stacks of gastronomic treats like olive oils, liquors, wines and preserves.

PROCIDA

Procida is just over 2 miles (3.5 km) long and has a population of around 11,000, making it the most densely populated island in Europe. Don't let this stat put you off as much of the population is crammed around Marina Grande, and for much of the year, Procida, unlike Ischia and Capri, is not overrun with visitors. Besides, there are plenty of green spaces and side lanes lined with handsome villas and market gardens to escape the holiday traffic. The island consists of volcanic craters created by the Phlegrean caldera system which now forms beautifully circular bays. A good introduction to Procida's charms is a walk around the medieval quarter above the Marina Grande, within the fortified walls of the Terra Murata and 7th-century Benedictine abbey. The scruffy and pastel-hued fishermen's dwellings with their array of arches make the intimate ports of Corricella and Chiaollella appear like the backdrops to a Neapolitan *presepe* (nativity scene) (see p. 78). Local traditions remain strong, making it the most down-to-earth of the islands – Procidiani you meet are friendly and generally keen to recommend a restaurant. This exuberance flows over during the island's main festivals, the Good Friday procession and Graziella celebrations. Children will be pleased to know that you are never far from a beach here – just be prepared for seeing the margins of beaches and harbours strewn with the odd piece of rubbish.

Essentials

Getting There

By Boat There are frequent ferry and hydrofoil services from Naples; Porta di Massa is the new port for ferries while Molo

Beverello and the quieter Mergellina handle the faster hydrofoil craft. Caremar 📞 *081 017 1998*; *www.caremar.it* and SNAV 📞 *081 761 2348*; *www.snav. it* are the main carriers. From Naples, the Caremar traghetto (ferry) takes 1 hr., the TMV (traghetto veloce: fast ferry) 40 mins and the *aliscafo* (hydrofoil) just 35 mins. During the *Stagione Alta* (High Season) adult prices are around 5€ for the ferry, 7€ for the fast ferry and 8€ for the hydrofoil. The SNAV hydrofoil costs 13.50€ for adults and 9€ for children. Most carriers also charge a few euros for each piece of large luggage.

There are also services from the port at Pozzuoli, should you be in the Campi Flegrei area. From Pozzuoli, the traghetto (ferry) takes 35 mins, the TMV (traghetto veloce: fast ferry) 25 mins and the *aliscafo* (hydrofoil) a mere 15 mins. During the *Stagione Alta* (High Season) adult prices are around 3€ for the ferry, 4€ for the fast ferry and 5€ for the hydrofoil. You can also take a SNAV hydrofoil to and from Procida and Ischia: Casamicciola.

Getting Around

On Foot Procida is a very small island, which makes it feasible to get to most places on foot. In reality the narrow streets and hilly terrain make this uncomfortable and dangerous when travelling with children.

By Bus/Taxi After dark you'll want to use taxis and/or buses. It's no fun walking down Procida's poorly lit main streets holding on to children, skirting around overflowing refuse bins and breathing in the exhaust fumes of speeding (or crawling at the height of summer) traffic. Four SEPSA-run **bus routes** 📞 *081 542 9965*; *www.sepsa.it* cover just about all the island. Bus tickets cost 1€. Taxis and mini-taxis are relatively inexpensive and indispensable when carrying luggage. There's a taxi rank at Marina Grande (📞 *081 896 8785*)

Visitor Information

For the latest info head to the Ufficio di Turismo, Via Roma 📞 *081 810 968*; *www.infoischia procida.it*/ *www.procida.net* near the ferries at Marina Grande.

Fast Facts

Banks Banco di Napoli is at Via Vittorio Emanuele 158, 📞 *081 810 1489*.

Chemist Farmacia Madonna Delle Grazie is at Piazza dei Martiri 1, Corricella 📞 *081 896 8883*.

Hospital & First Aid For medical assistance 📞 *081 810 0510*/ 📞 *081 810 1213*.

Laundry Terza Annunziata is at Via Vittorio Emanuele 69 📞 *081 896 8651*.

Post There's a post office at Via Libertà 34 📞 *081 896 0711*.

Family-friendly Events

The Good Friday Procession

Dates back to 1627 and has origins in the Spanish tradition of the mysteries: pious representations of Christ's suffering made by local children are carried through the streets and then an 18th-century wooden statue of the dead Christ is taken to the lofty lanes of the Terra Murata carried by a dozen white-robed locals. The following morning a funereal procession takes place, accompanied by much trumpeting.

Festa della Madonna delle Grazie

This festival involves a colourful religious procession and feasting.
2nd July.

La Sagra del Mare (the Festival of the Sea)

Culminates in a beauty pageant of local girls in traditional garb and the naming of the Graziella – inspired by Alphonse de Lamartine's book of the same name.
Late July.

La Sagra del Pesce Azzurro

Much fish and wine are consumed at this Corricella event.
Mid-August.

What to See & Do

First impressions of Procida are a good indication of the island's slightly shabby but intimate appeal. Marina Grande (aka Porto Sancio Cattolico or simply "Sent Co" by the *Procidiani*) at the northeastern tip of Procida is the principal harbour and where your boat arrives. An expanse of sticky pitted flagstones spreads before you, frequently dotted with that characteristic Neapolitan scene: vehicles parked or moving in all directions. Each morning workaday types getting their espresso and *cornetto colazione*-fix and visitors laden with luggage are joined in the bars (Bar Capriccio at Via Roma 99, has tables outside) by an influx of schoolchildren off the boat from Ischia. A ramshackle row of tall pastel-hued buildings lines the marina, filled with eye-pleasing arches and picturesque imperfections. These fishermen's dwellings were designed to shelter fishing boats and now endearingly frame loggias and doorways. A hotchpotch of bars and restaurants with outdoor seating stretches along the ground floors of these vaulted Via Roma buildings.

The island's main shopping street, Via Principe Umberto, leads to Piazza dei Martiri, which contains the bulbous, baroque beauty of the Chiesa della Madonna delle Grazie. The square also contains a memorial to 12 *Procidani* – Republican martyrs who were killed during a Royalist backlash to a 1799 uprising. A climb to the oval citadel Terra Murata (meaning "walled land"), the highest point of the island at 300ft (91m), affords superb views of the Marina di Corricella and beyond. Here you'll find the Terra Casata and

Best Beaches

They may not be entirely litter-free but the beaches of Procida have their child-friendly charms. Near Marina Grande is the **Spiaggia della Silurenza**, which has nearby bars, restaurants and beach facilities. Daredevil local youngsters jump off the *Cannone* shoreline (Big Cannon: named after an historic cannon placed on the rocks): take care as there are jagged rocks here. Off Piazza Marina Grande is the smaller **Spiaggia della Luna**, which is less popular with families. Some 200 steps accessed on Via dei Bagni, off Piazza San Giacomo take you down to the dark coarse sands of **Spiaggia di Chiaia**. The **Pozzo Vecchio Beach** is enclosed within a semicircular bay and is reached from Via Battisti. **La Spiaggia del Ciraccio** ★ is Procida's longest expanse of sand and is near the island's campsites. The most popular beach is a continuation of Ciraccio and is around the corner from the charming Chiaiolella harbour. Afternoon winds keep both these beaches cool and excellent for wind-surfing. There are two bathing establishments, La Capannina ☎ *081 896 0253* and Lido di Procida ☎ *081 896 7531*; *www.lidodiprocida.com* with all the facilities needed for a family day on the beach: parasols, cabins, pedalos, sun loungers, bars and restaurants.

Castello d'Avolos, a medieval *cittadella* (citadel) and castle turned prison built in the 1560s by the Catalan House of Aragon. Other photogenic sights include the imposing noble residence **Palazzo De Iorio,** a belvedere offering fine views and the...

Abbazia di San Michele Arcangelo ★ ★ AGES 4 AND UP

Via Terra Murata. ☎ *081 896 7612; www.abbaziasanmichele.it*

This church was built in the 11th century and ransacked several times by Saracen pirates in the 15th and 16th centuries. Chuntering children should be gobsmacked by the coffered ceiling, gold leaf flourishes and an equally exuberant inlaid marble altar. Don't miss Nicola Russo's painting *Saint Michael Protects*

the Island which depicts Procida's patron saint halting a 1535 attack by Turkish pirates. According to the legend, St Michael came out of nowhere, appearing as a vision in the sky, stirred the calm seas and Saracen-helmsman Barbarossa Hayreddin Pasha's glance turned to a stare. The fabulous views, a museum telling the history of this strategic spot as well as exhibitions of mariners' ex-votos and 18th-century presepe (nativity) (see p. 78) figures should keep you busy for an hour and a half.

Open 9.45am–12.45pm and 3–6pm daily; closed Sun pm. **Admission** *Church free; Museum 2€.*

The charming fishing village, **Marina della Corricella** ★ ★ is a short hop from Piazza dei Martiri. Its array of pastel-coloured buildings and evocative alleyways were the backdrop of the heartstring-twanging film *Il Postino*, starring charismatic Neapolitan comedian Massimo Troisi. Children will enjoy nosing around the portside watching the fishermen tend to their boats and nets. The village's fairytale-like shapes, vivid colours and intimacy make it feel like you've entered a Neapolitan *presepe* (see p. 78).

At the south-western tip of Procida is the lively **Marina Chiaiolella** ★, known for its yachts, watersports and bar-restaurants. Children will lap up the laid-back atmosphere centring round a crescent-shaped harbour formed by a long-dead volcano crater. Nearby is a mezza-luna-shaped island with a 109m-high hump of Mediterranean scrub teeming with wildlife, known as the **Isola di Vivara** **www.isoladivivara.it**. This protected nature reserve is connected to Procida by way of a bridge.

Shopping

The granite-flagstone lanes of Procida are lined with chic boutiques like Capri but they do have down-to-earth stores for bona fide Procidiani where you can pick up a bargain. Amongst the evocative old ironmongers, hardware stores and local *alimentari* food stores are a few independent shops also worth a gander.

Besio Roberto Michele is a children's clothes shop that stocks fancy threads for *bambini*

(babies) and *ragazzi* (children). Via Vittorio Emanuele 211. ✆ *081 896 0427*.

Il Ghiottone Di Imputato M

Gluttons will be in heaven at this gastronomic establishment fit for fancy picnics, gifts and for the home larder. Via Vittorio Emanuele 15. ✆ *081 896 0349*.

Izzo Rosana is the address to pick up some funky Italian stationery for children. Via Vittorio Emanuele 36 ✆ *081 896 9118*.

CAFES, SNACKS & FAMILY-FRIENDLY DINING

Capri

Capri town's revered cafés may be crammed into the Piazzetta, but the real sweet and savoury treats can be found at Via Vittorio Emanuele 9, where the tempting smell of homemade ice cream cones at **Pasticcerria Buonocore** ★★ (see p. 197) will lodge itself in your olfactory memory for ever. As well as yummy ice cream, they do the lip-smacking lemon-and-almond caprilù cake and filled *panini*. It may be a tad pricey but it's a must-visit.

In Anacapri, **Bar Bucchetto**, Via G. Orlandi 38 is great for snacks, ice cream and atmosphere near the busy bus terminal and **Nautilus Café**, Via G. Orlandi 116 is perfect for refreshments and nibbles at the tranquil end of Anacapri's main lane and shopping drag.

Plenty of food options at the Piazzetta, Caprí

For cheap picnics, stock up on fresh ingredients at **Supermercato Super Capri** – Deco Via Matermania 1, Capri and **Supermarket Al.** Via Pagliaro 19, Anacapri.

Capri's FIND

Via Roma 38, 80073 Capri ☎ *081 837 3108; www.capris.it*

A short walk from the Piazzetta on the road to Marina Grande is a new, sleek and relaxing café-bar-restaurant with sublime views from its picture windows. Children will love the pizza and homemade ice cream; adults can sample exquisite pasta and seafood dishes including *tagliolini* pasta ribbons with courgettes and mussels, medallions of tuna and grilled swordfish. Another bonus is that the windows slide away to create an airy contemporary loggia – plus the air-con works –

which is a godsend at the height of summer. An open kitchen set-up provides a dash of culinary theatre and sense of occasion for all the family to enjoy.

Open *24 hours daily* ***Main Courses*** *8€–23€.* ***Credit*** *AmEx, DC, MC, V.* ***Amenities*** *Highchairs. Reservations accepted.*

Il Solitario

Via G. Orlandi 96, 80071 Anacapri ☎ *081 837 1382; www.trattoriail solitario.it*

Near the Santa Sofia church, a pergola shades happy locals and tourists feasting on flavoursome pizzas and classic Southern Italian dishes. It's been open since 1960 – when it was a favourite tavern of card-playing Anacapresi. The simply-prepared, good-value like peperoni ripieni (stuffed peppers), pasta al forno (oven-baked pasta) and ravioli capresi are a hit with the children. Chunks of beef, seafood dishes like polipo affogato (steamed octopus) and *dolci* like ricotta and pear cake please more mature palates.

Open *Noon-3pm and 7pm-midnight daily.* **Main Courses** *6€–19€.* **Credit** *DC, MC, V.* **Amenities** *Highchairs. Reservations accepted.*

La Rondinella ★★ FIND

Via G. Orlandi 295, 80071 Anacapri 📞 *081 837 1223*

Tucked away in a flowery tranquil lane opposite the Casa Mariantonia, La Rondinella (meaning The Little Swallow) is all about friendly service, fab food and laid-back dining. Book a table on the wonderful terrace or opt for a spot close by – within the spacious dining room. Children will be able to smell and see the pizza napoletana emerging from the kitchen. Adults don't miss out on the culinary fun: you can choose from a variety of classic Neapolitan dishes including the freshest seafood creations. The linguine al Scampo and frittura di gambero e calamaro (lightly fried prawns and squid) will have seafood lovers wanting to lick their plates clean.

Open *Noon–3pm and 7–11pm daily.* **Main Courses** *6€–19€.* **Credit** *AmEx, DC, MC, V.* **Amenities** *Highchairs. Reservations accepted.*

Ischia

Ischia Porto has a wealth of great caffè-pasticcerie including **Bar Ciccio** ★★, Via Porto 1 which has been open for over a century and does delicious ice creams, including healthy (organic, *doppio-zero* fat-free and gluten-free) options. The schoolchildren's favourite is **Bar Pasticceria Calise**, Via Sogliuzzo 69, which prepares classic *cornetti* including a wicked number with a crema e amarene (cream and sour cherries) filling. At Lacco Ameno, **Il Triangolo** (Via Roma, 📞 081 994 364) overlooks Il Fungo and serves refreshing *granite* (iced slush drinks) in lots of flavours including strawberry, melon, coffee and yoghurt. For a sneaky snifter in an ice cream, try the arancello and limoncello *gelati* at *Dolce è La Vita* in Sant' Angelo. Make up a picnic at Salumeria Manzi at Via Roma 16, which has meats, fruits, veg, cheeses, bread, etc..

Mezzanotte

Via Porto 72 80077 Ischia 📞 *081 981 653*

Mezzanotte offers superb value and atmosphere for families among the many restaurants along the flagstone quayside of the Riva Destra. There are two levels, which are popular with a youngish crowd at the weekends, who hang around the upstairs cocktail bar and on the harbour terrace. You can't go wrong with their version of the classic pizza, *la margherita*, topped with the creamiest *mozzarella di bufala*. Mums and dads may be tempted by a cheeky cheesecake or *panna cotta*.

Open Noon–3pm and 7pm–late daily. *Main Courses* 7€–22€. *Credit* AmEx, DC, MC, V. *Amenities* Highchairs. Reservations accepted.

Neptunus ★★

Via delle Rose, 11, Sant'Angelo d'ischia 80070; ☎ 081 999 702

The freshest ingredients and a magical terrace atmosphere make the Neptunus well worth plunging into for a couple of hours of family dining. An intimate outside area provides a stage for tarantella performances during the summer and looks onto the shoreline around picturesque Sant' Angelo. Giuseppe Jacono and his friendly team happily prepare child-friendly pasta dishes and serve some yummy desserts including a wickedly rich *torta caprese*.

Open Noon–3pm and 7.30pm–midnight daily. *Main Courses* 7€–22€. *Credit* AmEx, DC, MC, V. *Amenities* Highchairs. Reservations accepted.

Umberto a Mare ★

Via Soccorso 2, 80075 Forio d'Ischia ☎ 081 997 171; www.umberto amare.it

With spellbinding vistas of the Soccorso promontory shoreline and a sophisticated menu to boot, this well-established and revered restaurant near the Santa Maria delle Neve church is one for a special family occasion. The atmosphere is typically Neapolitan – relaxed and welcoming – and there are plenty of pasta options to please the children. Grown ups and teens can stretch their culinary experiences with innovative *piatti* like *ricciola*

fish served with sweet artichokes and fresh basil. Book a table by the window for the stunning sunset.

Open Noon–3.30pm and 7.30pm–11pm Tues–Sun. *Main Courses* 18€–35€. *Credit* AmEx, DC, MC, V. *Amenities* Highchairs. Reservations recommended.

Procida

Down by the main port at Marina Grande, **Bar Capriccio**, Via Roma 99 is a good bet for coffee, cool drinks and snacks close to the ferry. The venerable **Caffè Dal Cavaliere** ★★ at Via Roma 42 ☎ *081 810 1074*) makes the most of the island's famously pithy lemons in their creamy pastries *lingue di bue* (cow's tongues). At Marina Chiaiolella, **Ristorante-Bar-Pizzeria Il Galleone**, Via Marina Chiaiolella is a beguiling spot to imbibe café-bar drinks, pizzas and food including *bruschette,* inventive salads as well as grilled fish and meat dishes

Caracalè

Via Marina Corricella 62, 80079 Procida; ☎ 081 896 9192

Caracalè provides a pleasurable family dining experience amid the beguiling surroundings of an old fisherman's place down on the waterfront of Corricella. If the weather is fine children will love the fun atmosphere on the *banchina* (quayside). The amiable owners are happy to rustle up a tasty pasta dish or heaped salad for fussy palates. For the *vecchi* there are classic seafood dishes like fried sword fish with aubergine to savour.

Open *Noon–3pm and 7–11pm daily.* **Main Courses** *8€–16€.* **Credit** *AmEx, DC, MC, V.* **Amenities** *Highchairs. Reservations accepted.*

Sent' Cò

Via Roma 167, 80079 Procida ☎ *081 810 1120*

At Marina Grande, behind the church of Sancio Cattolico, or *Sent Cò* as the locals call it in their clipped dialect, is this no frills ristorante-pizzeria – it's big on atmosphere and welcomes children. The Catch of the Day – *il pescato del giorno* – is well worth asking about, as is their famed fish soup. Children may turn their noses up at the grown-up choice and may plump for the *pizze* and pasta dishes: their *oriecchiette* (small ear-shaped pasta) is often served with a *sugo* containing some of Procida's vitamin-rich seasonal (vegetables). Parents can encourage the children to *mangia le verdure*: eat your greens!

Open *Noon–3pm and 7–11pm Tues–Sun.* **Main Courses** *6€–14€.* **Credit** *DC, MC, V.* **Amenities** *Highchairs. Reservations accepted.*

FAMILY-FRIENDLY ACCOMMODATION

Capri and Ischia are both geared to tourists and visiting families. Capri is far pricier though, while Ischia offers more choice. There is less of a choice on Procida due to planning restrictions. Some of the islands' hotels can feel very crowded during the High Season, when swimming pools are mobbed so we've selected hotels that offer family-friendly facilities and a relaxing atmosphere.

Capri

INEXPENSIVE

Hotel La Tosca

Via D.Birago 5, 80073 Capri ☎ *081 837 0989;* **E:** *h.tosca@capri.it*

A warm welcome, excellent value, decent facilities and great location make La Tosca a great choice for families on a budget. It's near enough the buzz of the *Piazzetta* for enjoying the shops and restaurants yet alluringly ensconced down a quiet lane to offer guests some tweeting-bird, flower-filled tranquillity. Breakfasts are taken on the terrace where you can drink in views of the Faraglioni rocks. Guest rooms are simply furnished with lots of cool white walls. Bathrooms are little cramped though.

Rooms *11.* **Rates** *80€–150€ double. Breakfast included.* **Credit** *DC, MC, V.* **Amenities** *Babysitting service. Bar. Extra bed. Non-smoking rooms. TV lounge. WiFi.* **In room** *A/C. Shower/ bath.*

Stella Maris

Via Roma 27, 80073 Capri. ☎ *081 837 0452;* **E:** *albergostellamaris@ libero.it*

If you fancy staying for a night or two in chic but steep Capri town then this old *pensione* near the Piazzetta offers great value. The friendly family team have been welcoming families to Capri's busiest district for over 25 years now. There may not be a pool and rooms are a little cramped but you'll probably want to be out and about: buses to all the beaches and attractions depart from over the road and all the shops and restaurants are on your doorstep. The décor is a little on the kitsch side, especially in the charming lobby-cum-lounge where breakfast is served. The owners have access to a number of apartments so it's a good bet to email them with your requirements. If you are staying in the main building ask for a room around the back as the ones on the street overlooking the bus hubbub are noisy.

Rooms 20. **Rates** 80€–140€ double; 130€–260€ apartments/suites. Breakfast included. **Credit** DC, MC, V. **Amenities** Extra bed. Non-smoking rooms. **In room** A/C for additional charge. Fridge. Safe. Shower/bath. TV.

MODERATE-EXPENSIVE

Casa Mariantonia ★ ★ FIND

Via G. Orlandi 180, 80071 Anacapri ☎ *081 837 2923;* **www.casa mariantonia.com**

Superb family options are available at this tranquil, out-of-the-way Anacapri gem run by a friendly *famiglia* who have lived here for generations. The brand-spanking new (finished in 2007) and spacious suites/apartments are ideal for most sized groups; they are equipped with two bathrooms, a kitchen and an ample terrace overlooking lemon groves.

Six additional guest rooms provide cool, clean and calming accommodation for guests with babies and toddlers. Breakfasts are a little basic but overall Casa Mariantonia is a joy to stay in. Just over the road is the fabulous restaurant La Rondinella (see above) and there's a gym nearby. The amiable owners are always available for a friendly chat and tourist advice.

Rooms 6; 2 suites/apartments. **Rates** 140€–230€ double; 220€–330€ apartments/suites. Breakfast included. **Credit** DC, MC, V. **Amenities** Cots. Extra bed. Gym nearby (not included in price). Non-smoking rooms. **In room** A/C. Fridge. Safe. Shower/bath. TV. WiFi Internet.

Hotel Weber Ambassador

Via Marina Piccola 118, 80073 Capri ☎ *081 837 0141;* **E: www.hotel weber.com**

If you are after a room or family suite overlooking the famous Marina Piccola with access to a chic beach, then the Weber is an excellent choice. Rooms have tiled floors and a clean, functional look – some have fab little terraces overlooking the sea. A shuttle service takes guests to and from la Piazzetta from early morning to the wee early hours (7am–3am). Good news for active families: the hotel has access to lots of sports facilities, including a table tennis table, mountain bike hire, fishing rod hire, watersports (boat, canoe, diving, windsurf and sailing) hire and tuition, and can arrange various boat trips.

Rooms 68. *Rates* 110€–220€ double; 180€–300€ suite. Breakfast included in very high season *Credit* DC, MC, V. *Amenities* Babysitting service. Bar. Extra bed. Laundry service. Non-smoking rooms. Restaurant. Sports and watersports facilities. *In room* A/C. Fridge. Safe. Satellite TV. Shower/bath.

VERY EXPENSIVE

J.K.Place ★★

Via Prov. Marina Grande 225, 80073 Capri, ☎ *081 838 4001; www.jkcapri. com*

If you are going to splurge in *molto cool* Capri this is the place to wet your wonga. Capri's first classy Inn – the Hotel Continental – was opened in this handsome whitewashed 19th-century palazzo but how things have changed... Two pools (indoor and outside) for the children, serene spa facilities and treatments for the adults, sumptuous interiors and your very own concierge make for a memorable stay. It feels more like a luxury home than a hotel. Teens keen on art, design and fashion will be inspired by the elegant pieces and stacks of art books scattered around the public areas. It's perhaps less toddler-friendly as there are quite a few pricey vases around. J.K.'s selection of games, DVDs and CDs should keep children quiet if they cry "bored!" Pristine marble-mosaic bathrooms complete the luxurious yet practical guest room fittings. The restaurant serves classic Mediterranean dishes and child-friendly snacks on the panoramic terrace or in the stylish yet homely dining room.

Rooms 22. *Rates* 500€–700€ double; 700€–2200€ suites and family rooms. Breakfast included. *Credit* AmEx, DC, MC, V. *Amenities* Babysitting. Bar. Cots. Disabled access. Dry cleaning service. Extra bed. Gym. Non-smoking rooms. Pool (indoor and outdoor). Restaurant. Spa. *In room* A/C. Fridge. Internet access. Safe. Shower/bath. TV/DVD/Satellite.

Ischia

INEXPENSIVE

Hotel Europa

Via A.Sogliuzzo 25 80077, Ischia Ponte ☎ *081 991 427; www.hotel europaischia.it*

Hotel Europa is close to Ischia Ponte and Ischia Porto's myriad attractions, and the beach is *un piccolo salto* (a short hop) away. The amiable family who opened the hotel in the 50s are happy to organise child-friendly boat trips and excursions around the island. A decent choice of guest rooms and facilities are all there for a very reasonable outlay. Children and adults alike will love relaxing in the naturally thermal pool. Mums and dads can indulge in the massages and spa treatments available. Pay a bit extra for a Superior Room and you'll get all the in-room facilities plus a balcony.

Rooms 34. *Rates* 85€–120€ double. Discounts for babies and children sharing parents' room. Breakfast included. *Credit* DC, MC, V. *Amenities* Bar. Cot (10€). Dry cleaning service. Extra bed (1/2 adult rate for 2-12 years). Internet. Laundry service. Non-smoking rooms. Parking. Restaurant. Spa treatments. Thermal pool (outdoor). *In room* A/C. Fridge. Safe. Satellite TV. Shower/bath.

Hotel Continental Mare

Via B. Cossa 25, 80077 Ischia ☏ *081 982 577; www.continentalmare.it*

Two fabulous pools make this hotel near Ischia Porto a child-friendly find – the lower, thermal pool is set within the lush grounds and is great for small children while the more spacious upper pool is ideal for stronger swimmers and adults seeking a quiet-ish spot for a sunbathe, read and nap. The head waiter Luigi is the epitome of efficiency and charm as are much of the staff. Dining here is a pretty good value option – especially the buffet lunch – although you may want to dine out some nights. There are various room options available but don't expect lavish interiors. Access to the pebbly beach is via some steps and is not suitable for younger children. The hotel is a little out of the way and you'll have to be a moderately fit family to tackle the path to and from Ischia Porto. This path is not suitable for toddlers. An alternative is the bus stop on the main road above the hotel or easier still a 12€ taxi ride.

Rooms 57. *Rates* 130€–240€ double; 190€–330€ suites and family rooms. Breakfast included. *Credit* AmEx, DC, MC, V. *Amenities* Bar. Dry cleaning service. Extra bed. Internet. Laundry service. Non-smoking rooms. Parking. Pools (outdoor). Restaurant. Spa treatments at sister

View from Hotel Continental Mare, Ischia

hotel. *In room* A/C. Fridge. Safe. Satellite TV. Shower/bath.

Hotel Parco Smeraldo Terme ★★

Spiaggia dei Maronti, 80070 Barano d'Ischia ☏ *081 990 127; www.hotel parcosmeraldo.com*

The hotel is right by the steaming fumaroles of Maronti beach – just about the most beguiling spot on Ischia – and this establishment compliments the stunning location with some top-notch family-friendly facilities. Ask for a room facing the sea and pay a little extra for wonderful views and the chance of enjoying a cool breeze on your very own balcony. Another bonus is that you can use most of the beach facilities for free and there are restaurants along this fabulous stretch of large-grained, darkish volcanic sand. There are lots to keep all the family stimulated and pampered: subtropical gardens with a fish pond made for relaxing and reading in, a tennis court, a *Wellness Centre* with two pools (including one with hydromassage) and spa treatments. The only downside is that being splendidly isolated in paradise means getting to the island's other attractions takes some effort.

Rooms 64. *Rates* 180€–210€ double; 200€–300€ suites and apartments (with kitchenettes). Breakfast included. *Credit* AmEx, DC, MC, V. *Amenities* Access to beach (free use of loungers and deckchairs). Bar. Cots (20€). Disabled access. Dry cleaning service. Extra bed (3–6 years 40% off adult tariff; 7–12 30% off adult tariff; over-13s 20% off adult tariff). Laundry service. Non-smoking rooms. Thermal pool (outdoor) and two indoor spa pools. Restaurant. Spa and wellness centre. *In room* A/C. Fridge. Internet access. Safe. Shower/bath. TV/DVD/Satellite.

Procida

Campeggio Punta Serra

Via Serra 4, 80079 Procida ☎ *081 896 9519/896 0195; E: campeggioserra@ simail.it*

For families after a place to plonk a tent or caravan, or to rent a bungalow amid tranquil woods, the Punta Serra campsite (open June–Sept) is a good value choice. Among the six campsites on the island this one offers the most shade, which is a heavensent trait in the summer. The Pozzo Vecchio beach, which appeared in the film *il Postino* is

a short walk away. The bungalows are simply furnished, with a kitchenette, fridge and adjoining bathroom with a shower. Sizes vary, so some bungalows can house families of up to six. There's a bar selling snacks and a games room for children. Lots of activities and entertainment for the family are organised.

Rates 60€–160€ bungalow sleeping 2–6. *Credit* DC, MC, V. *Amenities* Bar. Cots. Games room. Internet access. Non-smoking rooms. Restaurant. Shop.

Hotel Celeste

Via Rivoli 6, 80079 Procida ☎ *081 896 7488; www.hotelceleste.it*

If you don't demand luxury but appreciate value and a canny location then Hotel Celeste ticks most of the boxes for families. It's ideal for groups wanting to be close to the beach, bars and restaurants as La Marina di Chiaiolella, la Spiaggia di Ciraccio and the Vivara nature reserve are all within walking distance. Most of its variously-sized, functional rooms have a balcony or terrace with table and chairs.

Rooms 35. *Rates* 60€–120€ double; 80€–160€ triple; 110€–210€ quadruple. Breakfast included. *Credit* DC, MC, V. *Amenities* Bar. Cots. Extra bed (see prices above). Internet access. Non-smoking rooms. Restaurant (in the high season mainly). *In room* A/C. Shower/bath. TV.

Hotel La Casa sul Mare

Via Salita Castello 13, 80079 Procida ☎ *081 896 8799; www.lacasasul mare.it*

Island Film Locations

Procida: Il Postino (The Postman): Fans of this Italian classic will spot Marina Corricella (where Mario first sets eyes on his Beatrice) and Pozzo Vecchio beach (where the poet Pablo Neruda teaches Mario the postman about metaphors).

For historic elegance and sublime views this 18th-century house in the heart of the *borgo antico* – near the fortified medieval complex of the Terra murata – tops the lot. Rooms are clean with cool hues, tiled floors and balconies with table and chairs – perfect to sit back and enjoy the views. It may be in a hilly location (so a bit tricky for toddlers and manoeuvering a buggy) but the hotel provides a shuttle service to the beach. Given the topography, position and layout this intimate hotel is perhaps more suited to families with older children.

*Rooms 10. **Rates** 100€–180€ double. Breakfast included. **Credit** DC, MC, V. **Amenities** Babysitting. Bar. Cots. Extra bed (45€ surcharge). Internet access. Laundry service. Non-smoking rooms. Parking. Shuttle bus to beaches. **In room** A/C. Fridge. Safe. Satellite TV. Shower/bath.*

Hotel La Vigna ★

*Principessa Margherita 46, 80079 Procida ☎ 081 896 0469; **www. albergolavigna.it***

The red-hued, crenellated exterior gives the hotel the appearance of a *castellino*. As its name suggests, the place is set within vineyards, which is a bonus for vino-afficionados, especially when they experience a wine tasting in the bar or better still on the panoramic roof terrace. The young owners have created a wonderful atmosphere and exquisite guest rooms with contemporary style: the Malvasia suite is a good choice for a small family and even has a luxury onsite bath set within exotic wood. Another bonus for a mum and dad is the spa and treatment area offering massages and therapeutic baths – they even use their wine in a special body massage and face mask. The restaurants, shops and transport links at Marina Grande are within easy each.

*Rooms 14. **Rates:** 90€–210€ double; 130€–260€ suites suitable for families. Breakfast included. **Credit** DC, MC, V. **Amenities** Babysitting. Bar. Cots. Disabled access. Extra bed (2–12 years 15% surcharge; over-12s 30% surcharge). Internet access. Laundry service. Non-smoking rooms. Parking. Spa and wellness centre. **In room** A/C. Fridge. Safe. Shower/bath. TV.*

The Insider

This section has an essential English–Italian vocabulary with some pronunciation guidance. A list of useful menu terms follows, which we hope you enjoy using – be brave and have a good go at ordering food – the Neapolitans are generally very encouraging of people trying to speak Italian. Remember though that most of the natives speak a different language altogether – *il napoletano* – so even if you understand some Italian you probably won't be able to decipher the clipped dialect words spoken around Campania.

For those keen on learning some Italian, get hold of a copy of *Italian for Children* (Contemporary Books), which is a fun CD/book course for youngsters and adults wanting to learn the basics. Teach Yourself do some well-thought-out introductory language books including a good vocabulary for beginners. The free BBC Italian language pages at *http://www.bbc.co.uk/languages/italian* are well worth delving into. For details about Italian language courses and cultural events, contact your nearest Italian Cultural Institute: in London (39 Belgrave Square SW1X 8NX. *020 7235 1461; www.icilondon.esteri.it*); Dublin (11 Fitzwilliam Square East, Dublin 2. *00 353(1) 662 0509*) or Edinburgh (82 Nicolson Street, Edinburgh EH8 9EW *0131 668 2232*).

USEFUL TERMS & PHRASES

Greetings & Pleasantries

English	Italian	Pronunciation
Thank you	**Grazie**	*graht*-tzee-yey
You're welcome	**Prego**	*prey*-go
Please	**Per favore**	*pehr* fah-*vor*-eh
Good morning or Good day	**Buongiorno**	bwohn-*djor*-noh
Good evening	**Buona sera**	*Bwohn*-ah *say*-rah
Good night	**Buona notte**	*Bwohn*-ah *noht*-tay
Hi/bye	**Ciao**	Chow
How are you?	**Come sta?**	*koh*-may *stah*
Very well	**Molto bene**	*mohl*-toh *behn*-ney
Good-bye	**Arrivederci**	ahr-ree-vah-*dehr*-chee
What's your name?	**Come si chiama?**	Ko-may see kee-ah-ma
My name is...	**Mi chiamo...**	mee kee-ah-mo
Excuse me (to get attention)	**Scusi**	*skoo*-zee
Excuse me (to get past someone)	**Permesso**	pehr-*mehs*-soh

English	Italian	Pronunciation
I don't understand	**Non capisco**	nohn ka-*pee*-sco
I don't speak Italian	**Non parlo italiano**	non par-lo ee-tal-yah-no
Correct	**Giusto**	*jew*-stoh
No, I don't want . . .	**No, non voglio . . .**	no, non *vohl*-yo

Nationalities

English	Italian	Pronunciation
I'm . . .	**Sono** . . .	*so*-no . . .
English	**Inglese**	een-*glaze*-eh
Irish	**Irlandese**	ear-lahn-*dayz*-eh
Scots	**Scozzese**	scot-*tzeh*-zeh
Welsh	**Gallese**	gah-lah-zeh
Australian	**Australiano**	a'ws-tra-lee-*ah*-no
New Zealander	**Dalla Nuova Zelanda**	dah-la nu-*wo*-va zee-*lahn*-dee-yah
American	**Americano**	ah-mehr-ee-*kahn*-oh
Canadian	**Canadese**	kahn-ah-*dayz*-eh

Family & Friends

English	Italian	Pronunciation
Mother	**la madre**	la mah-dreh
Father	**il padre**	eel pah-dreh
Dad	**il papà, il babbo**	ell paa-pa, eel bah-bbo
Mum	**la mamma**	lah-mah-mah
Children	**i figli**	ee fee-ylee
Baby (boy/girl)	**un/una bambino/a**	oo/oona bam-bee-noh/nah
Son/Daughter	**il/la figlio/a**	eel/lah fee-yl-eeo/fee-yl-ah
Brother	**il fratello**	eel frah-teh-llo
Sister	**la sorella**	la so-reh-lla
Husband	**il marito**	eel mah-ree-toh
Wife	**la moglie**	la mo-yl-ee-eh
Grandparents	**i nonni**	ee noh-nnee
Friend	**un/una amico/a**	oon/oonah a-mee-koh / a-mee-kah
Friends	**gli amici**	ylee a-mee-chee
Boy	**un ragazzo**	oon ra-gah-dzz-oh
Girl	**una ragazza**	oo-nah ra-gah-dzz-ah

Directions

English	Italian	Pronunciation
Where is . . .?	**Dovè . . .?**	doh-*vey*
the station	**la stazione**	lah stat-tzee-*oh*-neh
a hotel	**un albergo**	oon ahl-*behr*-goh
a restaurant	**un ristorante**	oon reest-ohr-*ahnt*-eh
the bathroom	**il bagno**	eel *bahn*-nyoh
To the right	**A destra**	ah *dehy*-stra
To the left	**A sinistra**	ah see-*nees*-tra
Straight ahead	**Avanti (or sempre diritto)**	ahv-vahn-tee (*sehm*-pray de*reet*-toh)

Shopping & Transactions

English	Italian	Pronunciation
I would like . . .	**Vorrei . . .**	vohr-*ray*
Do you have . . .?	**Ce l'hai . . .?**	cheh lie
How much is it?	**Quanto costa?**	*kwan*-toh *coh*-sta?
This one	**Questo**	*kway*-sto
That one	**Quello**	*kwel*-loh
Too expensive	**Troppo costoso**	*troh*-poh koh-*sto*-zoh
I would like to change . . .	**Vorrei cambiare . . .**	vohr-*ray* kahm-bee-*yar*-eh
cash	**contanti**	cone-*tahn*-tee
credit card	**carta di credito**	*kar*-tah dee *creh*-dee-toh
Deposit	**Deposito**	deh-*po*-zee-toh
Market	**Mercato**	mehr-*kah*-toh
Supermarket	**Supermercato**	*su*-pehr-mehr-kah-toh
I want to buy . . .	**Vorrei comprare . . .**	vohr-*ray* coam-*prar*-eh

Numbers

1	**uno**	(oo-noh)		11	**undici**	(oon-dee-chee)
2	**due**	(doo-ay)		20	**venti**	(vehn-tee)
3	**tre**	(tray)		21	**ventuno**	(vehn-toon-oh)
4	**quattro**	(kwah-troh)		22	**venti due**	(*vehn*-tee *doo*-ay)
5	**cinque**	(cheen-kway)		30	**trenta**	(*trayn*-tah)
6	**sei**	(say)		40	**quaranta**	(kwah-*rahn*-tah)
7	**sette**	(set-tay)		50	**cinquanta**	(cheen-*kwan*-tah)
8	**otto**	(oh-toh)		60	**sessanta**	(sehs-*sahn*-tah)
9	**nove**	(noh-vay)		70	**settanta**	(seht-*tahn*-tah)
10	**dieci**	(dee-ay-chee)		80	**ottanta**	(oht-*tahn*-tah)

90	**novanta**	(noh-*vahnt*-tah)	5,000	**cinque mila**	(*cheen*-kway *mee*-lah)
100	**cento**	(*chen*-toh)			
1,000	**mille**	(*mee*-lay)	10,000	**dieci mila**	(dee-*ay*-chee *mee*-lah)

Time

English	Italian	Pronunciation
When?	**Quando?**	*kwan*-doh
Yesterday	**Ieri**	ee-*yehr*-ree
Today	**Oggi**	*oh*-jee
Tomorrow	**Domani**	doh-*mah*-nee
Morning	**Mattina**	mah-*tee*-nah
Afternoon	**Pomeriggio**	pohm-mehr-*ree*-joe
Evening	**Sera**	*seh*-rah
1 hour	**Un'ora**	oon-*or*-rah
7 hours	**Sette ore**	set-tay *or*-reh
What time is it?	**Che ore sono?**	kay *or*-ay *soh*-noh

Days of the Week & Months of the Year

English	Italian	Pronunciation
Monday	**Lunedì**	loo-nay-*dee*
Tuesday	**Martedì**	mart-ay-*dee*
Wednesday	**Mercoledì**	mehr-cohl-ay-*dee*
Thursday	**Giovedì**	joh-vay-*dee*
Friday	**Venerdì**	ven-nehr-*dee*
Saturday	**Sabato**	*sah*-bah-toh
Sunday	**Domenica**	doh-*mehn*-nee-kah
January	**Gennaio**	Jeh-*nneye*-oh
February	**Febbraio**	Feh-*breye*-oh
March	**Marzo**	*Martz*-oh
April	**Aprile**	A-*pree*-lay
May	**Maggio**	Mah-*jee*-oh
June	**Giugno**	*Jew*-ny-oh
July	**Luglio**	*Loo*-lee-oh
August	**Agosto**	A-*gos*-toh
September	**Settembre**	Se-*ttem*-breh
October	**Ottobre**	O-*ttoh*-breh
November	**Novembre**	No-*vem*-breh
December	**Dicembre**	Dee-*chem*-breh

Travel

English	Italian	Pronunciation
What time does . . . leave?	à che ora parte	ah kay *or*-ah *par*-teh
the train	il treno	eel *tray*-no
the intercity bus	il Pullman	eel *pool*-mahn
the city bus	l'autobus	*lout*-toe-boos
the ferry	il traghetto	eel tra-*get*-toh
the ship	la nave	lah *nah*-vey
I want to go to . . .	Voglio andare . . .	*vohl*-yo ahn-*dar*-eh
Stop or station (bus or train)	Fermata	fehr-*mat*-tah
Ticket	Biglietto	beel-*yeh*-toh
Passport	Passaporto	pahs-sah-*por*-toh
What time do you open/close?	à che ora aprite/ chiudete?	ah kay *or*-ah ah-*pree*-teh/ kee-you-*deh*-teh

Useful Terms at the Chemist with Children

English	Italian	Pronunciation
Chemist	farmacia	farr-mah-*chee*-ah
Cold	affreddore	a-frreh-*ddoh*-reh
Sore throat	mal di gola	mal dee *goh*-lah
Headache	mal di testa	mal dee *teh*-sta
Stomach ache	mal di stomaco	mal dee *sto*-mah-koh
A children's painkiller containing paracetamol	Tachipirina	tah-key-pee-*ree*-nah
Vomit	Vomito	*vo*-mee-tto
Diarrhoea	Diarrea	Dee-ah-*rreh*-ah

Baby Stuff

English	Italian	Pronunciation
Dummy	ciuccio	*choo*-chee-o
Nappies	pannolini	pah-nno-*lee*-nee
Baby-changing table	fasciatoio	fash-ee-a-*toy*-o
Baby chair	seggiolino	se-gee-o-*lee*-noh

Hotel Booking

English	Italian	Pronunciation
A single room	**Una singola**	oo-nah *seen*-goh-lah
A double with one big bed and a cot	**Una doppia matrimoniale e una culla**	oo-nah *doh*-pee-yah ma-tree-moan-ee-*y'all*-eh eh oo-nah *koo*-lah
A double with two beds	**Una doppia con due letti**	oo-nah *doh*-pee-yah con *doo*-ay let-tee
with a private bathroom	**con bagno**	con *bahn*-yoh
Half board	**Mezza pensione**	meh-dzz-ah pehn-see-*oh*-neh
Full board	**Pensione completa**	Pehn-see-*oh*-neh com-*pleh*-ta

Eating

English	Italian	Pronunciation
Breakfast	**Prima colazione**	*pree*-mah coh-laht-tzee-*ohn*-ay
Lunch	**Pranzo**	*prahn*-zoh
Dinner	**Cena**	*chay*-nah
Snack	**Merenda/spuntino**	meh-rehn-dah/ spoon-*tee*-noh
Have you got a table for four?	**Avete una tavola per quattro?**	Ah-*veh*-te oo-nah *tah*-voh-lah purr *kwah*-troh
I'd like to reserve a table	**Vorrei riservare una tavola**	vor-*ray* ree-sair-*vah*-reh oo-nah *tah*-voh-lah
The bill, please	**Il conto, per favore**	eel kon-toh *pehr* fah-*vor*-eh
Vegetarian	**Vegetariano/a**	veh-jeh-tar-ee-*ah*-noh/nah
I'm allergic to . . .	**Sono allergico à . . .**	so-no ahl-*lair*-gee-koh ah
nuts	**noci**	*no*-chee
peanuts	**arachidi**	ah-*rah*-kee-dee
milk	**latte**	*la*-teh
shellfish	**molloschi**	*mohl*-loh-skee
I can't eat meat/pork	**Non posso mangiare carne/suino**	non po-so mahn-*giar*-eh *car*-neh/soo-*ee*-no
I can eat	**Posso mangiare**	poh-so mahn-*giar*-eh
fish	**pesce**	*peh*-shay
chicken	**pollo**	*pol*-loh
duck	**anatra**	*ah*-nah-tra
beef	**manzo**	*mahn*-zoh
steak	**bistecca**	bee-*steh*-kah

English	Italian	Pronunciation
lamb	**agnello**	ahn-*yell*-oh
boar	**cinghiale**	cheen-*g'yah*-leh
venison	**cervo**	*chair*-voh
sausage	**salsicce**	sahl-*see*-chay
eggs	**uova**	*woh*-veh
salad	**insalata**	een-sah-*lah*-ta
vegetables	**verdure**	vair-*doo*-ray
aubergine	**melanzane**	meh-lahn-*zahn*-eh
courgettes	**zucchini**	zoo-*keen*-ee
bell peppers	**pepperoni**	pep-pair-*oh*-nee
fruit	**frutta**	*froo*-tah
water	**acqua**	*ah*-kwah
fizzy/still	**frizzante/naturale**	free-*zahn*-teh/nah-too-*rah*-leh
tap water	**acqua dal rubinetto**	*ah*-kwah dahl roo-bee-*net*-toh
beer	**birra**	*bee*-rah
red wine	**vino rosso**	*vee*-no *rohs*-so
white wine	**vino bianco**	*vee*-no bee-*yahn*-koh
bread	**pane**	*pah*-neh
butter	**burro**	*boo*-roh
ice	**ghiaccio**	ghee-*yah*-cho
bottle	**bottiglia**	boh-*teel*-yah
fork	**forchetta**	for-*ket*-tah
glass	**bicchiere**	bee-key-*air*-eh
spoon	**cucchiaio**	koo-key-*yai*-oh
knife	**coltello**	kohl-*tell*-loh
oil	**olio**	*oh*-lee-oh
pepper	**pepe**	*peh*-pay
plate	**piatto**	pee-*yaht*-toh
cream	**crema**	*kray*-ma
salt	**sale**	*sah*-leh
cup	**tazza**	*taht*-zah
sugar	**zucchero**	*zoo*-cair-oh
rare	**al sangue**	ahl *sahn*-gway
well done	**ben cotto**	ben *koh*-toh
baked	**al forno**	ahl *fore*-noh
fried	**fritto**	*free*-toh

grilled	alla griglia, alle brace	ah-la *gree*-ylia, ah-lay *brah*-chay
steamed	al vapore	ahl vah-*pohr*-ay
stuffed	ripieno	ree-pee-*yay*-no
boiled	bollito	boh-*lee*-toh
roasted	arrosto	ah-*roh*-sto
the menu	la carta	lah *kar*-tah
fixed-price menu	menu à prezzo fisso	men-*you* ah *pret*-zoh *fees*-soh

USEFUL WEBSITES & TELEPHONE NUMBERS

There are lots of handy resources and travel websites out there for families travelling to Northern Italy. Here are some you might find useful.

Airlines

The major airlines flying to Naples International Airport (aka Capodichino) are:

Alitalia
UK 0870 544 8259/Ireland 01 677 5171
www.alitalia.co.uk/ www.alitalia.ie

Aer Lingus
Eire 0818 365 000/ UK 0870 876 5000
www.flyaerlingus.com

British Airways
0870 850 9850
www.britishairways.com

Flybmi
0870 6070 555/ 01332 64 8181
www.flybmi.com

easyJet
0905 821 0905
www.easyjet.com)

For cheap flights check out *LowFareFlights.co.uk* and *www.flightmapping.com* which do price comparisons for you.

Tourist Boards: Information about Naples & the Campania Region

For advice about all aspects of travelling to Italy, contact the Italian Tourist Board: ENIT (1 Princes Street, London W1B 2AY free from UK and Ireland *0800 0048 2542; www.enit.it*). The regional tourism websites vary in quality; some have excellent content and even direct you to recommended hotels and local operators:

Amalfi:
www.amalfitouristoffice.it

Capri:
http://www.capritourism.com/

Ischia & Procida:
www.infoischiaprocida.it

Napoli:
www.www.inaples.it

Sorrento:
http://www.sorrentotourism.com/

For general info about Naples and the Campania region go to *www.frommers.com* and *www.discoveritalia.com*.

Hand-painted ceramics

Independent Advice with Customer Feedback about Hotels, etc

There are many interactive sights full of candid reviews, pictures, advice and even video clips from travellers – these are great for checking if sights, restaurants and hotels are all they are cracked up to be. The biggest resource is *www.Tripadvisor.com* followed by *www.virtualtourist. com*. Other useful sites include *HolidayWatchdog.com*; *Holidays-uncovered.com*; and the excellent *www.slowtrav.com*, which has insightful entries from travellers who seek out the more obscure and interesting places.

Tour Operators & Specialist Travel Companies

Good places to start on the web are the big travel sites *expedia.co. uk* and *opodo.co.uk*. For decent hotel rates, check out *www.price line.co.uk*. For all manner of speciality holidays, go to *www.info hub.com*, *www.responsibletravel. com* and *www.specialtytravel. com*. Classy hotels and apartments can be found at *www. andandoslowtravel.com*. Other operators worth investigating are *www.directholidays.co.uk*; *Thomsonfly.com*; *Thomas Cook. com*; *lastminute.com*; *www.tele textholidays.co.uk*; *www.travel counsellors.com*.

Always check independent reviews of hotels before you book though to avoid disappointment: the descriptions on many websites like *www.last minute.com* are often way off the mark.

Sporty, adventure and walking breaks for families can be found at *www.activitybreaks.com*; *www.responsibletravel.com*; *www. ramblersholidays.co.uk www. exodus.co.uk*.

Villa Rental, Agriturismi, Camping & Hostelling

To rent a villa or apartment have a look at *www.rentvillas.com*; *www.homelidays.com*.

Agriturismi vary in quality and rusticity, but you are almost always certain to get fab local food and superb value for families. These Italian websites are well worth a gander: *www.agriturist.it*; *www.agriturismo.net*; *www.agriturismo.com*.

UK tour operators specializing in camping holidays include *www.eurocamp.co.uk*; *www.key-camp.co.uk*. For details about all kinds of campsites go to these Italian webpages: *www.federcampeggio.it*; *www.easycamping.it*; *www.camping.it www.campeggi.com*. Youth hostelling is a budget option worth considering (*www.ostellionline.org*).

An even cheaper way of finding suitable family accommodation is to swap your house with someone in Italy: check through the listings at *Homeexchange.com* and *homelink.org.uk*. *matching houses.com* enables house swaps for families with special needs.

Luggage: Send it in Advance

Avoid carrying heavy suitcases and other bulky items like prams and sporting equipment by arranging to send them to your destination in advance. Go to *firstluggage.com* or *carrymy luggage.com* for a quote. *babies travellite.com* will even send baby essentials like food and nappies to your destination.

Medical Information & Useful Medical-related Services

For medical information go to *FCO.gov.uk*; Ireland: *www.foreign affairs.gov.ie*.

Colourful boats on the beach

Families with children who have special needs may like to contact parents whose children have similar conditions to swap travel tips at: *youreable.com* and *disabledfriends.com*. Prepare an identity bracelet that has all the details of a child's medical condition, required treatments and doctor's name at *medicalert.org.uk*.

Train Travel

To plan train journeys go to Ferrovia Italiana (*www.trenitalia.com*) or the new site *www.italiarail.co.uk* where you can buy tickets. If you're planning to travel through France or other countries on the way to Italy check out *www.raileurope.com*.

Driving & Car Rental in Italy

There are lots of resources on the web for car drivers. For details about the Italian motorway network and advice about driving on those crazy Italian roads, check out *www.autostrade.it* and *www.driving.drive-alive.co.uk*. For advice and general guidelines about fitting children's car and booster seats, check out *www.childcarseats.org.uk*. The leading car hire company websites and their phone numbers are: *www.avis.co.uk* (☎ 0844 581 0147); *www.budget.co.uk* (☎ 0844 581 2231); *www.2.hertz.co.uk* (☎ 08708 448 844). For cheap car rental deals go through: *www.carjet.co.uk* (☎ 08702 67 67 67); *www.easyautos.co.uk* (☎ 08700 540 205); *www.autoeurope.com* (☎ 0800 358 1229); *www.alltravelitaly.com*, UK ☎ 0800 018 6682/Ireland ☎ 1800 200 115). Remember to book well in advance for the best deals.

Travelling with Children

For advice and top tips about family travel, these websites are worth checking out: *Holiday TravelWatch.com*; *www.travellingwithchildren.co.uk*; *www.travelforkids.com*; *www.babygoes2.com*; *www.deabirkett.com*.

It may be in Italian but the website *www.bambinopoli.it* is worth trying to navigate as it has lots of valuable info about child-friendly hotels, museums and even has a list of babysitting agencies.

Index

A

Abbazia di San Michele Arcangelo (Procida), 218
Accommodations
  Amalfi Coast, 185–188
  best, 10
  Campi Flegrei, 108–110
  The Islands, 223–228
  Naples, 84–88
  ratings system for, 26
  Sorrentine Peninsula, 185, 187–188
  Vesuvius region, 146–148
  websites for, 25–28, 238, 239
Active families, activities for
  best, 6–7
  Campi Flegrei, 96–97
  Capri, 200
  Ischia, 208
  The Islands, 190
  Li Galli, 166
  Naples, 75
  Sorrento, 158, 159
The Aeneid (Virgil), 101
Agano Crater (Naples), 96–97
Agriturismo, 7, 26, 38, 115, 117, 145, 154
Air travel, 25, 26, 31–33, 237
Alcohol, 41
Amalfi, 168–171, 181, 185–186
  accommodations, 185–186
  church, 169, 170
  dining, 181
  events, 168
  museums, 169–170
  shopping, 170, 171
Amalfi Coast, 38–39, 150–151, 163–180
  accommodations, 185–188
  beaches, 166, 167
  best attractions for children, 153
  castles and palaces, 173–174, 177
  churches, 166–167, 169, 170, 172–173, 177
  dining, 180–184
  events, 165, 168
  festivals, 172, 176
  map, 12, 150
  museums, 169–170, 177–180
  nature walks, 6–7

Paestum, 175–176, 178–180
Positano, 165–168
Ravello, 171–174
Salerno, 171–178
shopping, 167–168, 170, 171
views, 165–166
Amphitheatre (Pompeii), 141–142
Anacapri, 193, 198
Anfiteatro (Pompeii), 141–142
Anfiteatro Flavio (Pozzuoli), 99–100
Animal attractions
  Agriturismo La Ginestra (Vico Equense), 154
  Lo Zoo di Napoli (Campi Flegrei), 7
  at Vesuvius, 115
  Villa Comunale Gardens and aquarium (Naples), 69–70
Antiques shopping, 76
Apartment rentals, 28, 185
Archaeological sites and museums. *See also* Greek ruins; Roman ruins
  Boscoreale (Vesuvius), 142
  Boscoreale-Antiquarium Nazionale Uomo e Ambiente nel Territorio Vesuvio (Villa Regina), 143
  Museo Antiquarium Equano (Vico Equense), 154
  Museo Archeologico dei Campi Flegrei (Baia), 100
  Museo Archeologico Nazionale (Paestum), 179–180
  Museo Archeologico Provincale (Salerno), 177
  Museo Civico Archeologico di Pithecusae (Ischia), 211
  Museo del Mare (Ischia), 209
  Museo Narrante del Santuario di Hera Argiva (Paestum), 180
  Parco Archeologico di Baia, 100
  Sanctuary and Church of Santa Restituta (Ischia), 211

Architectural terms, 137
Architecture
  best, 3–4
  Cappella di Sansevero (Naples), 59
  Casa Rossa (Capri), 197
  Castel dell'Ovo (Naples), 64–65
  Castello d'Avolos, 218
  Castel Nuovo (Naples), 65–66
  Certosa di San Giacomo (Capri), 197
  Chiesa della Madonna delle Grazie (Procida), 217
  Church of Santa Maria del Carmine (Ischia), 214
  Church of Santa Maria della Sacca (Ischia), 214
  Duomo (Naples), 59–60
  Duomo di San Matteo (Salerno), 177
  Galleria Umberto I (Naples), 66–67
  Il Santuario della Madonna del Soccorso (Forio), 212
  Museo Archeologico Nazionale (Naples), 3
  Museo di Capodimonte (Naples), 3–4
  Museo Nazionale di Capodimonte (Naples), 73–75
  Piscina Mirabilis (Bacoli), 101–102
  San Domenico Maggiore (Naples), 61–62
  Santa Chiara (Naples), 63, 64
  Terra Casata (Procida), 217–218
  Villa Malaparte (Capri), 202
  Villa San Michele (Anacapri), 199–200
Arco Naturale walk (Capri), 202–203
Area Marina Protetta di Punta Campanella (Sorrento), 159
Arienzo beach (Positano), 167
Art galleries, 4, 71–72, 75. *See also* Religious art
A Sfogliatella Di Ercolano (Naples), 56